The Cook It and Freeze It Book

THE COOK IT AND FREEZE IT BOOK

by
Margaret Deeds Murphy

HAWTHORN BOOKS, INC.
PUBLISHERS / New York

To my mother, my Aunt Edith, and
Miss Margaret Fedde

THE COOK IT AND FREEZE IT BOOK

Library of Congress Catalog Card Number: 71-158030

ISBN: 0-8015-1754-0

2   3   4   5   6   7   8   9   10

Design by Ellen E. Gal

Contents

INTRODUCTION   ix

PART I. FOODS TO FREEZE

1. GENERAL FREEZING INFORMATION   3
   What Foods Are Frozen? · Packaging · Preparation
   for Freezing · Refreezing Thawed Foods

2. MEAT   10
   General Instructions for Freezing Uncooked Meat
   · Cooking Frozen Meat · Recipes

3. POULTRY   32
   General Instructions for Freezing Uncooked
   Poultry · General Suggestions for Roasting Poultry ·
   General Suggestions for Broiling Poultry · Recipes
   · General Instructions for Freezing Cooked Poultry
   · Recipes

4. FISH AND SHELLFISH   54
General Instructions for Freezing Fish and Shellfish
• Recipes

5. GAME   94
General Instructions for Freezing Game • Recipes

6. FRUIT   107
General Instructions for Freezing Fruit • Directions
for Packing Fruit • Suggestions for Serving Frozen
Fruit • Recipes

7. VEGETABLES   124
General Instructions for Freezing Vegetables • Suggestions for Serving Frozen Vegetables • Recipes

PART II. COURSES TO FREEZE

8. APPETIZERS   151
General Rules for Freezing Appetizers • Recipes

9. STOCKS AND SOUPS   162
General Rules for Freezing Homemade Stocks and
Soups • Recipes

10. BREADS   173
General Rules for Freezing Breads • Notes on
Making Bread • Freezing Unbaked Dough • Recipes

11. MAIN DISHES AND LEFTOVERS   200
General Rules for Freezing Main Dishes • Pro-
cedures for Reheating Frozen Main Dishes •
Freezing Leftovers • Recipes

12. SALADS   211
General Rules for Freezing Salads • Recipes

13. SANDWICHES   218
    General Rules for Freezing Sandwiches • Flavored
    Butters for Sandwiches • Sandwich Combinations
    and Cold Fillings That Freeze Well • Recipes

14. COOKIES   226
    General Rules for Freezing Cookies • Recipes

15. DESSERTS   237
    General Rules for Freezing Desserts • Recipes

APPENDIX: FREEZING BITS AND PIECES   263

INDEX   266

Introduction

Most of us want to be creative in our cooking but as thrifty as possible about our food bills. Or if we garden, we may have produce in excess of what can be eaten fresh. Or the market has such delicious bargains that we bought quantities too large to be used immediately. These are all legitimate reasons for freezing foods.

Freezing is the most modern way for the homemaker to preserve foods. It means that one can savor peaches in dead winter when the pocketbook cannot afford fresh peaches imported from far places. A freezer makes it possible to prepare all or part of a fancy dinner and save much last-minute frenzy when entertaining. The freezer is as versatile as you.

A freezer is a marvelous helper. It can also be a repository for a lot of foods you don't remember you have. It can save money; it can allow you to serve fresh blueberries in January or a beef stew in the time it takes to defrost and heat to serving temperature. Using a freezer is like playing the piano. It can produce some perfectly gorgeous music or some very discordant notes, but like playing the piano, you are in control. What you put in comes out.

First . . . what is a freezer? A freezer is a separate piece of equipment or a separate section of the refrigerator where food can be frozen and stored at 0° or lower. The freezer section of a refrigerator-freezer combination is isolated from the refrigerator section by a solid divider and has either a separate outside door or an inner insulated door. Some refrigerator freezers and ice-cube compartments are not intended to provide this low temperature (0°) and are intended for only short-term storage of already frozen foods and not for freezing. They can be identified by the fact that they do not have *separate, insulated* doors.

The storage capacity of freezers is given either in pounds of food stored or in cubic feet, both of which confuse me. So I always look at it practically. If a freezer is big, it holds a lot of food. If it is smaller, it holds less. If you have a large freezer, you can probably freeze all the things you want. If you have one that is smaller, you may have to make choices. A big freezer can get you into a lot of trouble with your food budget because it is very easy to lose or forget things in the back or bottom, depending on whether it is an upright or chest type. The only way I know to avoid this is to try to keep similar foods stored together so you'll have some visual idea of how much you have *and* to keep a running inventory in a book as foods are put in and taken out.

For the record, however, roughly 35 pounds of food can be stored in each cubic foot of usable space. This estimate is dependent on the size and the shape of the packages. For example, more nice neat little boxes or cartons can be packed into a given space than clumsy big frozen turkeys or soup bones or odd-shaped contents of casseroles.

Using your food freezer facilities in this manner will make them serve you, rather than you serve them.

One of the most common mistakes novices at food preservation make is to overproduce or underproduce. You end up with trillions of peaches and no blueberries. The best way to avoid this trap is to make a plan at the beginning of the year based on the number in the family, likes and dislikes in food, and kinds of facilities for preserving. This plan does not have to be inflexible. It can be as flexible as: "60 pints of fruit (be sure to get some sour cherries for pies) and 120 pints of vegetables (more beans and corn, and get broccoli to freeze this year)."

No more food should be preserved by freezing than can be reasonably used up by the storage time indicated in the directions. The longer foods are kept, the more deterioration in quality. Since freezing foods is work, it is not very wise to spend time preserving food that will not be eaten at its peak. Next season will be bargain time again in the market, and you'll either add to the amount already frozen or sadly remember that to *really* save money you must use up the leftovers.

Planning is particularly important with freezer preservation, as it is easy to let a bargain in meats, for example, carry one away. But again, buy only what can be used in a reasonable time. Also remember that if the freezer is full of bargain meats, there won't be room for luscious in-season raspberries, corn, or other favorite foods.

Another caution is to avoid overloading yourself with work at one time, unless you have plenty of willing hands to help. Even though you may save a few cents by purchasing green beans by the bushel, it may be a wiser purchase to pay slightly more for a half bushel and less work all at one time.

PART I
FOODS TO FREEZE

1 General Freezing Information

WHAT FOODS ARE FROZEN?

Freezing food depends a great deal on the size of the freezer and the likes and dislikes of family members. It also depends on the circumstances under which one lives.

A homemaker who has a large garden or lives in an area where roadside stands or farmers' markets sell vegetables in season at bargain prices may freeze vegetables in great quantities. An urban dweller who has no access to these bargains will fill the freezer with other kinds of foods.

A sight-seeing trip through the freezer section of the supermarket will give a pretty good idea of what can be frozen, which is just about anything. The one thing to remember is that what comes out of the freezer will be no better than what went in.

In choosing what to freeze, one should remember that

3

freezing as a form of food preservation is not inexpensive. The purchase price of the freezer, the cost of running it, and the cost of materials used for packaging all indicate that one should choose wisely in the selection of foods to freeze. One should not forget, however, that freezing is the most versatile form of food preservation.

PACKAGING

There are many forms of packaging for use in freezing. Your choices will vary with the kinds of food you choose to freeze. It is recommended that a homemaker just beginning a freezer program not make too extensive an investment in freezer packaging materials until she has had the opportunity to experiment and decide how she is going to use the freezer.

For example, perhaps the freezer will be used primarily for cuts of meat which can be wrapped in freezer wrap or for casseroles that are frozen in the dishes in which they are to be reheated. This kind of freezing will not require any expensive outlay in freezer containers.

The primary purposes of freezer packaging are to exclude air from the food, to keep it clean and sanitary, and to separate the different kinds of food. The air in freezers is dry because any moisture is frozen and deposited on walls and freezing coils. Improperly packaged foods allow the dry air in the freezer to extract moisture from the frozen foods. This results in what is called freezer burn. The food develops dry spots and becomes discolored. It lowers the quality of the food, and, of course, the longer the food is stored, the poorer the quality becomes. Containers or packaging must be airtight and moisture- and vapor-proof so that no liquid or air can get in or out.

Never save money on packaging materials. As a general rule one should not try to reuse containers in which cottage cheese, yogurt, or similar items are purchased. They are not waxed or coated heavily enough to be suitable for freezing.

Packaging comes generally classified as rigid or nonrigid. These descriptions give an idea of what to look for.

RIGID CONTAINERS

Rigid containers are glass, plastic, tin, aluminum, or waxed or plasticized fiber board containers. Each has its own advantages. Glass containers, particularly wide-mouthed, are easy to use and easy to maintain and can be reused over and over. Plastic is lightweight and takes some care in maintenance (can be warped by dishwasher drying heat). Tins with plastic closures are easy to maintain and reuse. Lightweight aluminum containers may not be reusable. Waxed or plasticized fiberboard containers are light, and many can be stored in a small space. Reuse is limited.

Rigid containers are used for fruits, vegetables—both liquid and dry pack—soups, meats, and poultry.

Inexpensive heat-proof dishes can go from freezer to preheated oven. They *cannot* be used on top of the range or under the broiler.

Pyroceram, a more expensive glass-ceramic product, can be taken from the freezer to the top of the range as well as under the broiler.

A new chinalike tableware has bowls that can also go from freezer to a preheated oven but not to range top or broiler.

NONRIGID CONTAINERS

Nonrigid containers include films such as moisture- and vapor-proof cellophane, aluminum foil (heavy-duty or freezer), pliofilm, polyethylene, and laminated papers. These come on rolls and can be cut the length desired to cover the food being frozen.

Also in this category are plastic or nylon bags, which can be used separately or as inserts for cardboard containers. (to make stacking in the freezer easier).

Film or bags are properly used with freezer tape or other sealing device to insure the seal. Plastic bags are also available which can be heat sealed. Use these as directed on the package label.

There is on the market a sealing device for use with heavy

pliofilm bags. These bags are "boil in the bag"—heavy and excellent to use for reheating cooked foods without fuss or mess. They are also efficient for fruits, vegetables, and other uncooked items.

In the recipes that call for freezer wrap, this can be heavy-duty aluminum foil, moisture- and vapor-proof cellophane, or other of the plastic wraps.

GENERAL TIPS

Rigid containers should come with a closure that is an adequate seal. If there is any question about the seal being airtight, cover the edge of the lid and onto the container with freezer tape.

Always leave an empty space at the top of a rigid container to allow for expansion of the frozen food. The space should be from ½ to 1 inch, or in the case of glass containers with a narrow top opening, ¾ inch for pints and 1½ inches for quarts. If this is not done, the expanding food might push off the lid or break the glass container.

In using film or bags, exclude as much air as possible, and seal packages airtight. Freezer tape, metal twists, or rubber bands can be used for sealing. With aluminum foil a "drugstore" fold can be used. This consists of bringing the two cut edges up together and folding down twice or whatever number of times is necessary to make a tight package around the food to be frozen.

If you like to feel even more secure, buy stockinette—a knitted tube which stretches—and put this over odd-shaped packages. Cut it to fit, and tie each end with a knot. The object of using stockinette is to avoid getting holes in the packaging over the food.

As far as I'm concerned, labeling is almost as important as sealing. Once the food is in the freezer and frozen, it is practically impossible to tell what it is without a label unless it is something as identifiable as a whole turkey or chicken. The date is equally important. Food does not keep indefinitely in a freezer, and it is only good sense to use up the oldest food first. I do not like to write directly on the package if I am using a rigid container. Most marking inks cannot be washed off, and so the original mark is indelibly left on the container. I put a piece of freezer tape on the container and write on that. After the container is emptied the freezer tape can be easily pulled off and the container washed, ready for reuse and relabeling.

Incidentally, I have discovered that masking tape works just as well as freezer tape and is much less expensive.

Buy a marking pen that will write on almost any surface. Write the name of the food, the date, and any directions for reheating. This way there will be no confusion when ready to use. Crayons can also be used, but a marking pen is better.

PREPARATION FOR FREEZING

Decide in advance of freezing which type of packaging you need for best efficiency, and have sufficient clean containers and/or freezer wrap and sealing materials and marking pen ready at hand.

A trick I have learned when using cellophane for freezing is to put a length of waxed paper about as long as the pieces of cellophane that will be needed on the counter top. Measure cellophane on the waxed paper. It will not curl or stick and is much easier to handle. Place whatever is being frozen on the cellophane, and wrap and seal. The waxed paper is ready for the next measured piece of cellophane.

If foods contain a lot of liquid, a wide-mouthed canning funnel will be very handy to eliminate spills onto the outside of the rigid containers, eliminating clean-up work.

Factories produce things efficiently because the experts set up a production line. If you are freezing a great quantity at one time, the only way to get it done with the least amount of work possible is to set up your own production line. Line up your work in the order that it needs to be done so that you can go from one job to the next without confusion. Also, now is a good time to teach yourself to do as much as possible while sitting down. As one who learned the hard way, after a foot operation, and who has continued to carry on the habit, I can guarantee less fatigue.

One of the reasons commercially frozen foods are of such high quality is fast freezing. Temperatures around minus 40° freeze the food very quickly, and in other processes temperatures as low as minus 109° or minus 320° can be used. In fast freezing package items are put singly on a belt or tray and frozen quickly. This maintains a firm cell structure in the frozen foods and prevents them from becoming "mushy" when cooked.

These are conditions we can't re-create at home, but we can approximate them to the extent that our equipment allows with the following rules.

1. Chill well any foods before they go into the freezer for freezing. This can be done before or after packaging according to the directions.

2. Do not stack foods to be frozen. The packages should be laid on shelves or the bottom of the freezer or on coils, so that all four sides can be in contact with frigid air. Only enough foods to freeze solid in less than 24 hours should be put into the freezer at one time. When frozen throughout, the packages can be stacked in the proper section of the freezer.

If you've never frozen foods before, you will probably have many questions which will be answered as we go along in the various categories.

REFREEZING THAWED FOODS

There have been a million words written regarding whether frozen foods that have fully or partially thawed could be refrozen, and it seems that every homemaker has a different understanding of those million words.

Perhaps an explanation of how the confusion arose will help dispel it. But first: *You can refreeze foods that have fully or partially thawed as long as no spoilage has begun.* (The odor and appearance of the food are indicators of spoilage; so is the length of time it has been defrosted.) *But* don't expect the same quality as in the original frozen food.

And this is how it all began. All foodstuff, raw or cooked, is composed of tiny cells with varying percentages of liquid enclosed within the cells. In the freezing process the liquid is frozen and expands. In commercial fast freezing the liquid freezes so fast that less expansion occurs than in home freezing. (If you doubt this expansion, feel the tops of ice cubes in the ice tray.)

Each time food is frozen, thawed, and refrozen, expansion and breakdown of the cells occur. This results in cooked food that is softer (sometimes vegetables are even "mushy") in texture—not nearly the quality of the original frozen food.

The beginning of this controversy goes back to the origin of commercially frozen foods. As the process was developed, it was not as "fast-freeze" as it is today. Couple this with inadequate storage at both the grocer's and in the home, and you can see why the first frozen foods after cooking could be pretty poor.

So with some justice homemakers were told not to refreeze frozen foods that had been defrosted.

However, the two keys are: 1. Foods can be refrozen if no spoilage has occurred. 2. Remember that the quality of the cooked food is not as good after it is defrosted and refrozen.

When defrosting and refreezing have occurred, it might be wise to mark this on the containers.

If power fails, keep the freezer closed. Tape a sign across the door so everyone who might use the freezer will be aware of the emergency. Most freezers if not opened will keep a temperature below 32° F. for about 2 days. If the emergency lasts longer, use dry ice to keep the freezer temperature low, or arrange to have the food transferred to another freezer, packing food packages in newspaper, which acts as an insulator, if they are to be transported any distance.

2 Meat

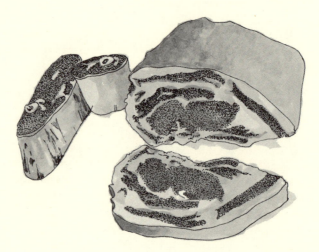

GENERAL INSTRUCTIONS FOR
FREEZING UNCOOKED MEAT

Since meat is the largest expenditure of the food budget and freezes very satisfactorily, it is wise buying to purchase meat bargains when they are available. Always buy the best quality meat you can afford and package it in family-size units. Never freeze meat in the package in which it is purchased, unless special arrangements have been made with the meatman to wrap the meat in freezer wrap.

Never skimp on packaging materials. Buy the best available, and always wrap meats securely.

Since meat is such a big expenditure, planning should go into its purchase. It is unwise, for example, for a small family to purchase a side or even a quarter of beef. The

10

price per pound may sound tempting, but one should remember that that price covers bone, fat, desirable and less desirable cuts of meat. Unless you are an expert at cutting and boning and have a large freezer space to devote to meat only, it is rarely a bargain to buy meat in this manner.

It is much wiser to watch the grocery ads for bargains on the cuts your family prefers and buy and freeze them.

If, however, you have the facilities to handle a quarter or half of beef, there will be about a 25 percent loss in fat and bone so that you would add ¼ more to the quoted price to know the true cost. Don't forget to include any charge for cutting and wrapping the meat. The forequarter of a 300-pound side of beef yields about 118 pounds, or 76 percent, of usable cuts, and the hindquarter about 100 pounds, or 70 percent.

When freezing a large number of packages of meat at one time, always chill the meat very well before it goes into the freezer. For the fastest freezing in a home freezer, turn the freezer control to lowest temperature to speed up freezing and help prevent warming of other foods in the freezer.

Put only 2 pounds per cubic foot of total storage space in to freeze at one time. Place the unfrozen packages against a refrigerated surface, not touching any of the already frozen foods.

ROASTS

Wrap roasts in freezer wrap, conforming wrapping material as closely to shape of meat as possible. Seal, label, and date. If meat is to be stored over a long period of time, it is wise to buy stockinette and cover packages with that in order to prevent damage.

Always label roast with weight and preferred cooking method, such as roast or braise, as well as the name of the cut, such as prime rib or shoulder roast. This little extra information will be more than welcome several months after the meat is frozen.

Storage Time for Roasts:

Beef	8 to 12 months
Fresh pork	4 to 8 months
Veal	4 to 8 months
Lamb	8 to 12 months

CHOPS

Chops should be individually wrapped for ease in separating to defrost and then overwrapped with freezer wrap. A family-size unit is most practical. Seal, label, and date.

Storage Time for Chops:

Fresh pork	3 to 4 months
Veal	3 to 4 months
Lamb	3 to 4 months

STEAKS

Wrap with freezer wrap, conforming as much as possible to the shape of the steak. Seal, label, and date. Be sure to give weight or number of servings. If individual steaks are frozen, wrap each individually and then overwrap. This helps to separate for defrosting.

When freezing meats with bone, such as steaks or chops, should the bone protrude, cover it with several thicknesses of aluminum foil to prevent the bone from making a hole through the wrap.

Storage Time for Steaks:

Beef	8 to 12 months
Fresh pork	4 months
Veal	4 months
Lamb	4 months

GROUND MEATS

It is best to package ground meats in individual servings. Either wrap individually or put 2 pieces of freezer wrap between each meat patty (for ease in separation to defrost), and overwrap with freezer wrap.

It is best to omit salt in ground meats to be frozen. Sausage, however, may have the other spices added.

Storage Time for Ground Meats:

Beef	2 to 3 months
Fresh pork	2 months
Unsalted pork sausage	2 months
Veal	2 to 3 months
Lamb	2 to 3 months

STEWING MEATS

Cut meat into stew-size cubes, and freeze in family-size units. Package or wrap the meat. Seal, label, and date.

Storage Time for Stewing Meats:

Beef	2 to 3 months
Fresh pork	2 months
Lamb	2 to 3 months

CURED MEATS

Cured meats such as hams, bacon, frankfurters, and sausages lose quality rapidly in the freezer. If it is necessary to freeze them, they should be used as soon as possible.

Storage Time for Cured Meats: 1 month

VARIETY MEATS

Liver, heart, tongue, etc., may be frozen, but not as successfully as the remainder of the animal.

The liver may be partially frozen, sliced to suit taste, then repackage with 2 thicknesses of freezer paper between slices, overwrapped with freezer wrap, sealed, labeled, and dated.

Wrap heart, tongue, and other variety meats in freezer wrap, after first trimming, ready to cook. Seal, label, and date.

Storage Time for Variety Meats: No longer than 4 months.

COOKING FROZEN MEAT

Frozen meat can be cooked either frozen or defrosted, and there are many opinions on the subject, differing widely. My personal preference is to defrost the meat when possible and cook as one would if the meat were just purchased.

If this is not convenient, add additional cooking time, at least ⅓ more to the cooking method being used, as it will be necessary to defrost the meat as well as cook it.

Thaw meat in the refrigerator or at room temperature. The refrigerator is preferable. Roasts require 5 to 8 hours per pound. At room temperature allow 2 to 3 hours per pound, with some loss of juices.

Treat thawed meat the same as fresh. Cook as quickly as possible, and store under refrigeration.

IN FOIL

A great deal of coverage has been given to the method of wrapping meat, fish, or chicken to be frozen in heavy-duty foil and then cooking from the frozen state in the foil wrap. This is possible and many times practical. It is well to remember, however, that it is a special kind of cooking which does not produce the same results as standard methods: The foil-wrapped food will be braised rather than truly broiled or roasted.

RECIPES

BEEF

BEEF FILLET GRETÉ WITH BÉARNAISE SAUCE

3 tablespoons butter
1 beef fillet (about 1½–2 pounds)
½ pound fresh mushrooms, finely chopped

¼ cup finely chopped onions
¼ cup finely chopped fresh parsley
1 tablespoon tomato juice

After Freezing:

1 cup Béarnaise Sauce (below)

Heat butter in skillet, and brown fillet quickly on all sides. Remove from skillet, and cool.

Add mushrooms, onion, and parsley to butter remaining in skillet (or add more butter if needed), and sauté for 2 or 3 minutes. Stir in tomato juice. Cool.

To Freeze: Slice cooled fillet in thin slices. Put a tablespoon of the mushroom mixture between each slice, and arrange on freezer foil. Wrap tightly. Seal, label, and date. Freeze.

To Serve: Unwrap package on oven-proof platter. Heat in a 425° F. oven for 30 minutes or until hot. Serve with Béarnaise Sauce.

Makes 4 servings.

Storage Time: Up to 6 months.

Béarnaise Sauce

3 egg yolks
1 tablespoon wine vinegar
1 tablespoon tarragon vinegar
1 sprig fresh parsley
1 teaspoon dried tarragon

½ teaspoon salt
⅛ teaspoon freshly ground black pepper
½ cup butter
½ cup boiling water

Put egg yolks, wine vinegar, tarragon vinegar, parsley, tarragon, salt, pepper, and butter in blender. Blend until smooth, about 5 seconds. Remove cover, and gently pour in ½ cup boiling water.

Pour mixture into top of double boiler, and cook over hot, not boiling, water, stirring constantly, until sauce is consistency of soft custard. Keep Béarnaise Sauce over warm water. Or it can be made in advance, refrigerated, and reheated.

Makes 1 cup sauce.

BRACCIOLI

4 pounds bottom round of beef	2 teaspoons basil
1 pound salt pork	2 teaspoons oregano
¾ cup diced ham	½ cup olive or vegetable oil
½ cup finely chopped fresh parsley	3 cups well-seasoned tomato sauce

Ask butcher to cut bottom round into 12 pieces, trim off all fat, and pound meat slices very thin. Chop salt pork and ham together until very fine. Add parsley, basil, and oregano, and mix. Spread mixture on slices of bottom round. Roll slices into small tight rolls, and secure with string. Heat vegetable oil in skillet, and brown meat rolls on all sides. Pour off any excess oil. Add tomato sauce, and cook meat over low heat until tender, about 1 hour.

Makes 12 servings.

To Freeze: Cool. Put as many rolls as would serve family unit in oven-proof dish or freezer container. Add sauce. Wrap with freezer wrap. Seal, label, date, and freeze.

To Serve: Heat rolls in 425° F. oven about 45 minutes

or until hot and bubbly. If necessary, add additional tomato sauce. Remove strings before serving.

Storage Time: Up to 2 months.

SAVORY BEEF BIRDS

4 pounds bottom round of beef
2 teaspoons salt
¼ teaspoon freshly ground pepper
⅛ teaspoon ground cloves

6 slices bacon
4 whole carrots, peeled
4 pieces celery
4 tablespoons oil
2 cups Beef Stock (page 163) or bouillon

After Freezing:
½ cup Beef Stock (page 163) or bouillon

Ask butcher to cut bottom round into 12 pieces, trim off fat, and pound meat slices very thin. Sprinkle with salt, pepper, and cloves. Cut bacon slices in half crosswise, and put ½ slice bacon, a piece of carrot, and a piece of celery on each piece of meat. Roll meat around filling, and secure with string. Heat oil in skillet, and brown meat on all sides. Add 2 cups Beef Stock or bouillon, cover, and simmer about 1 hour.
Makes 12 birds.

To Freeze: Cool. Wrap rolls individually, and overwrap in family-size units. Seal, label, date, and freeze.

To Serve: Unwrap rolls needed. Place in skillet with ½ cup Beef Stock or bouillon, cover, and cook over low heat until heated through, 30 to 35 minutes. Remove strings before serving.

Storage Time: Up to 2 months.

BEEF POT ROAST

4- or 5-pound beef pot roast,
   defrosted
5 or 6 slices salt pork
2 tablespoons brandy
1 cup Beef Stock (page 163)
2 cups dry white wine
½ teaspoon thyme
1 bay leaf
½ teaspoon freshly grated or
   ground nutmeg
1 teaspoon salt
¼ teaspoon freshly ground
   pepper
5 carrots, peeled
8 small white onions

Remove all fat from beef. Cover with salt pork, and tie in place. Brown on all sides in a deep casserole or roasting pan. Add brandy, stock, and wine. Season with thyme, bay leaf, nutmeg, salt, and pepper. Cover and simmer over low heat until tender, about 3 hours. Add carrots and onions, and continue cooking another ¾ to 1 hour. Remove salt pork from pot roast. Slice meat, and serve with pan gravy, carrots, and onions.

Makes 6 to 8 servings.

STEAK CHATELAINE

4 tablespoons soft butter
4 tablespoons cooked
   marrow *
½ teaspoon salt
⅛ teaspoon freshly ground
   pepper
¼ teaspoon freshly grated or
   ⅛ teaspoon ground
   nutmeg
1 tablespoon lemon juice
2 tablespoons finely chopped
   shallots
1 tablespoon chopped fresh
   parsley
2-pound sirloin steak,
   defrosted

Mix the butter with marrow, salt, pepper, nutmeg,

* Buy marrow bones. Boil in a small amount of water for 30 to 40 minutes. Cool. Remove marrow, and mash. Measure and use as directed.

lemon juice, shallots, and parsley. Trim the fat from the steak, and broil to desired doneness. A 1-inch-thick steak 3 inches from source heat: 15 minutes rare, 20 minutes medium rare. Turn once. Spread with butter mixture, and return to broiler for 1 minute or until hot. Slice to serve.
Makes 4 servings.

BEEFSTEAK VENEZUELA

2½ pounds round steak, par-
    tially defrosted
5 tablespoons olive oil
¾ cup sliced onion
1 clove garlic, crushed

2 bay leaves, crushed
2 teaspoons salt
½ teaspoon freshly ground
    pepper

While meat is still partially frozen, cut into strips ¼ inch thick, 1 inch wide, and about 3 inches long. Heat oil in a large skillet. Add beef, and cook and stir for several minutes. Add onion, garlic, bay leaves, salt, and pepper, and continue to cook and stir until meat is crisp and browned. Serve with steamed rice.
Makes 6 servings.

GROUND BEEF

When ground beef is a meat-counter special, buy as large a quantity as you can easily handle, and spend a day preparing ground beef recipes for the freezer. You will be happy you did!

To Prepare for Freezing: It is very practical to sauté ground beef until lightly browned. Pour off excess fat, and cool. Then pack into freezer containers in measured amounts, and label, date, and freeze.

If no scale is available to weigh the ground beef before it is sautéed, 1 pound of relatively fat-free ground beef when cooked measures about 2 cups.

TOMATO MEATBALLS

1 ½ pounds ground beef
   chuck
1 ½ teaspoons salt
½ teaspoon freshly ground
   pepper
2 tablespoons finely minced
   onion
1 egg, beaten
4 tablespoons flour

2 tablespoons butter
2 cups sieved canned
   tomatoes
½ teaspoon Worcestershire
   sauce
¼ teaspoon Tabasco sauce
½ teaspoon dry mustard
1 tablespoon sugar

After Freezing:

¼ cup freshly grated
   Parmesan cheese

Lightly mix ground beef with salt, pepper, onion, and egg. Form into balls, and roll in flour. Heat butter in skillet, and brown floured meatballs. Add tomatoes, Worcestershire and Tabasco sauces, mustard, and sugar. Cover and simmer over low heat 15 minutes.
Makes 6 servings.

To Freeze: Chill. Pack meatballs and sauce into containers. Cover. Label, date, and freeze.

To Serve: Defrost in skillet over low heat. If necessary, add ½ cup water. When defrosted and hot, add ¼ cup grated Parmesan cheese. Serve with spaghetti.

Storage Time: Up to 2 months.

MAGGIE'S MEAT LOAF

1 ½ cups soft bread crumbs
   (about 2 slices bread)
1 cup (1 8-ounce can) tomato
   sauce
1 egg

1 ½ teaspoons salt
1 teaspoon Worcestershire
   sauce
1 small onion, grated
2 pounds ground beef chuck

Combine soft bread crumbs with tomato sauce, egg, salt, Worcestershire, and onion. Mix well. Add beef, and stir until blended with crumb mixture. Mix lightly so the meat does not pack any more than necessary. Spoon meat mixture into a greased 9 x 5 x 4-inch loaf pan, and smooth top. Bake in a 375° F. oven for 1 hour and 15 minutes.
Makes 10 servings.

To Freeze: Cool. Cut meat loaf into serving slices, and insert a piece of aluminum foil between each slice. Over-wrap whole loaf with aluminum foil. Seal, label, date, and freeze.

To Use: The package may be opened and as many slices removed as needed. Defrost and serve cold, or wrap in aluminum foil, place on a baking sheet, and heat in a 400° F. oven for 15 minutes or until hot.

Storage Time: Up to 2 months.

INDIVIDUAL BARBECUED MEAT LOAVES

½ cup dry bread crumbs
¾ cup milk
1 egg
¼ cup grated onion
1 teaspoon salt
⅛ teaspoon freshly ground
    pepper

1 pound ground beef chuck
2 tablespoons brown sugar
1 tablespoon vinegar
3 tablespoons catsup
½ teaspoon dry mustard
½ teaspoon Worcestershire
    sauce

Combine bread crumbs with milk, egg, onion, salt, and pepper. Mix well. Lightly stir in ground beef. Pack into buttered 2½-inch muffin pans. Mix brown sugar with remaining ingredients, and spoon over meat in pans. Bake in a 350° F. oven for 30 minutes.
Makes 6 servings.

To Freeze: Cool. Remove meat loaves from pan. Wrap

individually with freezer wrap. Seal, label, and date. Freeze. Store together in a box or plastic bag.

To Serve: Place unwrapped meat loaves on baking sheet. Heat in 400° F. oven about 30 minutes.

Storage Time: Up to 3 months.

SWEDISH CABBAGE ROLLS

1 medium head firm cabbage
1 pound ground beef chuck
½ pound ground lean pork
1 cup fine dry bread crumbs
½ cup finely diced onion
2 tablespoons beef broth
1 cup cooked rice

⅛ teaspoon nutmeg
⅛ teaspoon cinnamon
1 teaspoon salt
¼ teaspoon freshly ground
  pepper
2 tablespoons butter

After Freezing:
½ cup Beef Stock (page 163)

Trim the outer leaves from cabbage as necessary. Cut out its core. Steam the cabbage in a small amount of boiling salted water until leaves are wilted, about 5 minutes. Carefully cut off leaves. Mix the ground beef and pork with the bread crumbs, onion, beef broth, and rice, and season with the nutmeg, cinnamon, salt, and pepper. Shape into egg-size rolls, and place 1 in the center of each cabbage leaf. Fold over the ends and sides, and secure with toothpicks. Heat the butter in a skillet, and brown the cabbage rolls. Cover and cook over very low heat, adding beef broth if necessary, for 30 minutes.

Makes about 8 servings.

To Freeze: Wrap chilled rolls individually in freezer wrap. Store in containers, or overwrap together with freezer wrap. Seal, label, date, and freeze.

To Serve: Put frozen rolls in skillet. Add a small amount of Beef Stock. Cover. When defrosted, continue to simmer slowly about 15 minutes.

Storage Time: Up to 2 months.

SOPHISTICATED SPOONBURGERS

1 pound frozen pre-cooked
   ground beef
1 teaspoon onion salt
1 pint sour cream

¼ pound mushrooms, sliced
½ cup water
Dash Angostura bitters
6 buns, split and toasted

Combine frozen ground beef with onion salt, sour cream, mushrooms, and water in a saucepan. Cook, covered, over very low heat until meat is defrosted and mixture is hot. Add Angostura bitters.
Serve on buns. Makes 6 servings.

LAMB

DEVILED LAMB CHOPS

12 shoulder lamb chops
6 tablespoons soft butter
½ cup prepared mustard

3 teaspoons paprika
3 teaspoons grated onion

To Freeze: Freeze lamb chops, but do not wrap. Mix butter with mustard, paprika, and onion. Spread on both sides of frozen chops. Wrap each individually, and overwrap in family-size units. Seal, label, date, and return to freezer.

To Serve: Place frozen chops under broiler 4 inches

from source of heat. Broil about 8 to 10 minutes on each side for medium to well-done lamb chops. For rare chops broil 5 minutes on each side.

Makes 6 servings.

Storage Time: Up to 2 months.

ROAST LEG OF LAMB

1 6½-to-7½-pound leg of
    lamb, defrosted
2 garlic cloves, peeled
1 teaspoon salt

1 teaspoon crushed rosemary
⅛ teaspoon freshly ground
    pepper

Wipe lamb, and make a slit next to bone at each end of leg. Push a garlic clove into each slit. Rub outside of lamb with a mixture of salt, rosemary, and pepper. Place on rack in roasting pan, and bake in a 325° F. oven. For well-done lamb, bake 30 minutes per pound, or until meat thermometer registers 175° F. For rare lamb, bake 20 minutes per pound, or until meat thermometer registers 150° F.

Makes 6 servings plus leftovers.

PORK

VERMONT PORK PIE

2 pounds ground lean pork
1½ cups chopped onion
2 cups chopped celery
2 cups Chicken Broth
    (page 167)
2 teaspoons salt

¼ teaspoon freshly ground
    pepper
1 teaspoon poultry seasoning
⅛ teaspoon cloves
2 cups soda-cracker or saltine-
    cracker crumbs
Pastry for 2 9-inch pies

Combine the pork with the onion, celery, and Chicken Broth. Sauté in a skillet over low heat for 15 to 20 minutes. Add salt, pepper, poultry seasoning, and cloves, and remove from heat. Add cracker crumbs, mix well, and cool. Divide pastry into 4 parts. Roll out 1 part, and fit as bottom crust of 1 pie shell. Then roll out second part, and fit as bottom crust of second pie shell. Add pork filling to each pie shell. Roll out remaining 2 parts of pie pastry, and cover each pie. Seal and flute edges.

Each pie makes 6 servings.

To Freeze: Wrap pies in freezer wrap. Seal, label, and date. Freeze.

To Use: Defrost and bake in a 425° F. oven for 45 minutes or until nicely browned. Serve hot, cut in wedges.

Storage Time: Up to 2 months.

BARBECUED SPARERIBS

2 tablespoons butter
¾ cup coarsely chopped
   onion
1 large clove garlic, minced
2 tablespoons wine vinegar
2 tablespoons lemon juice
¼ cup firmly packed light-
   brown sugar
2 teaspoons salt
½ teaspoon freshly ground
   black pepper
2 teaspoons dry mustard

½ teaspoon Tabasco sauce
1 bay leaf
¼ teaspoon oregano
¼ teaspoon basil
¼ teaspoon thyme
2 cans (8-ounce) tomato
   sauce
¼ cup water
6 pounds pork spareribs
Salt
Freshly ground pepper

Heat butter in saucepan, and sauté onion until soft. Combine onion and butter with garlic, vinegar, lemon juice, brown sugar, salt, pepper, mustard, Tabasco sauce, bay leaf, and herbs with 1 can tomato sauce in blender. Blend 30 seconds or until smooth, and return to saucepan. Add remaining can of tomato sauce and water, and simmer over low heat 15 minutes.

Meanwhile, trim as much fat as possible from spareribs. Cut between ribs to make individual ribs for serving. Place spareribs on rack in large baking pan, sprinkle lightly with salt and pepper, and bake at 425° F. for 30 minutes. (Either use Teflon-lined baking pans or line other pans with aluminum foil to facilitate cleaning.) Reduce heat to 350° F. Brush ribs with barbecue sauce, and continue baking for another hour. Baste with sauce about every 10 minutes. Ribs should be browned and crusty when done.

Makes 12 servings.

To Freeze: Cool. Wrap in serving-size packages. Label, date, and freeze.

To Serve: Heat in 425° F. oven about 20 to 30 minutes.

Storage Time: Up to 6 weeks.

PORK CHOPS

To Prepare Pork Chops for Freezing: Trim excess fat from chops. Render pork fat in skillet, lightly frying. Dip pork chops in flour, and quickly brown both sides in pork fat. Cool. Wrap chops individually. Overwrap packages of a number according to size of family, that is, 1 or 2 chops per person. Label and date. Freeze.

Storage time: Up to 4 months.

ORANGE BAKED PORK CHOPS WITH YAMS

3 fresh yams, peeled and cut into ½-inch slices
½ cup firmly packed brown sugar
6 prebrowned frozen pork chops
6 orange slices, peeled
½ teaspoon ground cloves
⅔ cup fresh orange juice

Arrange yams in bottom of buttered casserole. Top with brown sugar. Arrange pork chops on top of yams and brown sugar. and add 1 orange slice to each pork chop. Mix cloves and orange juice, and pour over chops and yams. Cover and bake in a 350° F. oven for 1 hour. Remove cover, and bake 15 minutes longer, basting several times with orange and brown-sugar sauce.

Makes 6 servings.

PORK CHOPS TAPPAN

3 tablespoons butter
¾ cup diced onion
½ cup diced celery
½ cup diced carrot
4 prebrowned frozen pork
    chops

1 cup Chicken Broth
    (page 167)
1 teaspoon salt
½ teaspoon freshly ground
    pepper
½ teaspoon thyme

Put butter in skillet, and lightly sauté onion, celery, and carrot. Arrange the pork chops on top of the vegetables, and add Chicken Broth. Season with salt, pepper, and thyme. Simmer until tender, approximately 45 minutes.

Makes 4 servings.

IOWA PORK CHOPS

4 prebrowned frozen pork
    chops
⅔ cup uncooked long-grain
    rice
3 cups water
4 slices tomato
4 slices onion

4 green pepper rings
1 teaspoon salt
½ teaspoon freshly ground
    pepper
½ teaspoon thyme
½ teaspoon basil

Arrange pork chops in buttered casserole. Add rice to 3 cups boiling water, and boil for 5 minutes. Meanwhile, arrange 1 slice tomato, 1 slice onion, and 1 green pepper ring on each pork chop. Spoon rice and water over pork chops. Season with salt, pepper, thyme, and basil. Cover and bake at 350° F. for 1 hour. Uncover and bake 15 minutes longer. Add ½ cup water if necessary.

Makes 4 servings.

PORK CHOPS IN TOMATOES

2 cups canned whole
    tomatoes
1 clove garlic, finely minced
1 onion, sliced
1 teaspoon basil
½ teaspoon oregano
¼ teaspoon Tabasco sauce

½ teaspoon sugar
1 teaspoon salt
½ teaspoon freshly ground
    pepper
4–6 prebrowned frozen pork
    chops

Combine in a large skillet the tomatoes, garlic, onion, basil, oregano, Tabasco sauce, sugar, salt, and pepper. Cook over medium heat, stirring occasionally, until mixture begins to boil. Add 4 to 6 pork chops. Cover and simmer over very low heat until tender, about 45 minutes. Serve with steamed rice.

Makes 4 to 6 servings.

VEAL

VEAL PROFILE

4 pounds veal steak, cut into
    1-inch cubes
Flour (about ⅓ cup)
2½ teaspoons salt
¼ teaspoon freshly ground
    pepper

½ cup butter
2 medium onions, grated
2 bay leaves
2 teaspoons Worcestershire
    sauce
3 cups hot water

After Freezing:

2 pints sour cream

Dip cubes of veal into flour seasoned with salt and pepper. Heat butter in skillet, and brown veal pieces on all sides. Add onion, bay leaves, Worcestershire sauce, and water to skillet. Cover and simmer over low heat about 1 hour.

Makes 12 servings.

To Freeze: Chill. Put meat and gravy in 2 containers. Cover, label, date, and freeze. Mark on each container to add 1 pint sour cream when heated.

To Serve: Cook meat over low heat, covered, until defrosted and tender, about 45 minutes. Just before serving stir in sour cream. Reheat, but do not boil. Serve with cooked spinach noodles or egg noodles.

Storage Time: Up to 3 months.

3 Poultry

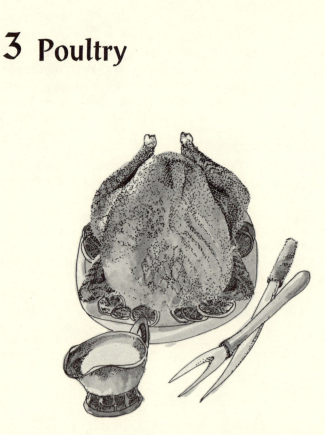

GENERAL INSTRUCTIONS FOR
FREEZING UNCOOKED POULTRY

Before freezing uncooked poultry, you should prepare it for the intended cooking method. Freeze only fresh poultry of good quality. Handle quickly during processing, and observe sanitary conditions.

Wrap each piece of poultry individually for freezing so that when the poultry is used, the frozen pieces can be easily separated for defrosting. Nothing is more frustrating, for example, than to try to separate 2 halves of a broiler which are solidly frozen together. Individual wrapping eliminates this.

32

WHOLE BIRDS

If the birds are purchased in a market, already dressed, be sure to remove the package of giblets and neck inside the bird. Wash bird well inside and out under running water. Dry inside and out. Fasten wings under back of bird, and wrap body closely in freezer wrap. Secure with tape. Label, date, and freeze.

If home-raised poultry is being frozen, remove feathers, and draw bird. Wash well, and chill thoroughly before wrapping to freeze. Holding 12 hours at a temperature below 40° F. is the recommended length of time to chill before freezing.

Note: Do not stuff birds before home freezing. (Commercially frozen stuffed birds are prepared under conditions that cannot be duplicated in the home.)

To Use: Remove freezer wrappings, place on tray, and cover loosely. Thaw in refrigerator. Thawing may be speeded up by putting bird in a water-tight bag and immersing in cold water.

TIMETABLE FOR THAWING WHOLE BIRDS IN REFRIGERATOR

Chickens	4 pounds and over	1–1½ days
	Less than 4 pounds	12–16 hours
Rock Cornish Game Hens	1–1½ pounds	8–9 hours
Ducks	3–5 pounds	1–1½ days
Geese	4–14 pounds	1–2 days
Turkeys	18 pounds and over	2–3 days
	Under 18 pounds	1–2 days

Storage Time: Chicken, Rock Cornish Game Hen, and Turkey up to 12 months.
Duck and Goose up to 6 months.

CUT-UP POULTRY

All poultry can be halved and/or quartered before freezing. If one cuts up a great deal of poultry, a pair of poultry shears to use for cutting bones is a worthwhile investment. Otherwise, work on a clean cutting board with a well-sharpened knife.

To disjoint chickens, remove bag of giblets and neck. Lay chicken on back on cutting board. Cut off wings. Cut off legs and thighs. Cut leg and thigh apart. Starting at vent end, cut crosswise toward neck to remove breast. Breast may be split lengthwise or wishbone section cut across front of breast, and remainder of breast split. (This depends somewhat on size of chicken; with smaller chickens, split breast lengthwise.) Cut back into 2 pieces. Wash cut-up pieces well, and dry.

To Freeze: Wrap pieces individually in freezer wrap. Pack in family-size portions into plastic bag or overwrap. (Whether back pieces are wrapped for freezing to fry or separately for broth depends on family tastes.) Label, date, and freeze.

To Use: Remove pieces from bag, unwrap, place on tray, cover loosely, and defrost in refrigerator. Medium-size chicken cut in pieces will take about 1½ hours. Once frozen raw chicken is fully or partially defrosted, it can be used for any recipe calling for raw chicken.

Storage Time: Up to 12 months.

HALF OR QUARTER BROILERS

Choose well-formed broilers weighing from 2 to 3 pounds. Remove packages of giblets and neck from inside bird. Lay bird on back, and cut through breast meat and bone from neck to vent. Spread bird open. Cut along backbone on both sides, and remove. Clip off wing tips. Small birds may be frozen in halves. Cut larger birds into quarter just below rib cage.

To Freeze: Wash and dry cut-up bird. Press wings against body, and wrap each piece individually. Store family-size servings in freezer bag, or overwrap together. Label, date, and freeze.

To Use: Thaw in refrigerator. Separate individually wrapped pieces. Remove wrapping, and place on tray in refrigerator. Cover loosely. Defrosts in about 3 to 4 hours.

Storage Time: Up to 12 months.

HALVED OR QUARTERED LARGER CHICKENS OR TURKEYS

In halves or quarters, cut through breast meat and bone from vent to neck. Remove backbone as instructed in directions for broiler (page 34). Cut off wing tips. Wash and dry pieces.

To Freeze: Wrap separately with freezer wrap. Store number of pieces in plastic bags according to use. Label, date, and freeze.

To Use: Thaw in refrigerator as suggested for broiler. Large turkeys require about 1 day; chicken halves 3 to 9 hours.

Storage Time: Up to 12 months.

HALVED AND QUARTERED DUCKS OR GEESE

Proceed as for larger chickens and turkeys.

Storage Time: Up to 6 months for geese and ducks.

CHICKEN BREASTS

When special prices are available on chicken breasts, buy and freeze for future use, or make up into some of the recipes in the cooked poultry section (pages 43–53). Breasts can be boned and frozen or frozen with bone in. Wash and dry well.

To Freeze: Wrap each breast separately for easier defrosting, overwrap, label number of breasts in package, date, and freeze.

To Use: Thaw in refrigerator. Separate breasts, remove wrappings, place on tray, cover loosely. Will be defrosted in about 3 to 4 hours.

Storage Time: Up to 12 months.

CHICKEN LIVERS

To Freeze: Freeze chicken livers separately from giblets. Do not freeze in units larger than 1 pint. Pack into a freezer container, label number of livers, date, and freeze.

To Use: Defrost in refrigerator. One pound livers defrosts in about 5 hours. Use same as fresh chicken livers.

Storage Time: Up to 6 months.

GIBLETS

To Freeze: Always freeze giblets separately. Wash, cut off and discard tough muscle section of gizzards, and dry well. Place in plastic bags. Label with approximate number of gizzards and hearts, and seal and freeze.

To Use: Frozen giblets may be put into water to simmer until tender, up to several hours, depending on size of bird from which taken. Season with salt, whole black pepper, celery, and onion. Use strained broth as liquid for gravy. Cut up giblets, and add to gravy.

Storage Time: Up to 6 months.

BACKS, NECKS, AND WING TIPS

Do not discard backs, necks, and wing tips. Make into broth as directed on page 167 at once, or wrap in freezer wrap, label, date, and freeze to use later. Protect against punctures in freezer wrap by placing several thicknesses of freezer foil over protruding bones.

Storage Time: Up to 12 months.

GENERAL SUGGESTIONS FOR
ROASTING POULTRY

Temperature should be 325° F. for chicken, turkey, duck, and goose.

ROASTING TIME PER POUND

Roasting Chicken	Under 4 pounds	30 minutes
	4 pounds and over	22–25 minutes
	Internal thermometer reading: 185° F.	
Turkey	6–8 pounds	3–3½ hours
	8–12 pounds	4–4½ hours
	12–16 pounds	5–5½ hours
	16–20 pounds	5½–6½ hours ·
	20–24 pounds	6½–7 hours
	Internal thermometer reading: 185° F.	

For duck and goose follow temperature and time chart recommended for chicken.

To roast unstuffed chicken from frozen state: Wrap frozen bird tightly in heavy-duty foil, using drugstore wrap. Place on rack in pan. Roast in a 425° F. oven 25 to 30 minutes per pound. Open foil last 30 minutes, and brush bird with butter several times.

BASIC STUFFING

The recommended rule of thumb is 1 cup stuffing per pound of poultry.

½ cup melted butter
½ cup chopped onion
1 cup chopped celery
4 cups stale bread cubes
1 teaspoon salt

⅛ teaspoon freshly ground pepper
1 teaspoon poultry seasoning
⅛ teaspoon thyme

Heat butter in skillet. Add onion and celery, and sauté over low heat until tender but not browned. Add bread cubes and season with salt, pepper, poultry seasoning, and thyme. Sauté and stir until bread cubes are lightly browned.
Makes about 4 cups stuffing.

Stuffing Variations

Mushroom: Cook 1 cup chopped fresh mushrooms with onion and celery.

Oyster: Cook 1 cup drained chopped oysters with onion and celery.

Chestnut: Boil, peel, and chop ½ pound chestnuts. Add with bread cubes.

Fruit: Omit onion, and add 1½ cups coarsely chopped steamed apricots, pitted prunes, or apples.

Sausage: Sauté ¼ pound freshly ground pork sausage, and add. Hot or sweet Italian sausage is especially good.

Ham: Dice ¼ pound piece of prosciutto. If prosciutto is not available, baked Virginia ham may be substituted.

GENERAL SUGGESTIONS FOR
BROILING POULTRY

Remove freezer wrap from broiler, and immerse broiler in marinade (see the following recipes) while it defrosts. This time-saving method gives flavorful cooked chicken. The marinade will solidify on the frozen chicken but will liquefy as the chicken defrosts.

To broil halves or quarters: Place on broiler rack 3 inches from source of heat. Broil 15 minutes, skin side down; turn and broil 15 minutes, skin side up. Brush with marinade several times during cooking.

Fast flavor trick: Mix 2 tablespoons each garlic, onion, and celery salts and paprika with 2 tablespoons olive or vegetable oil. Brush on chicken, and broil as directed. (With this marinade there is no need to brush during cooking.) Makes enough for 2 halves or 4 quarters.

RECIPES

CHICKEN

MARINADE ROCKPORT

1 cup olive or vegetable oil
1 teaspoon grated lemon rind
½ cup lemon juice
¼ cup crumbled blue cheese
½ teaspoon salt
2 tablespoons Worcestershire
   sauce
⅛ teaspoon Tabasco sauce
1 frozen broiler chicken,
   halved or quartered

Combine oil, lemon rind, lemon juice, and blue cheese. Season with salt and Worcestershire and Tabasco sauces.

Mix well. Marinate chicken in this mixture for 6 to 12 hours, before broiling. Baste with marinade during broiling process. Makes 1¾ cups marinade.

HERBED MARINADE

1 cup olive or vegetable oil
½ cup cider vinegar
1 teaspoon salt
1 teaspoon paprika
2 teaspoons onion salt

2 teaspoons crushed basil
½ teaspoon crushed thyme
1 frozen broiler chicken,
    halved or quartered

Combine oil, vinegar, salt, paprika, onion salt, basil, and thyme, and mix well. Put frozen broiler in marinade, and defrost. Marinate it for 6 to 12 hours. Baste with marinade while broiling.
Makes 1½ cups marinade.

MARINADE MONTEREY

¾ cup olive or vegetable oil
1 clove garlic, crushed or
    minced
3 tablespoons prepared hot
    mustard
1 teaspoon chili powder
½ teaspoon granulated sugar

2 tablespoons lemon juice
2 teaspoons salt
¼ teaspoon freshly ground
    pepper
1 frozen broiler chicken,
    quartered or disjointed

Combine oil, garlic, mustard, chili powder, sugar, lemon juice, salt, and pepper. Put cut-up frozen chicken pieces in marinade, and defrost. Marinate 1½ to 3 hours. Baste with marinade while broiling.
Makes about 1 cup marinade.

HONG KONG BAKED CHICKEN

8 chicken quarters
¼ cup sesame seeds
⅓ cup peanut oil
2 tablespoons grated onion
½ clove minced garlic
½ teaspoon salt

1 teaspoon freshly grated
    ginger or ½ teaspoon
    ground ginger
2 teaspoons soy sauce
⅛ teaspoon chili powder
1 teaspoon granulated sugar

Place the chicken quarters skin side down in a buttered baking dish. Mix together the sesame seeds, peanut oil, onion, garlic, salt, ginger, soy sauce, chili powder, and sugar, and brush chicken with about half of the mixture. Bake in 375° F. oven for 30 minutes. Turn chicken, and baste well. Bake about 30 minutes longer, basting frequently.

Makes 8 servings.

BAKED TEXAS CHICKEN

½ teaspoon salt
1 teaspoon paprika
¼ teaspoon freshly ground
    pepper
1 teaspoon chili powder
½ teaspoon ground cumin

2 cups finely crushed corn
    chips
1 3½-pound fryer, cut up and
    defrosted
¼ cup olive or vegetable oil

Add salt, paprika, pepper, chili powder, and cumin to corn chips, and mix well. Brush chicken with oil, and coat with crumb mixture. Arrange, skin side down, in buttered baking pan. Bake in a 375° F. oven for 30 minutes. Turn chicken pieces, and bake 20 to 25 minutes longer or until tender.

Makes about 4 servings.

CHICKEN BREASTS ELSIE

¼ pound chipped beef
8 small chicken breasts,
    boned
4 slices bacon, cut in half

½ cup sliced fresh mush-
    rooms
1 pint dairy sour cream
¼ cup chopped fresh parsley

Cut up beef, and arrange in bottom of flat buttered baking dish. Place chicken breasts on beef, skin side up. Place ½ strip bacon over each breast. Mix mushrooms with sour cream, and pour over chicken. Bake, uncovered, for about 1½ hours in a 300° F. oven. Just before serving, sprinkle with chopped parsley.

Makes 8 servings.

SHERRIED CHICKEN BREASTS

⅓ cup flour
1 teaspoon seasoned salt
¼ teaspoon freshly ground
    pepper
4 large chicken breasts,
    halved

¼ cup vegetable or olive oil
2 tablespoons butter
½ teaspoon crushed rose-
    mary
⅔ cup dry sherry

Mix flour with seasoned salt and pepper, and coat chicken breasts with flour mixture. Heat oil and butter in skillet. Add chicken, and brown lightly on both sides. Pour off any remaining fat. Sprinkle chicken with rosemary, and add sherry. Cover and simmer over low heat about 40 minutes or until tender.

Makes 8 servings.

GENERAL INSTRUCTIONS FOR
FREEZING COOKED POULTRY

Cooked poultry can be prepared especially for freezing, or you may freeze that leftover turkey or capon cooked for a holiday meal.

When especially roasted for freezing, cool the cooked bird quickly in the refrigerator. Do not stuff roasted poultry for freezing. Cut meat from bones. Pack white meat and dark meat separately, and package meat with as little air space as possible to lessen chances of rancidity during storage.

Cooked poultry may be frozen with or without gravy or broth.

Package pieces with broth or gravy in freezer containers.

Slices may be packaged in freezer wrap. Label and date before freezing.

To Use: Thaw sliced poultry in refrigerator. Poultry packed in gravy or broth may be heated in oven or on top of range.

Storage Time: Cooked poultry in broth or gravy up to 6 months. Sliced poultry up to 1 month.

RECIPES

CHICKEN

FRIED CHICKEN

Prepare fried chicken according to your favorite recipe. Cool quickly in refrigerator.

To Freeze: Wrap each piece individually, and place

enough for family-size serving in plastic bag, or overwrap. Seal, label, date, and freeze.

To Use: Unwrap chicken, place on buttered baking sheet, and heat in a 400° F. oven about 30 minutes or until thoroughly heated.

Storage Time: Up to 4 months.

GOLDEN CHICKEN

4 tablespoons butter
8 tablespoons flour
4 cups Chicken Broth
   (page 167)

12 cups cooked chicken or
   turkey
1 cup diced cooked ham
1 tablespoon salt
½ cup diced pimiento

After Freezing (for 1 container):

1 egg
1 cup dairy sour cream
¼ cup dry white wine

1 3-ounce can Chinese
   noodles

Melt butter, and add flour. Stir in Chicken Broth, and cook and stir until mixture boils. Add chicken and ham, and season with salt and pimiento.
Makes 16 to 24 servings.

To Freeze: Cool quickly. Spoon into 4 freezer containers. Label, date, and freeze.

To Serve: Defrost 1 container of chicken over low heat in saucepan. When hot, beat together egg, sour cream, and wine. Add to chicken mixture, and heat. Do not boil. Serve over Chinese noodles.
Makes 4 to 6 servings.

Storage Time: Up to 2 months.

CHICKEN FRIED RICE

2 cups diced cooked chicken
   or turkey
1 teaspoon salt
2 tablespoons soy sauce
⅔ cup peanut oil
4 cups uncooked long-grain
   rice

5 cups Chicken Broth
   (page 167)
1 cup chopped onion
1 cup thinly sliced celery
½ cup chopped green pepper

After Freezing (for 1 container):

2 tablespoons peanut oil   2 eggs

Mix chicken with salt and soy sauce, and let stand while preparing remainder of dish. Heat peanut oil in skillet, and add rice. Cook and stir until rice is lightly browned. Add Chicken Broth and chicken gradually to the rice in skillet. Cover and simmer 15 minutes. Stir in onion, celery, and green pepper.

Makes 16 servings.

To Freeze: Cool. Pack lightly into 4 quart containers. Label, date, and freeze.

To Serve: Defrost 1 quart container. Spoon into skillet with about 2 tablespoons peanut oil. Heat thoroughly over low heat. Beat eggs slightly. Push rice to one side, and fry (scramble) eggs until almost set. Mix in with rice.

Makes about 4 servings.

Storage Time: Up to 4 months.

CHICKEN KIEV

16 broiler chicken breasts
(about 8 pounds)
2 cups butter
3 tablespoons chopped fresh
parsley
3 tablespoons chopped fresh
chives
2 teaspoons ground rosemary

2 cloves garlic, finely minced
3 teaspoons salt
½ teaspoon freshly ground
pepper
3 eggs
3 tablespoons water
2 cups fine dry bread crumbs

Bone chicken breasts, and flatten with a rolling pin between pieces of waxed paper. Chill in refrigerator. Soften butter, and mix with parsley, chives, rosemary, garlic, salt, and pepper until well blended. Shape into 16 rolls, and freeze. When frozen, wrap chicken breasts around butter roll, and secure by tying with thread. Leave a length of thread long enough to find after cooking so that it may be cut and removed. Beat eggs lightly with water. Dip chicken breasts in egg mixture, then in bread crumbs. Let stand on rack 10 to 15 minutes for coating to set. Each roll is 1 serving.

To Freeze: Wrap each roll individually in freezer wrap, and seal. Freeze. Place in container to store to avoid damage. Label and date.

To Serve: Remove wrappings, and place on baking dish. Bake in a 425° F. oven for 35 to 40 minutes. Remove thread before serving.

Storage Time: Up to 2 months.

HOMEMADE CHICKEN PIE

9 cups cooked chicken (or turkey), cut in large pieces
¾ cup chicken fat
⅔ cup flour
6 cups Chicken Broth (page 167)

Salt and freshly ground pepper to taste
18 Pie Pastry Triangles or 18 Pie Pastry Circles (below)

Put chicken pieces in 3 flat round 6-cup casseroles or 18 1-cup casseroles. Heat fat with flour in saucepan. Gradually stir in Chicken Broth. Cook and stir until sauce begins to boil and thicken. Season with salt and pepper. Pour over chicken in casserole. Cover and cool. Top large casserole with Pie Pastry Triangles; individual pies with Pie Pastry Circles.

To Freeze: Chill. Overwrap complete casserole with freezer wrap. Seal, label, and date. Freeze.

To Serve: Remove wrap. Place in a 425° F. oven. Bake large pie 50 to 60 minutes or until top is browned and pie heated through. Bake individual pies at 425° F. for 40 minutes or until brown and hot.
Makes 3 large or 18 small pies.

Storage Time: Up to 3 months.

Pie Pastry Triangles

3 cups all-purpose flour
3 teaspoons baking powder
1½ teaspoons salt
¾ cup shortening

¾ cup hot water
¾ cup butter
1 teaspoon wine vinegar
3 egg yolks

Sift the flour, baking powder, and salt together. With a fork cut in the shortening. Combine hot water, butter, and vinegar, and cool. Beat in the egg yolks. Stir into flour mixture, just to blend. Chill. On a lightly floured board roll ⅓ of pastry ⅛ inch thick into a circle ½ inch smaller than circle size of a large round casserole. Cut into 6 triangles. Repeat with other two thirds of pastry.

Makes 18 circles.

Pie Pastry Circles

Follow instructions for Pie Pastry Triangles (above), but instead of rolling dough into a circle large enough for a large round casserole, make the circles (using a cookie cutter) just a little smaller than the tops of individual pies.

Makes 18 circles.

COLD CHICKEN MARGUERITE

4 2½-to-3 pound fryers,
   cut up
½ cup olive or vegetable oil
2 teaspoons salt
¼ teaspoon freshly ground
   pepper

2 teaspoons paprika
1 teaspoon tarragon
4 tablespoons butter
2 cups dry sherry

Cut up chickens, and save bony pieces for Chicken Broth (page 167). Put oil in flat baking dish. Add chicken pieces in single layer. Sprinkle chicken with salt, pepper, paprika, and tarragon, and dot with butter. Pour sherry over chicken. Bake in a 350° F. oven about 40 minutes or until chicken is tender and browned. Baste with sherry several times during cooking.

Makes 16 servings.

To Freeze: Chill. Wrap pieces individually with freezer wrap. Overwrap in family-size units. Seal, label, date, and freeze.

To serve: Defrost and unwrap chicken. Serve cold.

Storage Time: Up to 3 months.

CHICKEN LOTUS

3 frying chickens, cut up
½ cup flour
1 teaspoon salt
Dash freshly ground pepper
⅔ cup peanut oil
1½ cups diced onion
3 medium green peppers, diced
¾ cup soy sauce
3 cups sliced fresh mushrooms
3 cups diced fresh or canned pineapple
½ teaspoon ground cloves
1 teaspoon freshly grated ginger or ½ teaspoon ground ginger
3 teaspoons grated orange peel

Wash and dry chicken pieces, and coat with flour mixed with salt and pepper. Brown chicken on all sides in peanut oil, about 20 minutes. Divide chicken between 3 freezer dishes, and cool. Add onion and green pepper to oil, and sauté until tender but not browned. Add soy sauce, mushrooms, pineapple, cloves, ginger, and orange peel, and mix well.
Makes 12 servings.

To Freeze: Cool. Spoon sauce over chicken in 1-quart freezer dishes. Wrap, seal, label, date, and freeze.

To Serve: If frozen in oven-proof dishes, bake, covered, in a 425° F. oven for 40 minutes. Uncover and bake 15 minutes longer or until cooked through. If freezer dish is not oven-proof, defrost enough to remove chicken from pan, and transfer to a baking dish.

Each container serves 4.

Storage Time: Up to 6 weeks.

CHICKEN BREASTS PARVENU

8 chicken breasts
⅓ cup flour
1 teaspoon salt
¼ teaspoon freshly ground
    pepper
6 tablespoons butter

½ clove garlic, crushed
1 cup chopped onion
1 pound fresh mushrooms,
    sliced
2 cups dry vermouth

After Freezing:
½ pound white grapes

Bone, remove skin, and cut chicken breasts in half. Mix flour with salt and pepper, and coat chicken breasts. Heat butter in skillet, and brown chicken lightly on both sides. Remove from skillet. Cool. Add garlic, onion, and mushrooms to skillet. Simmer gently for 5 minutes. Add vermouth, and simmer 5 minutes longer.

Makes 8 servings.

To Freeze: Arrange chicken breasts in flat freezer dish in single layer. Pour sauce over chicken. Cool. Cover tightly. Label, date, and freeze.

To Serve: If frozen in oven-proof dish, bake, covered, in a 400° F. oven for 40 minutes. Uncover and cook 15 minutes longer, basting several times with sauce. If freezer dish is not oven-proof, defrost enough to remove chicken from pan, and transfer to baking dish. Serve garnished with icy-cold white grapes.

Storage Time: Up to 6 weeks.

CHICKEN BAHAI

3 2½-to-3-pound fryers,
   cut up
Flour (about ½ cup)
1 teaspoon salt
¼ teaspoon freshly ground
   pepper
½ cup peanut oil

2 cups orange juice
1½ cups pineapple juice
½ teaspoon freshly grated
   nutmeg or ground
   nutmeg
⅛ teaspoon cloves

After Freezing:

1 cup drained pineapple
   chunks

1 cup drained Mandarin
   oranges
1 cup chopped cashew nuts

Cut up chickens, and save bony pieces for Chicken Broth (page 167). Mix flour with salt and pepper. Coat chicken pieces in flour, and brown in skillet in hot oil. As pieces are browned, transfer to large casserole. Pour off remaining oil. Add orange and pineapple juices, nutmeg, and cloves to skillet. Scrape crust from bottom, and heat to boiling. Pour over chicken, and bake, covered, in a 350° F. oven about 40 minutes.
Makes 8 to 12 servings.

To Freeze: Cool. Divide chicken into 2 oven-proof dishes. Divide sauce evenly over each portion. Wrap, seal, label, date, and freeze.

To Serve: Bake chicken, covered, in 400° F. oven for 30 minutes. Remove cover, and to each casserole add ½ cup pineapple chunks, ½ cup Mandarin oranges, and ½ cup chopped cashew nuts. Continue baking 15 to 20 minutes longer or until chicken is thoroughly heated.
Each casserole makes 4 to 6 servings.

Storage Time: Up to 4 months.

4 Fish and Shellfish

GENERAL INSTRUCTIONS FOR
FREEZING FISH AND SHELLFISH

Because there are so many varieties of fish available in the United States, I am going to give general directions for various types and recipes for many varieties.

Fish freezes well. Since it spoils quickly, it should be frozen as soon as possible after being caught or purchased, and it should be handled in clean surroundings. A reminder: Freezing does not improve quality, it only preserves what is present.

Fish is categorized as "fatty" or "lean." Fatty fish includes sea bass, butterfish, halibut, eel, lake trout, mackerel, pompano, salmon, shad, smelt, sturgeon, tuna, and whitefish. Some of the lean fish are cod, catfish, bluefish, flounder, haddock, hake, perch, pickerel, swordfish, red snapper, black and white bass, spotted trout, pike, and pollack. Fatty fish should be used within 3 months after freezing; lean fish can be kept up to 6 months.

Fish may be frozen whole, as it comes from the water. It may be eviscerated only, with the head, tail, and fins left on, or they may be removed. Fish may be filleted without any bones or if large enough, cut crosswise into steaks or chunks. This versatility means that fish may be frozen for any recipe.

Whole or eviscerated whole fish may be glazed. This is done by freezing the fish, dipping it in cold water to get a coating of ice, freezing, and dipping again until a coat of the desired thickness is achieved. This retards evaporation of moisture from fish and also enables a sportsman to show off his prize catch. However, I'd still recommend packaging glazed fish in freezer wrap.

A trick I've learned from sportsmen makes use of the heavy plastic-coated paperboard of half-gallon milk cartons. After they are empty, open the top wide, and wash well. With scissors cut a piece off the top about ½ inch wide. (This makes a circle; do not cut.) Holding the opposite sides from the one used to pour the milk, pull the top down on the outside of the carton. Place the circular strip down around to hold the top down. The result is a fine carton for whole fish. To use it as a freezer container, clean fish, put into carton, and surround with finely crushed ice to hold fish in place. Then fill with cold water, close, secure top, and label, date, and freeze.

Because I always seem to have more time when I'm freezing fish than when I'm getting ready to cook it, I recommend that fish be frozen "pan-ready." However, in emergencies fish can be frozen "straight from the brook."

Fish should be defrosted in the refrigerator, or in an emergency in the package under *cold* running water. Because fish is delicate and easily overcooked, I prefer to defrost it before cooking. This gives you better control of the cooking and insures even cooking throughout. However, fish can be cooked from the frozen state.

GENERAL RULES

Freezing is an excellent way of keeping fish and shellfish. These general rules should be followed:

1. Freeze immediately while the fish is still fresh. Remember, freezing does not improve quality, and *only* fresh products should be frozen.

2. It is wisest to have the fish ready for preparation when frozen. Then it can be cooked from a frozen state if desired.

3. Keep the fish clean so it is not contaminated before going into the freezer.

4. Suit packaging of fish to the product. Always use moisture-proof, vapor-proof wrapping or containers.

5. Raw frozen fish keeps from 4 to 6 months at 0° F. or below.

6. Cooked frozen fish keeps 2 to 3 months at 0° F. or below.

7. Frozen fish should be either cooked from the frozen state or defrosted in the refrigerator. In an emergency the packaged fish can be defrosted under cold running water.

8. Fish should be tightly wrapped in freezer wrap, and sealed.

9. Always label frozen fish with amount in cups or pounds, and date.

10. In freezing several small fish in 1 package or several steaks (or even fillets) wrap the individual pieces in freezer wrap (or transparent wrap) before overwrapping. This way the pieces are easier to separate for defrosting.

11. Freeze in recipe or family-size units.

WHOLE FISH

Clean fish as follows:

1. Wash well.

2. Remove scales by gently scraping with dull side of knife from tail to head. Rinse fish.

3. Remove entrails. First slit fish belly from vent to

head, and remove entrails. Rinse. Fish can now be frozen if desired. Wrap in freezer wrap, using drugstore fold. Seal, label, and date. Or, before freezing, you may also:

4. Remove head by first cutting above the collarbone. Then break backbone over edge of table.

5. Remove back fin. Cut around fin with sharp knife so fin bones will not be left in fish.

6. Wash again.

FISH STEAKS

If the fish is large enough, it can be cut crosswise into steaks as thick as one wishes, generally 1 to 1½ inches. There will be the backbone and some rib bones in a fish steak.

FISH FILLETS

Cut fish lengthwise away from the backbone. Fish fillets should be completely boned.

FISH FILLETS

1 pound fish fillets (sole, perch, bass, halibut), thinly sliced
1 egg
1 tablespoon water

1 cup fine dry bread crumbs
Cooking fat or oil
Lemon slices
Tartar Sauce (page 81)

Wash and cut fillets into serving-size pieces. Mix egg with water. Dip fish fillets first in egg, then in bread crumbs. Let coated fillets dry on waxed paper for about 5 minutes. Heat about 2 inches of cooking fat or oil in skillet, and brown fish quickly. Remove from fat, and drain on absorbent paper.

Makes 3 servings.

To Freeze: Put cooled fillets on cookie sheet, and freeze until frozen solid. Remove and pack in containers with piece of freezer wrap between fillets. Label, date, and return to freezer.

To Use: Remove as many cooked fillets as needed. Place on a cookie sheet, and heat in a 425° F. oven 15 to 20 minutes or until thoroughly heated through. Serve with lemon slice and/or Tartar Sauce.

Storage Time: Up to 4 months.

FISH STOCK

If you have decided to fillet the fish, you will have bones with fish flesh still on them.

FISH STOCK

1 cup fish bones *	1 teaspoon salt
1 medium-size onion	1 small bay leaf
1 carrot, sliced	¼ teaspoon thyme
1 stalk celery, sliced	1 cup dry white wine
1 sprig parsley	1½ cups water
6 peppercorns	

In large saucepan combine fish bones with vegetables, seasonings, wine, and water. Cover and simmer 15 minutes. Remove fish from bones, strain liquid, and freeze the fish and liquid together for fish chowder or for recipes calling for fish stock.

* If fish bones are not available, use ½ cup ragged pieces trimmed off fish fillets.

RECIPES

SOLE, FLOUNDER, HADDOCK, COD, AND HALIBUT

FISH ROLLS WITH ANCHOVY SAUCE

2 pounds fish fillets (sole, flounder), defrosted
2 cups Fish Stock (page 58)
4 tablespoons butter
4 tablespoons flour

1 tablespoon anchovy paste
Salt and freshly ground pepper to taste
2 tablespoons chopped fresh parsley

Cut fillets lengthwise in strips 1 to 2 inches wide. Roll, starting at narrow end. Fasten with toothpick, or secure with thread. Pour Fish Stock into large skillet. Add fish rolls to stock, and bring just to boiling point. Simmer fish, covered, for about 8 minutes or until it flakes easily with a fork. Remove fish rolls to a hot platter. Remove toothpicks or thread. Keep hot. Melt butter in saucepan. Stir in flour, and cook until bubbly. Measure 2 cups Fish Stock, and gradually stir in with a wire whisk. Stir in anchovy paste. Continue stirring until mixture begins to boil and thickens. Season with salt, pepper, and parsley.

Makes 6 servings.

PROVINCETOWN FISH SOUP

2 tablespoons butter
1½ cups chopped onion
¾ cup chopped green pepper
2 cups canned tomatoes
1 teaspoon salt
2 cups diced potatoes

6 cups water
2 pounds boneless haddock or cod, defrosted
1 tablespoon vinegar
Pinch of saffron

Heat butter in large saucepan, and sauté onion and green pepper until tender but not browned. Add tomatoes, salt, potatoes, and water. Cover and cook 15 to 20 minutes or until potatoes are tender. Cut fish into small pieces, and add with vinegar and saffron to potato mixture. Cook, below boiling, another 10 minutes or until fish flakes.
Makes 6 to 8 servings.

To Freeze: Add only 3 cups water, and omit saffron. Cook 10 minutes. Add fresh fish, and simmer 5 minutes. Cool, ladle into container, and label. Mark container: "Add 3 cups water and a pinch of saffron." Freeze.

To Use: Empty into saucepan, and add 3 cups water. Cook, covered, over low heat until defrosted. Add pinch of saffron.

Storage Time: Up to 3 months.

HALIBUT MOUSSE WITH LOBSTER SAUCE

1 pound boneless halibut	¼ teaspoon Tabasco sauce
2 cups bread crumbs made from bread several days old	1 tablespoon lemon juice
	4 egg whites, stiffly beaten
	Mayonnaise
2 cups light cream, scalded	Lobster Sauce (page 61)
¾ teaspoon salt	

Defrost halibut, and put through finest blade of meat grinder. Combine bread crumbs, scalded cream, salt, Tabasco sauce, lemon juice, and halibut. Mix well. Cool to lukewarm. Fold beaten egg whites into halibut mixture. Spoon fish mixture into a 6-to-8-cup mold which has been rubbed with mayonnaise. Set mold in a pan of hot water, and bake in a 350° F. oven for 30 minutes or until mousse is firm. Unmold on platter, and serve at once with Lobster Sauce.
Makes 6 servings.

Lobster Sauce

½ pound fresh mushrooms,
    sliced
3 tablespoons butter
2 tablespoons flour
1½ cups light cream
3 egg yolks, lightly beaten

¼ cup dry sherry
1 cup diced precooked lobster
    meat, defrosted
½ teaspoon salt
Dash freshly ground black
    pepper

Sauté mushrooms in butter for 5 minutes. Stir in flour. Gradually stir in the cream, egg yolks, and sherry. Cook, stirring over very low heat, until mixture thickens. Stir in lobster meat. Season with salt and pepper.

Makes 3 cups sauce.

PORTUGUESE FISH AND CHIPS

½ cup cider vinegar
1½ cups water
1 clove garlic, finely minced
⅛ teaspoon ground cumin
⅛ teaspoon oregano
½ teaspoon salt
Dash freshly ground black
    pepper

2 pounds fish fillets (sole,
    flounder, haddock), de-
    frosted
½ cup cornmeal
Fat for frying
Frozen french-fried potatoes,
    prepared as directed on
    package

Combine vinegar, water, garlic, cumin, oregano, salt, and pepper, and mix well. Add fish fillets. Cover and marinate in refrigerator for several hours. When ready to serve, remove fish from vinegar solution. Dry on absorbent paper, and roll in cornmeal. Heat fat (about ¼ inch deep) in large skillet, and fry fish quickly, carefully turning to brown both sides. Serve with french-fried potatoes.

Makes 6 servings.

TROUT, PERCH, CATFISH, AND BASS

PAN-FRIED TROUT, PERCH, OR CATFISH

6 pan-dressed fish (trout, perch, or catfish), defrosted
¼ cup evaporated milk
1 teaspoon salt
Dash freshly ground pepper
½ cup flour
¼ cup cornmeal
1 teaspoon paprika
Bacon fat for frying

Wash and dry fish. Mix evaporated milk, salt, and pepper in a flat dish such as a pie plate. Mix flour, cornmeal, and paprika on waxed paper. Heat about ⅛ inch fat in a 12-inch skillet. Dip fish first in milk, then in cornmeal. Fry in hot fat, turning carefully to brown both sides, about 5 minutes on each side. If fish flakes easily with a fork, it is done.
Makes 6 servings.

BAKED STUFFED WHOLE FISH

1 3-to-5-pound whole fish (bass, trout, shad, salmon, catfish, or perch), defrosted
Salt
Freshly ground pepper
¼ cup butter
2 tablespoons finely chopped celery
1 tablespoon finely chopped onion
2 cups cubed day-old bread
2 tablespoons lemon juice
½ teaspoon thyme
1 tablespoon chopped parsley
½ teaspoon salt
2 tablespoons softened butter
Butter for basting
1 lemon, cut in wedges

The fish may have head and tail on or not, as one desires. Wash well and dry. Season inside of fish with salt and pepper. Heat butter in skillet, and sauté celery and onion until tender but not browned. Stir in bread cubes, lemon juice, thyme, parsley, and ½ teaspoon salt, blending well. Stuff into cavity of fish, and sew shut, or close with skewers. Brush outside of fish with softened butter. Grease and line pan with a strip of heavy-duty aluminum foil, and place fish on foil. Bake in a 400° F. oven about 10 minutes per pound or until fish flakes easily with fork. Baste several times with butter during baking. Fish should separate easily from bone. To serve, remove fish from pan by lifting on foil strip. Transfer to platter. Serve with lemon wedges.

One 3-pound fish will serve about 4 people.

Note: This is a basic recipe. The stuffing can be varied with such herbs or spices as one wishes or with the addition of finely chopped mushrooms, nuts, or water chestnuts.

BAKED BASS WITH SHRIMP STUFFING

1 pound cleaned shrimp
1 egg
¼ cup heavy cream
1 teaspoon salt
⅛ teaspoon freshly ground
   pepper

½ cup sherry wine
1 4-pound whole cleaned
   bass, defrosted
1 cup heavy cream
2 slices Bermuda onion
1 lemon, cut in wedges

Chop or grind shrimp coarsely. Mix with egg, ¼ cup cream, salt, pepper, and sherry. Spoon into cavity of bass, and fasten shut with toothpicks, or sew. Place in a buttered flat casserole, add additional cup cream, and bake at 375° F. for 30 minutes. Place onion around fish, and bake 15 minutes longer or until fish flakes easily. Serve with lemon wedges.

Makes 4 to 6 servings.

SALMON AND SWORDFISH

BAKED FISH STEAKS WITH CREOLE SAUCE

2 tablespoons butter
¼ cup chopped green pepper
¼ cup chopped onion
1 small garlic clove, finely
    minced
2 cups canned tomatoes

1 small bay leaf
¼ teaspoon ground cloves
½ teaspoon salt
½ teaspoon granulated sugar
2 pounds fish steaks (salmon,
    swordfish), defrosted

Heat butter in saucepan. Sauté green pepper, onion, and garlic until tender but not browned. Add tomatoes, bay leaf, cloves, salt, and sugar, and simmer 10 to 15 minutes. Arrange fish steaks in a flat buttered casserole. Pour creole sauce over fish. Bake in a 400° F. oven for 25 to 30 minutes or until fish can be flaked easily with a fork.

Makes 4 servings.

To Freeze: Use fresh fish steaks. Bake fish in a flat casserole lined with heavy-duty foil at 400° F. for 20 minutes. Cool. Freeze. Remove from casserole. Wrap top with foil. Overwrap with plastic wrap or plastic bag. Label, date, and return to freezer.

To Serve: Unwrap and return to casserole in which it was originally baked. Bake in a 425° F. oven for 35 to 40 minutes or until thoroughly hot and cooked.

Storage Time: Up to 1½ months.

Note: Baked Fish Steaks with Creole Sauce may be doubled. Bake one half for dinner at 400° F. for 30 minutes. Bake and freeze other half as directed.

POACHED SALMON STEAKS

2 pounds salmon steaks,
   frozen
2 tablespoons butter
¾ cup apple juice
1 teaspoon salt
1 small bay leaf
½ cup light cream

2 tablespoons flour
¼ pound fresh mushrooms,
   sliced
¼ cup dry white wine or
   vermouth
2 tablespoons chopped fresh
   parsley

Defrost salmon steaks, and cut into 6 portions. Melt butter in a skillet, and place fish in pan. Add apple juice, salt, and bay leaf. Cover and simmer for 5 to 7 minutes or until fish flakes easily with fork. Remove fish to hot platter, and keep hot. Discard bay leaf. Mix cream and flour to make a smooth paste. Add with mushrooms and wine to pan juices, and cook and stir until mixture boils and is thickened. Pour over salmon steaks. Sprinkle with chopped parsley.

Makes 6 servings.

BAKED SWORDFISH

¼ cup flour
1 teaspoon salt
⅛ teaspoon freshly ground
   pepper
2 swordfish steaks (about 3
   pounds), defrosted

1 sprig fresh dill, chopped, or
   1 teaspoon crushed dill
   seed
1 small onion, thinly sliced
4 tablespoons butter
½ teaspoon paprika
1 cup dry sherry

Mix flour with salt and pepper, and rub on both sides of swordfish steaks. Arrange 1 steak in casserole in which it will fit fairly neatly, allowing room for the sherry. Sprinkle with dill, and cover with onion slices. Dot with 2 tablespoons of butter. Place second steak on top of first. Dot with remaining butter, and sprinkle with paprika. Pour sherry around fish. Bake in a 425° F. oven for 30 minutes or until fish flakes easily with a fork. Baste several times with sherry. To serve, cut through both slices, so each person has a swordfish "sandwich."

Makes 6 servings.

SHRIMP

Shrimp may be frozen in the shell or peeled and deveined. It may be raw or cooked when frozen.

RAW SHRIMP IN THE SHELL

To Freeze: Wash well in several waters to remove sand. If there are heads on the shrimp, cut them off. Wash in brine (1 teaspoon salt to 1 quart water). Drain shrimp well. If the shrimp is to be frozen loose, spread drained shrimp on a baking sheet or other flat pan. Put into coldest place in freezer. Freeze. When frozen, package as desired, in plastic bags, containers, or wrap. Seal, label, and date. Return to freezer.

If shrimp is frozen loose, any amount can be removed that is needed, so size of package is not important.

Otherwise, drained shrimp can be packaged in family-size units. Seal, label, date, and freeze.

To Use: Drop frozen shrimp in boiling salted water. When water boils again, cook 5 minutes. Drain at once, and rinse in cold water.

Storage Time: Up to 6 months.

PEELED AND DEVEINED RAW SHRIMP

To Freeze: Peel, devein, and wash shrimp well. Drain. To freeze the shrimp loose, spread on a baking sheet or other flat pan. Put into coldest place in freezer. Freeze. When frozen, package as desired in plastic bags or wrap. Seal, label, and date. Return to freezer.

If shrimp is frozen loose, any amount can be removed that is needed, so size of packages is not important.

Otherwise, drained shrimp can be packaged in family-size units. Seal, label, date, and freeze.

To Use: Drop frozen shrimp in boiling salted water. When water boils again, cook 3 minutes. Drain at once, and rinse in cold water.

Storage Time: Up to 6 months.

COOKED SHRIMP

To Freeze. Remove shells, and devein shrimp. Wash well. Place in boiling, lightly salted water. Bring again to a boil, and cook 3 minutes. Drain and cool in cold water immediately. Drain well. To freeze loose, spread the cooked, cooled shrimp on baking sheet or other flat pan. Put into coldest place in freezer. Freeze. When frozen, package as desired in plastic bags or wrap. Seal, label, and date. Return to freezer.

If shrimp is frozen loose, any amount can be removed that is needed, to size of package is not important.

Otherwise, drained shrimp can be packaged in family-size units.

To Use: Defrost shrimp in refrigerator.

Storage Time: Up to 4 months.

SPICY SHRIMP

1 quart boiling water
2 tablespoons mixed pickling
    spice
½ teaspoon Tabasco sauce

½ teaspoon salt
1 pound raw frozen shrimp
    in the shell

To boiling water add mixed pickling spice, Tabasco sauce, and salt. Add frozen shrimp. When water boils again, cook 5 minutes. Let shrimp cool in spicy liquid.

Makes 3 to 4 servings.

BEER SHRIMP

1 pound raw frozen shrimp, shelled and deveined
1 sprig fresh dill
3 or 4 celery leaves
6 peppercorns
½ bay leaf
16 ounces beer (2 cups)

Put frozen shrimp in saucepan. Add dill, celery leaves, peppercorns, bay leaf, and beer. Bring to a boil. Separate shrimp as they defrost. Cook 3 to 5 minutes. Cool in liquid.

Makes 3 to 4 servings.

SHRIMP COCKTAIL

12 to 20 cooked, shelled shrimp
Lettuce
2 lemon wedges
Shrimp Cocktail Sauce (below)

Depending on the size of the shrimp, allow 6 to 10 shrimp for each serving. Arrange some shredded lettuce and a small lettuce leaf in a stemmed cocktail glass or on a small flat plate. Arrange shrimp on lettuce. Garnish with a wedge of lemon. Serve with Shrimp Cocktail Sauce.

Makes 2 servings.

Shrimp Cocktail Sauce

1 cup prepared chili sauce
2 tablespoons lemon juice
1½ tablespoons Worcestershire sauce
1½ tablespoons prepared horseradish
⅛ teaspoon Tabasco sauce

Combine chili sauce with lemon juice, Worcestershire sauce, horseradish, and Tabasco sauce. Chill well.

Makes about 1¼ cups sauce.

HOT LEMON SHRIMP

½ cup butter
3 cups shrimp, defrosted, cooked, peeled, and de- veined
3 tablespoons lemon juice

Dash Tabasco sauce
Dash tarragon
1 tablespoon chopped parsley
Salt and freshly ground pepper to taste

Melt butter in a flat pan or skillet. Add shrimp, and heat thoroughly. Stir in lemon juice, Tabasco sauce, tarragon, parsley, salt, and pepper. Heat. Serve as a first course on small plates. Pour sauce from skillet over shrimp.

Makes 6 servings.

SHRIMP REMOULADE

2 tablespoons wine vinegar
1 teaspoon salt
¼ teaspoon freshly ground pepper
6 tablespoons olive oil
2 tablespoons prepared hot mustard
2 teaspoons prepared horse- radish
⅓ cup finely minced shallots or finely minced scallions and their tops

1 teaspoon chopped fresh parsley, tarragon, and/or chervil
1 teaspoon anchovy paste
1 teaspoon chopped gherkins
1 teaspoon capers
½ teaspoon garlic salt
½ teaspoon paprika
3 cups shrimp, defrosted, precooked, peeled, and deveined

Mix wine vinegar with salt and pepper. Gradually beat in oil until all is blended. Blend in remaining seasonings, one at a time. Mix with shrimp. Marinate shrimp in remoulade suace for several hours to blend flavors. Serve on flat plates with crusty bread.

Makes 6 servings.

SHRIMP MARINARA

3 tablespoons olive oil
1 clove garlic, chopped
½ teaspoon oregano
½ teaspoon basil
2 cups canned tomatoes
½ teaspoon salt
Dash Tabasco sauce
½ cup dry white wine

3 cups shrimp, defrosted, precooked, peeled, and deveined
2 tablespoons freshly chopped parsley
1 pound linguini or thin spaghetti, cooked *al dente*

Heat olive oil in skillet. Add garlic, and sauté until light brown. Add oregano, basil, tomatoes, salt, Tabasco sauce, and wine, and simmer, covered, about 30 minutes. Add shrimp and parsley, and simmer 10 minutes longer. Serve over hot linguini.

Makes 4 to 6 servings.

SHRIMP AND RICE

4 slices bacon
1 cup uncooked long-grain rice
½ cup chopped onion
¼ cup chopped green pepper
¼ cup chopped celery
2 cups canned tomatoes

1 cup water
1 teaspoon salt
½ teaspoon chili powder
2 cups shrimp, defrosted, precooked, peeled, and deveined

Cut bacon into small pieces, and fry in a large skillet until almost crisp. Remove bacon. Add rice, and cook and stir until rice is browned. Add onion, and cook until tender but not browned. Stir in green pepper, celery, tomatoes, water, salt, and chili powder. Cover and simmer 15 to 20 minutes or until all liquid is absorbed and rice is tender. Stir in cooked bacon and shrimp, and heat.

Makes 6 servings.

SHRIMP SALAD

2 to 3 cups shrimp, defrosted, precooked, peeled, and deveined
2 tablespoons French dressing
1 cup finely diced celery
2 tablespoons capers
½ cup mayonnaise
Salt
Freshly ground pepper
Crisp lettuce
1 tomato, sliced
4 hard-cooked eggs, sliced

Cut shrimp into small pieces. In a bowl mix shrimp with French dressing. Cover and marinate in refrigerator for several hours. When ready to serve, lightly toss shrimp with celery, capers, and mayonnaise. Season with salt and pepper according to taste.

Serve on crisp lettuce leaves. Garnish with tomato and hard-cooked egg slices.

Makes 4 to 6 servings.

MOBILE PICKLED SHRIMP

2 pounds frozen raw shrimp in shell
½ cup chopped celery leaves
¼ cup whole mixed pickling spice
2 quarts boiling water
2 cups sliced onions
1½ cups vegetable or olive oil
1½ cups white vinegar
5 bay leaves
2 tablespoons capers with liquid
1½ teaspoons celery seed
1½ teaspoons salt
¼ teaspoon Tabasco sauce

Thaw, peel, and devein shrimp. Wash in cold water. Cook celery leaves and pickling spice together for 10 minutes in boiling water. Add shrimp, and simmer, covered, 3 to 5 minutes. Drain. In a glass or pottery bowl arrange layers of shrimp and onion. Combine oil, vinegar, bay leaves, capers, celery seed, salt, and Tabasco sauce, and pour over shrimp and onions in bowl. Cover and let stand in refrigerator overnight. Drain. Serve as an appetizer on shredded lettuce or in a bowl with toothpicks as an hors d'oeuvre.

Makes 10 servings.

SCALLOPS

Scallops, a member of the mollusk family, are a delicacy well worth freezing when they are at their peak in production and lowest in price. Bay or cape scallops are small and highly prized. Ocean scallops, which are larger and not so sweet in flavor, are also very good. The edible part of a scallop is the muscle. Cooked scallops can be frozen, but we recommend freezing them raw.

To Freeze Scallops Raw: Wash and pick any pieces of shell from raw scallops. Wash again in brine (⅓ cup salt per gallon water). Drain. Pack into containers or plastic bags of a size suitable for a family-serving unit. Seal, label, and date. Freeze.

To Use: Defrost scallops in refrigerator until they can be separated.

Storage Time: Up to 4 months.

SAUTÉED SCALLOPS

3 cups frozen raw scallops
¼ teaspoon salt
¾ cup fine dry bread crumbs
6 tablespoons butter

⅛ teaspoon Tabasco sauce
Lemon wedges or Tartar
    Sauce (page 81)

Defrost scallops, and sprinkle with salt. Coat with bread crumbs. Heat butter and Tabasco sauce in a large skillet. Add breaded scallops, and sauté quickly, turning to brown both sides, 5 to 6 minutes. Serve with lemon wedges or Tartar Sauce.

Makes 4 to 6 servings.

BROILED SCALLOPS

3 cups frozen raw scallops
⅓ cup soy sauce
⅓ cup lemon juice
⅓ cup vegetable oil

½ teaspoon seasoned pepper
2 tablespoons freshly
    chopped parsley

Make sure scallops are all approximately the same size, and defrost. Mix soy sauce with lemon juice, oil, and seasoned pepper. Add scallops, mix, and coat well. Marinate in refrigerator for several hours. When ready to cook, drain scallops and put in a shallow heat-proof pan. Broil 3 inches from source of heat about 3 minutes or until lightly browned. Sprinkle with parsley before serving.

Makes 4 to 6 servings.

BROTHER GIRARD SCALLOPS

3 cups sea scallops, defrosted
¼ cup honey
¼ cup prepared mustard

2 teaspoons curry powder
1 teaspoon lemon juice

Line a broiler-proof pan with aluminum foil. Arrange scallops in a single layer on foil. Mix honey with mustard, curry powder, and lemon juice. Brush scallops with mixture. Broil 3 inches from heat source for 5 minutes, basting and turning.

Makes 6 servings.

SCALLOP CHOWDER

1 quart frozen raw scallops
½ cup diced salt pork
1 cup diced onion
2 cups diced, peeled raw
    potatoes
Water
3 cups milk

½ teaspoon salt
¼ teaspoon freshly ground
    pepper
2 tablespoons butter
2 sprigs fresh parsley,
    chopped

Defrost scallops. If large scallops are used, cut into 4 pieces. In a large saucepan fry salt pork and onion together until salt pork is crisp and onions are tender. Add potatoes and water just to cover. Simmer, covered, about 20 minutes or until potatoes are tender. Add scallops, milk, and heat just to boiling. Keep below boiling point for about 15 minutes to blend flavors. Season with salt and pepper. When ready to serve, add butter and garnish with fresh parsley.

Makes 6 servings.

To Freeze: Prepare as directed until ready to add scallops. Cool. Add scallops. Freeze in containers. Label, and date. Note on lid to add 3 cups milk to container.

To Heat: Combine milk with chowder base in top of double boiler. Heat until chowder is defrosted and hot.

Storage Time: Up to 6 months.

SCALLOP CASSEROLE

4 cups frozen raw scallops
1 tablespoon grated onion
1 cup thinly sliced fresh
    mushrooms
4 tablespoons lemon juice
6 tablespoons butter, melted

1 teaspoon salt
⅛ teaspoon freshly ground
    pepper
Dash Tabasco sauce
¾ cup fresh bread crumbs

Defrost scallops, and cut into small pieces. Place in bowl. Mix in onion, mushrooms, lemon juice, butter, salt, pepper, and Tabasco sauce. Let stand for 30 minutes. Spoon into a buttered flat 6-cup casserole. Top with fresh bread crumbs.
Bake in a 425° F. oven for 25 to 30 minutes.
Makes 6 servings.

CLAMS

In some areas fresh clams are available all year round, so freezing is not necessary. On the other hand, if there is great seasonal variation in price, freezing may be economically feasible. Do not freeze clams in the shell except where indicated in recipes.
Broadly, clams are divided into hard-shell and soft-shell

clams. Locally they are called by various names. In New England, for example, there are quahogs *and* clams. Quahogs are hard-shell clams that are generally shucked, chopped, and used for clam chowder. Young hard-shells, known as littleneck and cherrystone clams, are used for clam cocktails. Surf clams (also called chowders, since they are mainly used for chowder) are another variety of hard-shell clams. On the Pacific Coast clam species include butter, littleneck, razor, and pizmo.

To Freeze: Save liquid. Remove from shell. Wash clams in lightly salted water, and drain. Package with liquid in family-size units. Seal, label, date, and freeze.

To Use: Always defrost clams in the refrigerator.

Storage Time: Up to 6 months.

CLAM COCKTAIL

Defrost enough clams so that there will be 6 or 8 per person. Arrange on bed of shredded lettuce in stemmed glass or on a small plate. Serve with Clam Cocktail Sauce (below).

Clam Cocktail Sauce

¾ cup catsup   2 tablespoons lemon juice
¼ cup prepared horseradish   ¼ teaspoon Tabasco sauce

Combine catsup with horseradish, lemon juice, and Tabasco sauce. Chill well.
Makes about 1 cup sauce.

CLAM PIE

4 cups sifted all-purpose   1⅓ cups shortening
    flour   ⅔ cup ice water
1½ teaspoons salt   Clam Filling (below)

Sift flour with salt. Cut in shortening with pastry blender or 2 knives until texture of cornmeal. Add water, and stir lightly to form a ball. Divide in half, and roll on floured board or pastry cloth into 2 circles to fit 2 9-inch pie plates. Fill with Clam Filling. Roll out remaining pastry to fit tops. Wet edges of bottom shell. Fit on top. Seal and flute edges. Makes 6 servings.

To Freeze: Put prepared pies in freezer. When frozen, wrap, seal, label, and date. Mark on label: "To Bake: 425° F. oven for 50 to 60 minutes."

To Serve: Pie can be baked from freezer or defrosted in refrigerator. Bake in 425° oven for 50 to 60 minutes or until pie is cooked and browned.

Storage Time: Up to 3 months.

Clam Filling

6 cups raw, ground quahog   1 cup evaporated milk
    clams   ½ teaspoon freshly ground
1 cup finely chopped onion   pepper
2 cups fine cracker crumbs   ½ teaspoon thyme
    (use Pilot crackers)

Combine clams with onion, cracker crumbs, and evaporated milk, and mix well. Season with pepper and thyme. Enough for 2 9-inch pies.

STUFFED BAKED CLAMS

2½ dozen cherrystone clam shells
1½ cups fine cracker crumbs
¼ cup finely minced shallots or onions
⅛ teaspoon freshly ground pepper
⅛ teaspoon Tabasco sauce
½ teaspoon oregano
½ teaspoon Worcestershire sauce
¾ cup prepared mayonnaise
3 cups chopped drained clams

Scrub clam shells well. Rinse and pat dry.

Mix cracker crumbs with onion, pepper, Tabasco sauce, oregano, Worcestershire sauce, mayonnaise, and clams. Fill shells with mixture. Place on a baking sheet or other flat pan, and freeze.

Makes 30.

To Freeze: Put frozen stuffed clams in a suitable container. Overwrap with freezer wrap. Seal, label, date, and return to freezer.

To Use: Place frozen clams on baking sheet. Bake at 350° F. for 12 to 15 minutes. If desired after baking they may be lightly browned under broiler for about 3 minutes.

Storage Time: Up to 6 weeks.

CLASSIC CLAM CHOWDER BASE

¼ pound salt pork
1 cup finely chopped onion
3 cups diced potatoes
2 cups boiling water

2 dozen raw chowder clams, chopped, including juice (about 3 cups chopped clams and juice)

After Freezing:

2 cups milk
2 tablespoons butter

Salt
Freshly ground pepper

Cut salt pork from rind, and dice into small pieces. In a saucepan fry salt pork until crisp. Add onion, and continue cooking until tender but not browned. Add potatoes and boiling water. Cover and cook until potatoes are just tender. Remove from heat, and add clams and juice, mixing well.
Makes 6 servings.

To Freeze: Cool. Spoon into 2 1-quart containers. Cover, label, and date. Freeze. Mark on container: Add 2 cups milk, 2 tablespoons butter, and salt and pepper to taste when reheating.

To Serve: Put frozen clam chowder base in top of double boiler. Add milk, butter, and salt and pepper to taste. Heat over boiling water.

Storage Time: Up to 3 months.

NEW ENGLAND CLAM CHOWDER

3 cups chopped frozen raw clams and juice	Water (about 2 cups)
⅓ cup diced salt pork	3 cups milk
¾ cup chopped onion	2 tablespoons butter
3 cups diced raw potatoes	Salt and freshly ground pepper to taste

Defrost clams. Do not drain. Cook salt pork and onion together in a saucepan until pork is lightly browned and onions are tender. Add potatoes and water to cover. Cover and cook until potatoes are tender, about 20 minutes. Add the milk, and bring just to the boiling point. Stir in clams and juice, and reheat. Do not boil. Let clam chowder stand over low heat for 15 to 20 minutes to blend flavors. When ready to serve, add butter, and season to taste with salt and pepper.
Makes 4 servings.

MANHATTAN CLAM CHOWDER

¼ pound diced bacon or salt pork
½ cup diced onion
2 cups diced potatoes
1 cup diced carrots
½ cup diced celery
1 small bay leaf
1 teaspoon thyme
⅛ teaspoon Tabasco sauce
1 teaspoon salt
Water (about 2 cups)
4 cups chopped raw clams, defrosted
2 cups canned tomatoes
2 teaspoons Worcestershire sauce

Cook bacon or salt pork and onion together in a saucepan until bacon is crisp and onion tender. Add potatoes, carrots, celery, bay leaf, thyme, Tabasco sauce, and salt. Add enough water to cover. Bring to a boil, and cook, covered, until vegetables are tender, about 15 to 20 minutes. Drain liquid from clams, and add enough water to make 5 cups. Add clam broth, tomatoes, and Worcestershire sauce to vegetables. Bring to a boil. Add clams, and cook just below boiling point for 10 to 15 minutes.

Makes 6 to 8 servings.

FRIED CLAMS

1 cup raw clams, defrosted
1 egg
1 tablespoon water
1 cup fine dry bread crumbs
Fat or oil for frying
Lemon wedges or Tartar Sauce (page 81)

Drain clams, and pat dry on towels. Beat the egg lightly with water. Dip the clams first in egg and then in the bread crumbs. Let stand on waxed paper for a few minutes to set coating. Heat fat (at least 3 inches deep) to 370° F., carefully put clams in hot fat, and cook until lightly browned. Drain on absorbent paper. Serve with lemon wedges or Tartar Sauce.

Makes 2 servings.

Tartar Sauce

1 cup mayonnaise
¼ cup drained sweet pickle
   relish
3 tablespoons chopped capers
1 tablespoon finely chopped
   onion

2 teaspoons prepared horseradish
2 tablespoons finely chopped
   parsley

Combine the mayonnaise with the pickle relish, capers, onion, horseradish, and parsley. Mix well. Chill 2 to 3 hours.

Makes 1¼ cups sauce.

FRIED CLAM FRITTERS

2 eggs, separated
1 cup sifted all-purpose flour
½ teaspoon baking powder
¼ teaspoon salt
2 teaspoons vegetable oil
½ cup milk

1 tablespoon lemon juice
1 pint defrosted raw clams,
   well-drained
Fat or oil for deep frying
Lemon wedges or Tartar
   Sauce (above)

Beat egg yolks until thick and lemon-colored. Sift the flour with baking powder and salt. Fold the flour, oil, milk, and lemon juice into the egg yolks. Beat egg whites until stiff but not dry. Fold the egg whites and clams into the flour mixture. Heat the fat (at least 3 inches deep) to 370° F.

Drop the clam mixture by the teaspoon into hot fat, and cook until lightly browned. Drain on absorbent paper. Serve hot with lemon wedges or Tartar Sauce.

Makes about 20.

WHITE CLAM SAUCE FOR SPAGHETTI

4 tablespoons butter
1 or 2 cloves garlic, minced
1 tablespoon flour
2 cups chopped raw clams, defrosted, and juice
4 tablespoons chopped fresh parsley
½ teaspoon salt
Dash freshly ground pepper
½ teaspoon thyme
½ teaspoon dried basil
1 pound thin spaghetti, cooked, drained, and tossed with butter

Heat butter in skillet. Add garlic, and cook for several minutes, but do not brown. Mix in flour, and cook until mixture bubbles. Stir in clam juice and parsley, and season with salt, pepper, thyme, and basil. Cook and stir over low heat for 5 minutes. Stir in clams, and heat through. Serve with hot spaghetti.

Makes 3 or 4 servings.

OYSTERS

Since oyster production has declined in recent years, it is a good idea to freeze oysters. Shucked oysters can be frozen raw if packaged in suitable containers. Oysters are graded by size and should be packed in little or no liquid. Small oysters are fine for oyster stew, scalloped oysters, or cocktails. Large oysters should be used for frying. Do not freeze oysters in the shell. However, if you wish to collect enough deep halves of oyster shells to save for serving oysters on the half shell, scrub well, dry, and store in plastic bags. Do not forget to wash after each use.

To Freeze: Check oysters for pieces of shell. Wash in lightly salted water. Drain. If oysters are to be used for making stew, they can be fairly high in liquid, since the liquid will help season the stew. If they are being used for fried oysters, remove excess liquid. Package oysters in suitable family units. Seal, label, and date. Freeze.

To Use: Always defrost oysters in the refrigerator.

Storage Time: Up to 6 months.

OYSTER COCKTAIL

Defrost oysters. Arrange 5 or 6, depending on size, on bed of shredded lettuce in stemmed glass or on small plate. Serve with Oyster Cocktail Sauce (below).

Oyster Cocktail Sauce

½ cup catsup
2 tablespoons tarragon
   vinegar
½ teaspoon paprika
¾ cup mayonnaise

½ teaspoon hot prepared
   mustard
¼ teaspoon garlic salt
Dash Tabasco sauce

To catsup add vinegar, paprika, mayonnaise, hot mustard, garlic salt, and a dash of Tabasco. Blend well with fork, and chill.
Makes 1½ cups sauce.

SCALLOPED OYSTERS

1 cup dry bread crumbs
1 pint raw oysters, defrosted
½ teaspoon salt
Dash freshly ground pepper

Dash Tabasco sauce
½ cup melted butter
½ cup light cream

Spread ⅓ of the bread crumbs in the bottom of a buttered 1-quart shallow casserole. Put ½ of the oysters on top of the bread crumbs, sprinkle with ½ of the salt, pepper, and Tabasco sauce. Repeat, ending with a layer of bread crumbs. Pour butter and cream over all. Bake in a 350° F. oven about 30 minutes or until hot.

Makes 4 to 6 servings.

OYSTERS CASINO

1 pint raw oysters, defrosted	2 tablespoons chopped chives
12 oyster shells	3 tablespoons dry bread
3 tablespoons chopped	crumbs
parsley	2 slices bacon, chopped

Drain oysters, and arrange shells in a layer in a flat oven-proof baking dish. Place oysters in shells. Sprinkle oysters with the parsley, chives, bread crumbs, and bacon. Bake in a 450° F. oven for 10 minutes or until bacon is crisp. Serve as an appetizer on the shells.

Makes 6 servings.

FRIED OYSTERS

12 large oysters, defrosted	1 cup fine dry bread crumbs
and drained	Fat or oil for frying
1 egg, beaten	Lemon wedges or Tartar
1 tablespoon water	Sauce (page 81)

Drain oysters, and pat dry on towels. Mix egg with water. Dip oysters first in egg and then in the bread crumbs. Allow to rest on waxed paper for a few minutes to set coating. Heat fat (at least 3 inches deep) to 370° F. Carefully put coated oysters in hot fat, and cook until lightly browned. Drain on absorbent paper. Serve with lemon wedges or Tartar Sauce.

Makes 2 servings.

OYSTER STEW

1 pint frozen raw oysters and
    their liquid
¼ cup butter
2 cups milk, scalded

2 cups light cream, scalded
½ teaspoon salt
Dash paprika

Defrost oysters. Heat butter in a saucepan, and add oysters and their liquid. Cook just until edges of oysters start to curl. Combine with hot milk, cream, and salt. Serve at once, or hold below boiling point for 15 to 20 minutes to blend flavors. Put a dash of paprika on each serving.

Makes 4 servings.

SAUTÉED OYSTERS

¼ cup butter
1 quart raw oysters, defrosted
    and drained
Oyster liquid
2 tablespoons diced celery
1 teaspoon salt

⅛ teaspoon freshly ground
    pepper
1 teaspoon paprika
Dash Tabasco sauce
2 tablespoons lemon juice
6 slices toasted bread

Melt butter in skillet. Add the oysters, the strained liquid, and the celery, and season with salt, pepper, paprika, Tabasco sauce, and lemon juice. Gently stir and sauté for about 4 minutes or until edges of oysters are curled and the mixture is thoroughly hot. Serve on toast.

Makes 6 servings.

LOBSTER

Lobster has always been considered a delicacy. Generally speaking, in home freezing, cooked lobster meat is taken out of the shell to be frozen, though I have frozen lobster tails and claws. A great deal depends on how much space you have in the freezer and how you wish to use the lobster.

When freezing cooked lobster meat, it is less expensive and easier to freeze larger lobsters than those used for broiling. At times during the year lobsters up to 6 or 8 pounds can be bought.

To Boil: Prepare a pot of water large enough to hold the lobster. Add salt (1 tablespoon to each quart of water). Bring to a boil. Pick up the lobster behind the claws, and plunge it headfirst into the boiling water. Boil rapidly until the lobster turns bright red, about 15 minutes. Remove at once, and plunge into cold water to cool. Split cooled lobster, and remove and discard stomach sac back of the head and the black intestinal vein. Pick out all the meat, and cut into suitable-size pieces.

To Freeze: Package in family-size units in plastic bags or containers. Seal, label, date, and freeze.

To Use: Always defrost cooked lobster meat in the refrigerator.

Storage Time: Up to 3 months.

When freezing cooked lobster claws or tails, wrap claws or tails in freezer wrap, and seal. Label, date, and freeze. Do not plan to keep more than a couple of months.

When freezing raw lobster, plunge lobster into boiling water just long enough to kill it. Remove, and freeze tail and claws in shell. Wrap in freezer wrap, and seal. Label, date, and freeze. Frozen raw lobster will keep up to 3 months. It should also be defrosted in refrigerator, or it can be cooked from the frozen state.

LOBSTER CANAPÉS

1 cup cooked lobster meat, defrosted
1 teaspoon lime juice
½ teaspoon onion salt
2 tablespoons chopped capers

¼ cup mayonnaise
24 thin cucumber slices
24 rounds white bread, buttered and toasted
½ teaspoon paprika

Chop lobster meat very fine. Mix with lime juice, onion salt, capers, and mayonnaise. Put a slice of cucumber on each round of buttered toast, and top with a tablespoonful of the lobster mixture. Sprinkle with paprika.

Makes 2 dozen canapés.

LOBSTER BISQUE

4 tablespoons butter
4 tablespoons flour
3 cups milk
1 cup cream
2 cups Chicken Broth (page 167)
¼ teaspoon nutmeg

2 cups diced cooked lobster meat
½ teaspoon salt
⅛ teaspoon freshly ground pepper
½ teaspoon paprika

Heat butter in saucepan. Add flour, and let cook until mixture begins to thicken and bubble. Add the milk, cream, and Chicken Broth, and season with nutmeg. Cook and stir with a whisk until bisque begins to boil and becomes thick and smooth. Add lobster meat, and heat. Season with salt and pepper. Simmer about 10 minutes. Serve with a dash of paprika over each bowl.

Makes 8 servings.

HOT LOBSTER

¾ cup butter
3 cups coarsely cut cooked
    lobster, defrosted
4 tablespoons dry white wine
⅛ teaspoon freshly ground
    pepper

Paprika
1 lemon, cut in wedges
2 tablespoons freshly
    chopped parsley

Heat the butter in a skillet over low heat. Add the lobster, and sauté 5 to 6 minutes or until lobster is thoroughly hot. Add the wine and pepper, and simmer 1 minute longer. Put into scallop shells or flat individual casseroles. Garnish with paprika, lemon wedges, and parsley.

Makes 6 servings.

LOBSTER THERMIDOR

4 tablespoons butter
1 teaspoon minced onion
1 cup sliced fresh mush-
    rooms
3 tablespoons flour
1 cup milk
1 cup heavy cream
½ teaspoon dry mustard
1 teaspoon celery salt
1½ teaspoons salt

⅛ teaspoon Tabasco sauce
2 egg yolks, slightly beaten
1 cup grated mild cheddar
    cheese
¼ cup sherry
1 tablespoon lemon juice
3 cups diced cooked lobster
    meat, defrosted
¾ cup buttered bread
    crumbs

Heat the butter in a saucepan. Add the onion and mush-rooms, and sauté for 5 minutes. Stir in the flour. Add the milk and cream, and season with mustard, celery salt, salt, and Tabasco sauce. Stir with a whisk over low heat until mixture boils and thickens. Add a little of the hot mixture to the egg yolks, and return to the sauce. Stir the cheese into the sauce. Add sherry, lemon juice, and lobster meat. Spoon into a buttered 2-quart casserole. Top with the bread crumbs. Bake in a 375° F. oven for 20 minutes or until lightly browned.

Makes 6 servings.

LOBSTER SALAD

3 cups diced cooked lobster
   meat, defrosted
2 tablespoons lemon juice
¼ teaspoon salt
1 cup diced celery

½ cup Blender Mayonnaise
   (below)
Salad greens
1 lemon, cut in wedges

Combine the lobster meat with the lemon juice, salt, celery, and Blender Mayonnaise. Chill in the refrigerator for several hours. Serve on crisp greens, and top with Blender Mayonnaise. Garnish with lemon wedges.

Makes 4 to 6 servings.

Blender Mayonnaise

1 egg
½ teaspoon salt
½ teaspoon dry mustard

2 tablespoons lemon juice
1 cup vegetable or olive oil

Combine the egg, salt, dry mustard, lemon juice, and

¼ cup of the oil in the blender. Cover and blend 30 seconds. Remove the cover, and gradually add the remaining oil.

Makes 1¼ cups mayonnaise.

CRAB

The crabs sold in the United States range from the soft-shell crab that Maryland is famous for to the Dungeness crab of the West Coast and the Alaska king crab. Most of us will freeze the crabs of our area or others when they are plentiful. Generally speaking, it is recommended that crab meat be cooked and taken out of the shell and frozen in a suitable container or freezer wrap. Soft-shell crabs which are served sautéed with their shells on are one exception. Some crab legs, such as King or Dungeness, are frozen cooked in the shell.

To Freeze Cooked Crab Meat: Boil live crabs for 10 to 15 minutes in a brine (½ cup salt to 1 gallon water). Cool rapidly. Pick out meat. Pack meat in suitable container in family-size unit. Seal, label, and date. Freeze.

Storage Time: Up to 3 months.

To Freeze Soft-Shell Crab: Kill crab by sticking point of knife between its eyes. Lift pointed ends of top shell, and scrape off the spongy material between body and shell. Remove tail. Wash thoroughly to remove any sand. Wash in a brine (½ cup salt to 1 gallon water). Drain. Wrap cleaned crabs in freezer wrap. Seal, label, and date. Freeze.

Storage Time: Up to 2 months.

To Cook: Defrost in refrigerator. Sauté defrosted crabs in a small amount of butter in skillet. Serve with lemon wedges. Two crabs per person is generally considered a serving.

Note: Before frying, crabs may be dipped in flour, corn-meal, or egg and crumbs if preferred. Crabs may be brushed with melted butter and broiled 8 to 10 minutes, turning to brown both sides.

CRAB-MEAT PUFF

2 eggs, hard-cooked
6 slices white bread
1½ cups milk
½ teaspoon salt
⅛ teaspoon freshly ground
    pepper

½ teaspoon dry mustard
1 cup cooked crab meat,
    defrosted
1 cup grated sharp cheddar
    cheese
¼ cup melted butter

Peel and finely chop eggs. Remove crusts from bread, and cut into ½-inch cubes. Mix the bread cubes with milk, and season with salt, pepper, and mustard. Put in a buttered 1½-quart casserole. Stir in the crab meat, cheese, and eggs. Pour melted butter over top. Bake in a 350° F. oven for 30 minutes or until firm.
    Makes 4 to 6 servings.

DEVILED CRAB

4 tablespoons butter
3 tablespoons chopped onion
3 tablespoons flour
1 teaspoon dry mustard
¾ teaspoon salt
1 cup Chicken Broth
    (page 167)
1 cup dry white wine

1 teaspoon Worcestershire
    sauce
Freshly ground pepper
3 cups cooked crab meat,
    defrosted
½ cup buttered bread
    crumbs
½ teaspoon paprika

Heat the butter in a saucepan, and sauté the onion until tender. Add the flour, mustard, and salt, and mix well. Stir in the Chicken Broth, wine, Worcestershire sauce, and pepper. Cook and stir with a whisk until mixture begins to boil, thickens, and becomes a smooth sauce. Fold in the crab meat. Spoon into a buttered flat 1½-quart casserole. Sprinkle the bread crumbs and paprika on top of mixture. Bake in a 375° F. oven for 10 to 15 minutes until bubbly and browned.
Makes 6 servings.

CRAB-MEAT SALAD

2 cups cooked crab meat, defrosted
2 tablespoons finely chopped green pepper
1 teaspoon grated onion
2 tablespoons lemon juice
3 tablespoons olive or vegetable oil
½ teaspoon salt
⅛ teaspoon Tabasco sauce
1 cup thinly sliced celery
½ cup Blender Mayonnaise (page 89)
3 eggs, hard-cooked
3 tomatoes
Crisp greens

Lightly mix crab meat with green pepper, onion, lemon juice, oil, salt, and Tabasco sauce. Cover and let stand in refrigerator for several hours. When ready to serve, mix with celery and Blender Mayonnaise. Peel and cut hard-cooked eggs into quarters lengthwise. Cut tomatoes into wedges. Arrange greens on salad plates. Pile crab-meat mixture in center of greens. Garnish each serving with ½ egg and ½ tomato.
Makes 6 servings.

HOT CRAB-MEAT SANDWICHES

1 10½-ounce can condensed
    cream of chicken soup
2 tablespoons chopped green
    pepper
1 tablespoon chopped onion
2 tablespoons lemon juice
1 teaspoon Worcestershire
    sauce

1 teaspoon prepared mustard
1 cup cooked crab meat,
    defrosted
8 slices bread
4 slices processed American
    cheese
8 thin slices tomato

Combine soup with green pepper, onion, lemon juice, Worcestershire sauce, and mustard. Heat to boiling. Stir in crab meat. Toast bread lightly. Spoon crab-meat mixture on 4 slices of toasted bread, and top each with cheese slice. Heat under broiler until cheese melts and crab meat is bubbly. Cut remaining toasted bread in half to form triangles, and place 1 on each side of crab-meat sandwich. Put a slice of tomato on each triangle of toast.

Makes 4 servings.

5 Game

GENERAL INSTRUCTIONS FOR
FREEZING GAME

Having been born into a family where hunting and fishing were a way of life and before freezers were invented, I found that pheasant four days in a row was no treat after the third day. To me, freezers are the greatest blessing that has happened to the sportsman, including electrically heated gloves!

The handling of game is a very personal thing, and hence, these words are offered, not as the end-all, but as a guide from my own experience and those of trusted associates. Many fastidious hunters recommend field dressing for birds and suggest filling the cavity with grass to keep it open and to aid cooling. Whether you field-dress birds or not, the birds should be laid out singly—not stacked—to aid in cooling. If at all possible, store birds in an iced chest until they can be processed.

Arguments go on forever when it comes to how long birds should be "hung." This is a process whereby the unplucked birds are hung by their heads in a cool, dry place for anywhere from 2 to 5 days before they are cooked. Supposedly this tenderizes and brings out the flavor in the birds.

However, there is no law that says you can't eat birds without hanging.

Ducks should be dry-plucked. Pheasants and small birds such as quail and squab should be scalded in 160° to 170° F. water and plucked.

The plucked and hung and dressed birds are ready for freezing.

To Freeze Game Fowl: Wrap in freezer wrap, and close with the drugstore fold, bringing the wrap up closely around the body. If several birds are frozen in 1 package, wrap each individually first, so that they can be more easily separated for defrosting. Seal, label, and date the package.

Storage Time: Up to 6 to 7 months.

Four-footed animals are also hung to age before freezing. If the game animal has little fat, it should not be hung too long. The standard time is 5 days, so reduce that time to 2 days for very "skinny" animals. Be sure that the carcass is well bled, and cut off any parts damaged by shells.

Cut the animal into steaks, chops, roasts, stews, or whatever suits your taste best.

To Freeze Four-Footed Animals: Always wrap meats so that the wrapping is close to the meat. Seal well, and mark the weight on the package, as well as the cut of meat, as a guide to cooking. Family-size units are most practical.

Storage Time: Up to 9 months.

Remember that most game (both birds and four-footed animals) is on the lean side. Age, of course, is also a factor. The older the animal is, the longer the cooking process. My own mother always cooked the game birds that my father and brothers brought home in a very simple manner, and most true lovers of game eschew it in any other fashion, claiming that to enjoy game is to enjoy the game flavor!

RECIPES

WILD DUCK

ROAST WILD DUCK

2 cleaned and dressed wild ducks, defrosted	4 slices salt pork
1 apple	Freshly ground black pepper
1 small onion	½ cup dry white wine

Wipe ducks with damp towel. Put half an apple and half an onion in each duck. Place on rack in a roasting pan. Cover breasts with slices of salt pork, and sprinkle ducks generously with pepper. Pour wine over ducks. Cover and bake in a 425° F. oven for 30 minutes. Uncover and bake another 15 to 20 minutes, basting with pan liquid until ducks are nicely browned.

Makes 4 to 6 servings.

To Freeze: If desired, ducks may be roasted and then frozen. Roast freshly killed (hung) ducks as directed. Cool. Wrap with freezer wrap. Label, date, and freeze.

To Serve: Roast duck may be defrosted and served cold, or it may be heated in a 425° F. oven for about 15 minutes.

Storage Time: Up to 4 months.

WILD DUCK MADEIRA

To Prepare for Freezing: Roast hung ducks which have been cleaned and dressed in a 500° F. oven for 15 minutes. Slice off breast meat into thin slices. Cool. Wrap in freezer wrap, separating slices with transparent wrap or foil. Label, date, and freeze.

Storage Time: Up to 4 months.

To Serve:

2 tablespoons butter	4 tablespoons currant jelly
12 slices Roast Wild Duck (page 96), defrosted	4 tablespoons Madeira wine
	Salt and pepper

Heat butter in a skillet or chafing dish. Add slices of duck, currant jelly, and wine. Season to taste with salt and pepper. Simmer until duck is throughly heated, approximately 15 to 20 minutes.
Serves 4.

WILD DUCKS CLARET

2 cleaned and dressed wild ducks, defrosted	½ bay leaf
1 teaspoon salt	3 whole allspice
⅛ teaspoon freshly ground pepper	1 sprig fresh parsley
½ cup brandy	¼ pound fresh pork fat
1 cup claret	1 tablespoon butter
1½ cups chopped onion	1 clove garlic, sliced
½ teaspoon thyme	½ pound fresh mushrooms, sliced

Cut the ducks into serving pieces, and put in an enamel or earthenware crock. Add the salt, pepper, brandy, claret, onion, thyme, bay leaf, allspice, and parsley. Cover and marinate the duck pieces in the refrigerator overnight or for 6 to 8 hours. Remove duck pieces from the marinade. Strain marinade, and reserve. Heat pork fat and butter in a casserole, and brown duck pieces. Add garlic, mushrooms, and reserved marinade. Cover, and simmer over low heat for 1¼ hours or until tender.

Makes 4 to 6 servings.

PHEASANT

CREAM-BRAISED PHEASANT A LA MRS. DEEDS

3 cleaned and dressed pheas-
    ants, defrosted
¼ cup flour
1 teaspoon salt

⅛ teaspoon freshly ground
    pepper
4 tablespoons butter
2 cups light cream (if not
    being frozen)

After Freezing:

2 tablespoons butter

2 cups light cream

Cut pheasants into serving pieces. Mix the flour with salt and pepper, and coat pheasant pieces with flour mixture. Heat the butter in a skillet, and brown the pheasant on all sides. Add the cream to the skillet. Cover and simmer pheasant over low heat until tender, about 1 hour.

Makes 6 servings.

To Freeze: Clean, dress, and cut fresh-killed (hung) pheasants into serving pieces. Dip in seasoned flour, and brown as directed in butter. Do not add cream. Cool. Wrap individual pieces in transparent wrap or foil. Overwrap in packages containing servings for 6. Label and date. Mark: Add 2 tablespoons butter and 2 cups light cream. Freeze.

To Serve: Unwrap individual pieces, and place in skillet. Add 2 tablespoons butter and 2 cups light cream. Cover and cook over very low heat until tender, about 1 hour. Turn pieces occasionally. This is for 6 servings.

Storage Time: Up to 4 months.

GROUSE

GROUSE WITH ORANGE SAUCE

4 cleaned and dressed grouse, defrosted
Salt
Freshly ground pepper
1 teaspoon grated orange rind
1 large California orange
2 tablespoons orange juice
¼ cup melted butter
1 teaspoon lemon juice
1 tablespoon orange liqueur (Grand Marnier or Cointreau)
4 slices bacon
4 tablespoons freshly chopped parsley

Defrost and wipe grouse inside and out with damp towel. Sprinkle inside and out with salt and pepper. Grate 1 teaspoon orange rind from orange. Cut 4 slices (¼ inch thick) orange from the center and reserve. Remove any remaining rind and the seeds. Squeeze 2 tablespoons juice from ends of orange. Mix the orange juice with the butter, orange rind, lemon juice, and orange liqueur. Cover breast of each grouse with an orange slice and a bacon slice. Fasten with toothpicks or string. Place breast side up on rack in pan, and bake in a 350° F. oven about 20 minutes, basting frequently with butter and fruit-juice mixture. Remove toothpicks or string. Sprinkle with chopped parsley.
Makes 4 servings.

WILD GOOSE

FRUIT-STUFFED WILD GOOSE

1 6–8-pound cleaned and
    dressed wild goose,
    defrosted
2 tablespoons lemon juice
½ teaspoon salt
⅛ teaspoon pepper

¼ cup butter
½ cup chopped onion
1 cup chopped apple
1 cup chopped dried apricots
3 cups soft bread crumbs
Thin slices salt pork

Wipe goose inside and out with damp towel. Sprinkle inside and out with lemon juice, salt, and pepper. Skewer the neck skin closed. Heat the butter in a skillet, and sauté the onion until soft but not browned. Stir in the apple, apricots, and bread crumbs. Spoon stuffing mixture into the cavity of the goose, and skewer the vent closed. Cover the breast of the goose with thin slices of salt pork. Roast in a 325° F. oven for 2½ to 3 hours. Baste the wild goose with pan drippings occasionally while it roasts.
Makes 6 servings.

RABBIT

CREAM-BRAISED RABBIT

1 wild rabbit, cleaned and
    dressed, defrosted
½–1 teaspoon thyme
3 tablespoons flour
½ teaspoon salt

1 tablespoon butter

⅛ teaspoon freshly ground
    pepper
4 tablespoons butter
1 cup light cream (if not
    being frozen)
After Freezing:
    1 cup light cream

Cut rabbit into serving pieces. Rub a little thyme into serving pieces. Mix flour with salt and pepper, and coat rabbit pieces with flour mixture. Heat butter in skillet, and brown rabbit on all sides. Transfer pieces to casserole. Add cream to skillet, and heat and stir to remove brown crust. Pour over rabbit in casserole, and bake in a 325° F. oven for 1 hour or until tender.

Makes 4 servings.

To Freeze: Clean, dress, and cut fresh-killed (hung) rabbit into serving pieces. Dip in seasoned flour, and brown as directed in butter. Do not add cream. Cool. Wrap individual pieces in transparent wrap or foil, and overwrap in packages containing servings for 4. Label and date. Mark: Add 1 tablespoon butter and 1 cup light cream to buttered casserole. Freeze.

To Serve: Unwrap individual pieces, and place in buttered casserole. Add 1 tablespoon butter and 1 cup light cream. Cover and bake in a 425° F. oven about 30 minutes. Uncover and bake 25 to 30 minutes longer or until tender.

Storage Time: Up to 4 months.

SHERRIED WILD RABBIT

2 cleaned and dressed wild
   rabbits
1 onion, sliced
2 carrots, sliced
2 stalks celery, sliced
3 sprigs fresh parsley
1 bay leaf
2 juniper berries (optional)
2 sprigs fresh thyme or ½
   teaspoon ground thyme

½ teaspoon ground sage
1 teaspoon salt
½ teaspoon freshly ground
   pepper
1 cup flour
1 teaspoon salt
½ teaspoon freshly ground
   pepper
½ cup butter

After Freezing:

¾ cup sherry wine

Cut the rabbits into serving pieces. Cover pieces with salt water (1 tablespoon salt per 1 quart water), and soak overnight. Drain. Put the rabbit pieces into a large kettle. Cover with water, and add the onion, carrot, celery, parsley, bay leaf, juniper berries, thyme, sage, salt, and pepper. Bring to a boil, and cook until tender. (This time varies with the ages of the rabbits, but start testing with a fork at 30 minutes. Do not overcook.) Remove the rabbit pieces from the broth, and drain well. Roll the rabbit pieces in flour seasoned with salt and pepper. Heat the butter in a large skillet, and brown the rabbit pieces quickly.

Makes 6 servings.

To Freeze: Cool. Wrap each piece of rabbit separately in transparent wrap, and overwrap all the pieces in 1 package. Label, date, and freeze.

To Serve: Unwrap pieces, and place in a buttered casserole. Add ¾ cup sherry wine, and bake rabbit in a 350° F. oven for 30 to 40 minutes or until hot and bubbly.

Storage Time: Up to 3 months.

SQUIRREL

BRUNSWICK STEW

3 cleaned and dressed squirrels, defrosted	¼ teaspoon freshly ground black pepper
2½ quarts water	1 cup chopped onion
1 teaspoon salt	4 cups canned tomatoes
½ cup diced bacon	2 cups diced peeled potatoes
⅛ teaspoon Tabasco sauce	2 cups frozen lima beans
1 teaspoon salt	2 cups frozen whole-kernel corn

Wash and cut squirrels into serving pieces. Put in kettle with water and salt. Bring to a boil. Skim liquid to remove foam. Cover and simmer 1½ to 2 hours or until squirrel is tender. Cool enough to remove meat from bones, and return meat to broth. Add the bacon, Tabasco sauce, salt, pepper, onion, tomatoes, potatoes, and lima beans. Simmer another hour. Add corn, and cook 10 minutes longer. Taste and correct seasonings if necessary. Serve in soup plates.

Makes 6 to 8 servings.

VENISON

ROAST RACK OF VENISON

Defrost the rack of venison in the refrigerator and then bring to room temperature. Place in a roasting pan, and either rub with butter or cover with slices of salt pork, held in place with string or skewers. Roast in a 325° F. oven 18 minutes per pound. (To calculate cooking time, a rack of venison weighs between 6 and 8 pounds.) If butter is used, baste occasionally during cooking. Let stand 10 minutes before carving. Serve with Port Sauce (below).

Port Sauce

1 cup port wine
1 tablespoon cornstarch
½ cup red-currant jelly

2 tablespoons lemon juice
1 teaspoon grated lemon rind

Combine port wine with cornstarch and currant jelly. Beat with a wire whisk until smooth. Then cook and stir until mixture begins to boil and thicken. Add the lemon juice and grated lemon rind, and blend.

Makes 1½ cups sauce.

MARINADE FOR VENISON ROASTS OR STEAK

½ cup vegetable or olive oil
1 cup chopped onions
1 cup chopped carrots
2 whole cloves
1 cup tarragon vinegar

½ teaspoon basil
½ teaspoon marjoram
1 teaspoon salt
¼ teaspoon freshly ground
    black pepper

Heat oil in saucepan, and sauté onions and carrots until tender but not browned. Add cloves, vinegar, basil, marjoram, salt, and pepper. Bring to a boil, cover, and simmer 5 minutes. Strain through a sieve. Use as marinade for venison. Leave the venison in the marinade for 8 hours, turning the meat every 2 hours. Use as a basting sauce for roasts or steaks.

Makes 2 cups marinade.

FROZEN VENISON STEW

6 pounds breast or shoulder
    of venison
Flour (about ¾ cup)
3 teaspoons salt

½ teaspoon freshly ground
    pepper
½ cup butter
8 cups Beef Stock (page 163)

After Freezing (for 1 container):

1 cup water
2 white turnips, peeled and
    diced

3 carrots, peeled and diced
2 medium onions, sliced
3 medium potatoes, sliced

Cut hung venison into cubes. Mix flour with salt and pepper, and coat venison with mixture. Heat butter in large skillet, and brown venison, a small amount at a time. Transfer to large saucepot as browned. Add additional butter to skillet if needed. When all the venison is browned, add 1 cup stock to skillet, and cook and scrape to remove brown crust. Add with remaining stock to venison in saucepot, and simmer, covered, until meat is tender, about 2 hours.

To Freeze: Cool rapidly. Package in 3 containers, dividing meat and liquid evenly between each container. Label, date, and freeze.

To Use: Empty contents of 1 container into saucepan. Add 1 cup water. Cover and cook over low heat until defrosted. Add the turnips, carrots, onions, and potatoes. Cook about 30 minutes or until vegetables are tender.
One container makes 6 servings.

Storage Time: Up to 4 months.

VENISON STEW

2 pounds frozen breast or shoulder of venison
¼ cup flour
1 teaspoon salt
¼ teaspoon freshly ground pepper
2 tablespoons bacon fat or butter

4 cups Beef Stock (page 163)
2 white turnips, peeled and diced
3 carrots, peeled and diced
2 medium onions, sliced
3 medium potatoes, diced

Defrost venison, and cut into cubes. Mix flour with salt and pepper, and coat venison with mixture. Heat fat in a large saucepan, and brown meat on all sides. Add the stock. Bring to a boil, and simmer, covered, 2 hours or until tender. Add the turnips, carrots, onions, and potatoes, and cook 30 minutes longer or until tender. Thicken gravy slightly with additional flour if desired.
Makes 6 servings.

APRICOT SAUCE FOR GAME

1 cup apricot preserves
¼ cup lemon juice
¼ cup water

2 teaspoons cornstarch
1 tablespoon sugar
2 tablespoons brandy

Mix apricot preserves with lemon juice, water, cornstarch, and sugar in a small saucepan. Stir to blend, then cook over moderate heat until mixture comes to a boil and is thickened. Add brandy. Serve with duck, venison, or goose.

Makes 1½ cups sauce.

6 Fruit

GENERAL INSTRUCTIONS FOR FREEZING FRUIT

It is extremely rewarding to be able to serve fresh frozen fruits from the freezer in the cold of winter. Plan to freeze as great a variety and as many containers as practicable in your freezer.

Always buy firm ripe fruits and berries, and sort out any overripe fruit. Fruits that are overripe are apt to become mushy in freezing. Those that are not ripe enough lack flavor when frozen, just as they do when fresh. Almost all fruits can be frozen, but follow directions for superior products.

Some fruits can be frozen without sugar (blueberries, cranberries, and strawberries for example), and others such as peaches are better when frozen with a sugar syrup or sugar. During the peach season I keep a jar of syrup with ascorbic acid in the refrigerator and then freeze a few jars of peaches whenever I get a special bargain. I do the same with other fruits in season.

DIRECTIONS FOR PACKING FRUIT

Syrup Pack: This is the best and easiest all-around method, especially if the fruits are to be used for dessert. As a rule it takes from ½ to ⅔ cup syrup per pint of fruit. Light, medium, and heavy syrup can be used, medium being the one recommended most. The proper proportions for the sugar syrup are as follows:

Light	2 cups sugar	4 cups water	yields 5 cups syrup
Medium	3 cups sugar	4 cups water	yields 5½ cups syrup
Heavy	7 cups sugar	4 cups water	yields 7¾ cups syrup

To make syrup, combine sugar and water in a saucepan. Stir over heat until sugar is dissolved. Bring to a boil, and boil 2 minutes. Cool.

Sugar Pack: If fruit is to be used for pies or other cooking, a sugar pack is practical. For a sugar pack place prepared fruit in a bowl. Sprinkle sugar over fruit, and mix gently to distribute evenly throughout fruit. Continue the gentle mixing until enough juice is drawn from the fruit to dissolve the sugar. Spoon into container for freezing. For reference in cooking note the amount of sugar used with fruit on the label (for example, ½ cup per quart).

Dietetic Pack: 48 ¼-grain saccharin tablets equals 1 cup sugar in sweetening power. Use the amount of water indicated in the yield of syrup with the saccharin. In other words, a light dietetic syrup would be made as follows. Dissolve 96 ¼-grain saccharin tablets in 5 cups water. In packing dietetic fruit follow directions for packing in regular syrup.

Use of Ascorbic Acid: Ascorbic acid (vitamin C) either alone or in combination with citric acid is used to prevent darkening of fruit and flavor changes during freezer storage.

Ascorbic acid in powder, crystalline, or tablet form may be purchased in drugstores or freezer supply stores. There are also commercial products on the market which should be used as directed on the container.

Ascorbic acid or the commercial product is added to the syrup for the syrup pack. (Dissolve in a small amount of cold syrup, and mix into the remainder of the syrup.) Store leftover syrup in the refrigerator.

In the sugar pack sprinkle the ascorbic acid dissolved in a small amount of water over the fruit before the sugar is added.

SEASONAL CHART FOR FRUIT

Apples	year round; peak fall and winter
Apricots	peak mid-June, July, mid-August
Bananas	year round
Blackberries	June, July, August
Blueberries	June, July
Boysenberries	June, July, August
Cherries	July
Cranberries	October, November, December
Dewberries	June, July, August
Figs	July
Loganberries	June, July, August
Melons	some available all year; peak summer and fall
Nectarberries	June, July, August
Peaches	peak July, August, September
Pineapple	year round; peak March through June
Plums	peak July, August, September, October
Raspberries	July
Rhubarb	April, May, June
Strawberries	year round; peak June, July
Youngberries	June, July, August

INSTRUCTION CHART FOR FREEZING FRUIT

Apples About 1½ pounds makes 1 pint; ½ bushel (24 pounds) makes 16 to 20 pints. Select crisp firm apples (McIntosh, Jonathan, winesap).

In syrup: Wash, peel, and core. Slice into thin slices. Pack in medium syrup with ½ teaspoon (1,000 milligrams) ascorbic acid added to each quart of syrup. Leave ½-inch headspace. Seal, label, date, freeze.

To Use: Defrost and use in salads, or cook apples in syrup until tender for sauce.

Storage Time: Up to 8 months.

In sugar: Prepare slices as above. Slice into salt water (2 tablespoons salt per gallon water). Drain. Steam-blanch (page 125) 2 minutes. Cool. Mix each quart apples with ½ cup sugar. Pack. Leave ½-inch headspace. Seal, label, date, freeze.

To Use: Defrost and use in pies, cobblers, or applesauce. Or use as fresh fruit in salads or dessert.

Storage Time: Up to 8 months.

Applesauce Wash apples well. Remove stem and blossom ends. Cut into quarters. Place in saucepan. Add ⅓ cup water per quart apples. Cover and cook until tender. Put through food mill or strainer. Sweeten to taste with ½ to ¾ cup sugar per quart applesauce. Pack into containers. Leave ½-inch headspace. Seal, label, date, freeze.

To Use: Defrost.

Storage Time. Up to 8 months.

Apricots About ⅔ pound makes 1 pint; ½ bushel (24 pounds) makes 30 to 35 pints. Select firm ripe fruit with good flavor.

In syrup: Sort, wash, halve, and pit. Peel if desired. If not peeled, blanch (page 125) 30 seconds. Cool, drain. Pack in medium syrup with ¾ teaspoon (1,500 milligrams) ascorbic acid added to each quart. Leave ½-inch headspace. Seal, label, date, freeze.

To Use: Defrost and serve as fresh apricot sauce, use in salad, or cook apricots in syrup until tender.

Storage Time: Up to 8 months.

In sugar: Prepare apricots as above. Dissolve ¼ teaspoon (500 milligrams) ascorbic acid in ¼ cup cold water, and sprinkle over each quart apricots. Mix each quart apricots with ½ cup sugar. Pack. Leave ½-inch headspace. Seal, label, date, freeze.

To Use: Defrost and use in pies, cobblers, or apricot sauce. Or use as fresh fruit in salads or dessert.

Storage Time: Up to 8 months.

Puree: Heat apricots in small amount of water until tender. Put through food mill or strainer. Add 1 cup sugar and ¼ teaspoon (500 milligrams) ascorbic acid dissolved in 1 tablespoon water to each quart puree. Pack into containers. Leave ½-inch headspace. Seal, label, date, freeze. (Other fruit purees are prepared in the same manner.)

To Use: Defrost and use in any recipe calling for puree.

Storage Time: Up to 8 months.

Bananas Bananas may be frozen to be used in cooking only. 1 large banana makes about 1 cup mashed banana. Choose ripe bananas.

Puree: Mash bananas, and mix at once with ¼ teaspoon (500 milligrams) ascorbic acid dissolved in 1 tablespoon water or 1 tablespoon lemon juice per cup. Pack into containers. Seal, label, date, freeze.

> To Use: Defrost and use in banana bread, muffins, cookies, or other baked or cooked products.

> Storage Time: Up to 4 months.

Whole: Package whole ripe bananas in the skin in plastic bags. Seal, label, date, freeze.

> To Use: Defrost. Peel, mash, and use at once in banana bread, cookies, muffins, or other baked or cooked products.

> Storage Time: Up to 2 months.

Blackberries, Boysenberries, Dewberries, Loganberries, Nectarberries, Youngberries About ¾ quart makes 1 pint; 1 crate (24 quarts) makes about 32 pints. Select firm, fully ripe berries.

In syrup: Pick over, wash, and drain. Pack berries into containers, and cover with medium syrup. Leave ½-inch headspace. Seal, label, date, freeze.

> To Use: Serve as berries with cream, on cereal, in any recipe calling for berries to be cooked, or in sauce.

> Storage Time: Up to 8 months.

In sugar: Prepare as directed above. Mix each quart berries with ¾ cup sugar. Pack. Leave ½-inch headspace. Seal, label, date, freeze.

> To Use: Use in pies or cobblers or any way fresh berries would be used.

> Storage Time: Up to 8 months.

Blueberries About ¾ quart makes 1 pint; 1 crate (24 quarts) makes about 32 pints. Select full-flavored ripe berries.

In syrup: Pick over and wash. Drain. Pack berries into containers, and cover with medium syrup. Leave ½-inch headspace. Seal, label, date, freeze.

To Use: Use as fresh berries or in recipes.

Storage Time: Up to 8 months.

Plain: Pick over berries. Pack in containers. Seal, label, date, freeze.

To Use: Wash frozen berries in colander. Use in pies or cobblers or as fresh berries.

Storage Time: Up to 6 months.

Cherries, Sour 1¼ to 1½ pounds makes 1 pint; ½ bushel (28 pounds) makes 18 to 20 pints. Select ripe fruit. Pick over cherries. Wash thoroughly. Remove stems and pits. Mix each quart fruit with ¾ cup sugar. Pack. Leave ½-inch headspace. Seal, label, date, freeze.

To Use: Use for pies or sauce.

Storage Time: Up to 8 months.

Cherries, Sweet Yield same as sour cherries.

Plain: Pick over cherries. Wash thoroughly. Remove stems and pits if desired. Pack in containers. Seal, label, date, freeze.

To Use: Defrost and use as fresh cherries in salads, desserts, fruit cups.

Storage Time: Up to 8 months.

In syrup: Pack prepared cherries in containers. Cover with medium or heavy syrup with ½ teaspoon (1,000 milligrams) ascorbic acid added to each quart. Leave ½-inch headspace. Seal, label, date, freeze.

To Use: Use as fresh cherry sauce, on ice cream, or in recipes.

Storage Time: Up to 8 months.

Cranberries ½ pound equals 1 pint; 1 box (25 pounds) makes 50 pints. Select firm deep-red berries with shiny skins. Pick over cranberries, and remove any stems. Wash and drain. Pack. Seal, label, date, freeze. *Note:* Cranberries can also be frozen in the box or bag in which they are purchased. They must then be picked over, stems removed, and washed before cooking.

To Use: Use for cranberry sauce or for any recipe that calls for fresh or cooked cranberries.

Storage Time: Up to 8 months.

Figs Select figs with tender flesh and skin and small seeds.

In sugar: Wash, sort, and cut off stems. Dissolve ¼ teaspoon (500 milligrams) ascorbic acid in ¼ cup water, and sprinkle over figs. Mix each quart fruit with ⅔ cup sugar. Pack into containers. Seal, label, date, freeze.

To Use: Use as fresh figs.

Storage Time: Up to 8 months.

In syrup: Prepare as above. Pack into containers. Cover with medium syrup with ¾ teaspoon (1,500 milligrams) ascorbic acid added to each quart. Leave ½-inch head-space. Seal, label, date, freeze.

To Use: Use as fresh figs.

Storage Time: Up to 8 months.

Juices Juices from such fruits as grapes, plums, and cher-ries can be extracted and frozen to use later. Wash and pick over fruit. Simmer with as little water as possible. Strain through cheesecloth. Cool and pack juice into containers, leaving ¾-to-1½-inch headspace, depending on size of container. Seal, label, date, freeze.

To Use: Use for punches, jelly-making, fruit gelatins.

Storage Time: Up to 8 months.

Melons (honeydew, canteloupe, etc.) 1 pound equals 1 pint. Select ripe melons having a good flavor. Cut in half, and remove seeds. Cut flesh of melon into balls, slices, or cubes. Pack into containers, and cover with light syrup. Leave ½-inch headspace. (Different kinds of melons can be mixed in the same pack if desired.) Seal, label, date, freeze.

To Use: Use as fresh fruit for dessert or in salads or fruit cups.

Storage Time: Up to 8 months.

Peaches and Nectarines 1 to 1½ pounds makes 1 pint; ½ bushel (24 pounds) makes 16 to 20 pints. Select firm, ripe fruit.

In syrup: Blanch 1 minute (page 125), peel, and pit. Pack either in halves or in slices. Cut into containers, and cover at once with light syrup, adding ½ teaspoon

(1,000 milligrams) ascorbic acid to each quart. Leave ½-inch headspace. Seal, label, date, freeze.

To Use: Serve as fresh peaches, or use in salads or dessert.

Storage Time: Up to 8 months.

In sugar: Prepare peaches as above. Slice or halve into bowl. Sprinkle at once with ¼ teaspoon (500 milligrams) ascorbic acid dissolved in ¼ cup water for each quart fruit. Mix each quart fruit with ⅔ cup sugar. Pack into containers. Leave ½-inch headspace. Seal, label, date, freeze.

To Use: Use as fresh peaches or in pie, cobbler, or other baked dishes.

Storage Time: Up to 8 months.

Pineapple 5 pounds makes about 4 pints. Select firm, ripe pineapple with good flavor.

Plain pack: Peel, core, slice, and dice. Pack prepared pineapple into containers. Seal, label, date, freeze.

To Use: Use as fresh pineapple for desserts or salads.

Storage Time: Up to 8 months.

In syrup: Prepare as directed above. Pack pineapple in container. Cover with light syrup. Leave ½-inch headspace. Seal, label, date, freeze.

To Use: Use as dessert or in salads or fruit cup.

Storage Time: Up to 8 months.

Plums, Prunes 1 to 1½ pounds makes 1 pint; ½ bushel (28 pounds) makes about 25 pints. Select firm, ripe, well-flavored fruit. Sort and wash. Leave whole, or pit and cut in halves or quarters. Pack into containers. Cover with light or medium syrup with ½ teaspoon (1,000 milligrams) ascorbic acid added to each quart. Seal, label, date, freeze.

> To Use: Use as fresh plums or prunes in desserts or salads. Cook for sauce, or use in baked dishes.

Storage Time: Up to 8 months.

Raspberries About ¾ quart makes 1 pint; 1 crate (24 pints) makes about 20 pints. Select firm ripe (but not over-ripe) berries.

In sugar: Mix each quart berries with 1 cup sugar. Pack. Seal, label, date, freeze.

> To Use: Serve as fresh berries, or use in any recipes.

Storage Time: Up to 8 months.

In syrup: Pack raspberries into containers. Cover with light or medium syrup. Leave ½-inch headspace. Seal, label, date, freeze.

> To Use: Serve as fresh berries or over ice cream or in recipes.

Storage Time: Up to 8 months.

Rhubarb About 1 pound makes 1 pint; 15 pounds, 15 to 20 pints. Select tender pink young stalks with good flavor.

In sugar: Wash well, and cut into 1-to-2-inch pieces. Blanch (page 125) 1 minute. Cool. Mix each quart cut rhubarb with ½ cup sugar. Pack. Seal, label, date, freeze.

To Use: Use for pies or sauce or in any recipe calling for fresh rhubarb.

Storage Time: Up to 8 months.

In syrup: Pack cut rhubarb prepared as above into containers. Cover with medium syrup. Leave ½-inch headspace. Seal, label, date, freeze.

To Use: Use in any recipe calling for fresh rhubarb.

Storage Time: Up to 8 months.

Strawberries About ⅔ quart makes 1 pint; 1 crate (24 quarts) makes about 34 pints. Select firm ripe berries.

In sugar: Wash and pick over. Remove caps. Pack whole or halved. Mix each quart berries with ¾ cup sugar. Pack into containers. Seal, label, date, freeze.

To Use: Use as fresh berries on cereal, in desserts or salads, or in recipes.

Storage Time: Up to 8 months.

In syrup: Pack prepared berries into containers. Cover with medium syrup, leaving ½-inch headspace. Seal, label, date, freeze.

To Use: Use as fresh berries on cereal or in desserts or salads.

Storage Time: Up to 8 months.

Plain: Freeze whole berries without sugar. Pack into containers. Seal, label, date, freeze.

To Use: Use as fresh berries or in recipes.

Storage Time: Up to 6 months.

SUGGESTIONS FOR SERVING FROZEN FRUIT

Serve frozen fruit while still a little icy. For variation, top peaches, apricots, raspberries, or strawberries with a scoop of orange sherbet.

Flavor fruits with wine or liqueur. Spoon a little sherry over peaches or apricots. Strawberries with kirsch is a famous combination. Try a little coffee liqueur on peaches or a dash of Cointreau on raspberries.

Mix raspberries with peaches.

Top peaches or strawberries with vanilla ice cream or a generous spoonful of butter-pecan ice cream on peaches.

Soak melon balls in flavored gin, such as orange or lemon gin. Serve icy cold.

RECIPES

APPLES

APPLES CRESTWICK

⅓ cup butter
4 cups sliced apples,
    defrosted
½ cup granulated sugar
½ teaspoon salt
¼ teaspoon cinnamon

¼ teaspoon nutmeg
¾ cup chopped walnuts
2½ cups coarse graham-
    cracker crumbs
2 tablespoons brown sugar
½ cup light cream

Melt butter in an 8 x 8 x 2-inch pan. Arrange the apple slices in the pan. Mix the granulated sugar with salt, cinnamon, and nutmeg, and sprinkle over apples. Combine the walnuts, graham-cracker crumbs, brown sugar, and cream, and spoon over apples. Bake in a 400° F. oven for 30 minutes or until apples are tender. Serve warm or cold.

Makes 6 to 8 servings.

CHERRIES

QUICK CHERRY DELIGHT

1 cup pitted sweet cherries, defrosted
½ cup granulated sugar

1 large banana, sliced
¼ cup broken pecan meats
½ cup heavy cream, whipped

Mix the cherries with the sugar, and let stand 10 to 15 minutes. Add the banana and pecans. Fold gently into whipped cream. Serve at once.

Makes 4 servings.

CRANBERRIES

CRANBERRY SAUCE

4 cups frozen cranberries
2 cups granulated sugar

1 cup water

Combine the cranberries with the sugar and water in a

saucepan. Bring to a boil, and cook, stirring occasionally, until all cranberries have popped. Chill.

Makes 4 cups.

NECTARINES

NECTARINES IN RED WINE

2 cups (8 to 10 halves)
    nectarines,* defrosted
¾ cup red wine

½ cup granulated sugar
½-inch stick cinnamon

Combine the nectarines, red wine, sugar, and cinnamon in a saucepan. Simmer until nectarines are tender, 10 to 15 minutes. Chill. Remove the stick of cinnamon. Serve nectarines with wine sauce.

Makes 4 to 5 servings.

PEACHES

BUTTERSCOTCH PEACHES

3 cups sliced peaches,
    defrosted
1 cup firmly packed light
    brown sugar

1 cup sifted all-purpose flour
½ teaspoon salt
½ teaspoon cinnamon
½ cup butter

Butter a 9-inch pie plate, and arrange peaches in dish. Mix sugar, flour, salt, and cinnamon in a bowl. Blend in the

* Peaches may be used.

butter with 2 knives or a pastry blender until a coarse mixture is formed. Spread over peaches. Bake in a 375° F. oven about 35 minutes. Serve warm or cold.

Makes 6 servings.

RASPBERRIES

RASPBERRY PANAMA

1 3-ounce package raspberry-
   flavored gelatin
1 cup hot water
¾ cup orange juice

1 cup heavy cream, whipped
1 cup crushed raspberries,
   defrosted

Dissolve the raspberry gelatin in hot water. Add the orange juice, and chill until mixture begins to thicken. Fold in the whipped cream and raspberries. Chill until set. To serve, spoon into sherbet glasses.

Makes 6 servings.

RHUBARB

RHUBARB SAUCE

3 cups frozen rhubarb
1 cup granulated sugar

¼ cup water

Combine rhubarb, sugar, and water in saucepan. Cover and cook over low heat until rhubarb is defrosted and mixture comes to a boil, stirring once or twice.

Makes about 3 cups.

Variations:

Add 1 cup frozen strawberries to hot cooked rhubarb. Makes about 3½ cups.

Add 1 tablespoon finely cut orange rind to rhubarb, and use ¼ cup orange juice instead of water. Makes about 3 cups.

7 Vegetables

GENERAL INSTRUCTIONS FOR
FREEZING VEGETABLES

Freeze vegetables while they are at peak flavor and lowest price. If freezer space is limited, it is well to remember that market supplies are now shipped year around from warm climates so that it is sometimes quite economical to freeze vegetables in what used to be considered "off season."

When it comes to experimenting, do not be too concerned with any hard and fast rules you may have heard. Freezing whole, peeled tomatoes has been a no-no for years. In fact, if they are to be used for cooking, they can be frozen to give that fresh tomato taste to dishes in midwinter. Celery and green peppers may be frozen to use for cooking. (Green peppers even for salads.) If you have any doubts about freezing an unusual vegetable, freeze a small amount and after

124

a week's storage use it as you normally would. Choose blanching directions for the vegetables that it most nearly resembles.

Directions are given for freezing cooked, dried black-eyed peas. Any long-cooking dried vegetable can be cooked slightly less than directed on the package and frozen. This enables you to have dried vegetables ready without having to remember to put them "to soak" the night before.

Preparing fresh vegetables for freezing: Wash well, and do whatever preparation is necessary to make them ready to cook at time of use. It is easier to pack vegetables of similar size together—asparagus spears or ears of corn, for example—so when necessary, sort vegetables for size. (Also in the case of vegetables like lima beans, if sorted to size, a more properly cooked dish will result, since all beans will require the same length of cooking time.)

Blanching: This is a process whereby the washed, ready-to-cook vegetables are dipped in boiling water for varying lengths of time to stop enzymatic action which can change the flavor of vegetables during freezer storage.

The most convenient method is to put vegetables into a wire basket and lower it into a kettle of boiling water. Roughly, allow 1 gallon water per pound of vegetables when blanching. Start timing when water reboils, and after the specified time is up, plunge vegetables immediately into cold water in a kettle or under running cold water in the sink. Stir vegetables so those in the center are cooled. More rapid cooling can be assured by the use of ice water.

Drain well and then pack in either rigid containers or plastic freezer bags. Seal, label, date, and freeze.

Directions are given in several places for steam blanching. To steam-blanch, use a large kettle with a tight lid. Put a rack in the bottom of the kettle which will hold food being steam-blanched out of water. Put water in bottom of kettle, and place about 1 pound of vegetables at a time in basket on rack. Bring water to a boil. Cover and steam required length of time. Cool as in hot-water blanching. Pack and freeze in same manner.

If desired, vegetables may be frozen loose. Place blanched

or steamed vegetables in a thin layer on a metal tray. Freeze
and then package.

It is not necessary to defrost vegetables before cooking.

SEASONAL CHART FOR VEGETABLES

Artichokes	year round; peak March, April, October, November, December
Asparagus	peak March, April, May, June, July
Beans, Lima	July through November
Beans, Snap or Wax	year round; peak during summer
Beets	year round; peak June, July
Broccoli	year round; peak November through April
Brussels Sprouts	begin in August; peak October, November, December; continue through March
Cabbage	year round; peak in fall and winter
Carrots	year round; peak in summer
Cauliflower	year round; peak January, February, March
Celery	year round
Corn on the Cob	peak May to October
Eggplant	year round; peak July, August, September
Greens	year round
Mushrooms	year round
Okra	year round; peak June through November
Onions	year round
Peas, Black-Eyed	June, July
Peas, Green	April, May, June
Peppers, Green, Sweet	year round; peak August, September, October
Potatoes, Sweet	come into market in September; available through the winter
Potatoes, White	year round
Pumpkins	mid-September, October, November
Squash, Summer	peak May, June, July, August, September
Squash, Winter	start in mid-September; available throughout winter

Squash, Zucchini	peak May, June, July, August, September
Tomatoes	year round; peak July, August, September
Turnips, White	year round
Turnips, Yellow	start in September; available throughout winter

INSTRUCTION CHART FOR FREEZING VEGETABLES

Artichokes Artichokes are usually purchased by piece. Select those with uniform green color, compact with tight-fitting leaves. Remove a layer of outer leaves, and wash well. Trim about 1 inch off top, and cut off stems. Blanch 7 minutes. Cool. Pack in rigid containers. Seal, label, date, freeze.

To Use: Cook artichokes in boiling water to cover about 30 minutes or until base can be easily pierced with fork. Add ¼ teaspoon salt for each artichoke and 1 tablespoon lemon juice to water.

Storage Time: Up to 6 months.

Asparagus About 1½ pounds is needed to make 1 pint, or 1 crate (12 2-pound bunches) will make 15 to 22 pints. Select tender young stalks. Sort according to thickness and length of stalks. Break or cut off tough ends. Remove scales with peeler or small sharp knife almost to tip end. Wash well. Blanch 2 to 4 minutes, depending on thickness of stalks. Cool. Freeze in stalk lengths or cut into pieces. Pack. Seal, label, date, freeze.

To Use: Cook in small amount of salted water 10 to 15 minutes or until tender. Time depends on size of asparagus.

Storage Time: Up to 6 months.

Beans, Lima About 2 to 2½ pounds purchased in the pod is needed to make 1 pint; 1 bushel (32 pounds) makes approximately 12 to 16 pints. Shell (if great variety in size, sort before washing) and discard any tough and immature beans. Wash. Blanch 2 to 4 minutes, depending on size of beans. Cool. Pack. Seal, label, date, freeze.

To Use: Cook in small amount of salted water 15 to 20 minutes or until tender. Time depends on size of beans.

Storage Time: Up to 6 months.

Beans: Snap, Green, and Wax ⅔ to 1 pound is needed to make 1 pint; 1 bushel (30 pounds) makes 30 to 45 pints. Cut off ends, and either pack whole or cut into 1-inch lengths. Blanch 3 minutes. Cool. Pack. Seal, label, date, freeze.

To Use: Cook in small amount of salted water 15 minutes or until tender.

Storage Time: Up to 9 months.

Beets 1¼ to 1½ pounds is needed for 1 pint; ½ bushel (26 pounds) will make 18 to 20 pints. Select young beets, not larger than 3 inches in diameter. Wash, and trim tops, leaving 3 inches of stem and root. Cook in boiling water until tender, 25 to 50 minutes, depending on size. Cool. Peel and slice or dice. Pack. Seal, label, date, freeze.

To Use: Reheat beets in small amount of water until defrosted. Season with butter, salt, and pepper.

Storage Time: Up to 6 months.

Beets, Harvard Cook beets as directed for freezing beets.

For each quart of diced cooked beets, combine ⅔ cup sugar, 1½ tablespoons cornstarch, ½ cup vinegar, and ½ cup water. Cook and stir until thickened and clear. Combine with beets. Cool. Pack. Seal, label, date, freeze.

To Use: Reheat over low heat. Add 1 tablespoon butter per pint and salt and pepper to taste.

Storage Time: Up to 3 months.

Broccoli 1 pound makes 1 pint; 1 crate (25 pounds), 24 pints. Select tight dark-green heads with tender stalks. Peel stalks, and trim. Soak in salted water (1½ tablespoons salt per gallon water) 30 minutes to remove insects. Split lengthwise so heads are not wider than 1½ inches. Wash well. Blanch 2 minutes. Cool. Pack. Seal, label, date, freeze.

To Use: Cook in small amount of salted water 15 to 20 minutes or until tender.

Storage Time: Up to 6 months.

Brussels Sprouts 1 pound makes 1 pint; 4 quart boxes will make about 6 pints. Select firm green heads. Trim as necessary. If necessary to remove insects, soak in salted water (1½ tablespoons salt per gallon water) for 30 minutes. Wash well, and sort for size. Blanch 3 to 5 minutes, depending on size. Cool. Pack. Seal, label, date, freeze.

To Use: Cook in small amount of salted water 10 to 15 minutes or until tender.

Storage Time: Up to 6 months.

Cabbage 1 pound makes about 1 cup. Remove outer leaves as necessary. Wash cabbage well. Discard core, and cut cabbage coarsely. Blanch 1 minute. Cool. Drain well. Pack. Seal, label, date, freeze.

To Use: Cook in small amount of water 5 minutes or until tender. Season to taste with butter, salt, and pepper.

Storage Time: Up to 6 months.

Carrots 1½ pounds makes 1 pint; ½ bushel (25 pounds) makes 16 to 20 pints. (These figures are for carrots with no tops.) Select tender young carrots. Peel. Small carrots can be frozen whole. Otherwise dice, slice, or cut into strips. Blanch whole carrots 5 minutes; others 2 minutes. Cool. Pack. Seal, label, date, freeze.

To Use: Cook in small amount of salted water 10 to 15 minutes or until tender.

Storage Time: Up to 9 months.

Cauliflower 2 medium heads will make 3 pints. Select firm white heads. Trim. Break into pieces about 1 inch across. If necessary to remove insects, soak in salted water (1½ tablespoons salt per gallon water) for 30 minutes. Wash. Blanch 3 minutes. Pack. Seal, label, date, freeze.

To Use: Cook in small amount of salted water 6 to 8 minutes or until tender.

Storage Time: Up to 6 months.

Celery Select stalks that are fresh and crisp and not too woody. Wash well. Dice. Blanch 1 minute. Cool. Pack in recipe-size units (¼, ½ cup, etc.). Seal, label, date, freeze.

To Use: Use as fresh celery in recipes where celery is to be cooked.

Storage Time: Up to 3 months.

Corn, on the Cob Select tender ears of same size. Remove husks and silk. Trim off cob and tip end as necessary. Blanch 7 to 11 minutes, depending on size of ear. Cool. Pack into containers, or wrap each ear individually in freezer wrap. Seal, label, date, freeze.

To Use: Heat in small amount of water until just hot.

Storage Time: Up to 6 months.

Corn: Whole Kernel, Cream Style 2 to 2½ pounds is needed for 1 pint; 1 bushel (35 pounds) makes 14 to 17 pints. (Figures are for corn in husk.) Select ears with plump tender kernels. Husk, remove silk, and wash. Blanch 4 minutes. Cool. Cut kernels off ⅔ depth of kernel for whole-kernel corn. Do not scrape ear. For cream-style corn, cut halfway into kernel, and scrape ear. Pack. Seal, label, date, freeze.

To Use: Bring to a boil in a very small amount of water, and cook 1 to 2 minutes.

Storage Time: Up to 9 months.

Eggplant 1 medium-size eggplant, cubed, makes about 1½ pints. Select heavy, firm, dark-color eggplants. Peel and slice ¼ inch thick. Dice or cut into strips for french-frying. Put at once into solution of 3 teaspoons lemon juice to 1 quart water for 30 seconds. Blanch by steaming over boiling water 5 minutes. Cool. Pack. Seal, label, date, freeze.

To Use: Use cubed eggplant as fresh in any recipe calling for cubed eggplant. Or steam in a small amount of water until tender and serve with tomato sauce.

French-fried: Partially defrost eggplant strips. Dip in egg and crumbs. Brown in shallow fat on all sides.

Storage Time: Up to 4 months.

Greens 1 to 1½ pounds is needed for 1 pint; 1 bushel (12 pounds) makes 8 to 12 pints. Select tender fresh greens. Remove any heavy stems. Soak in salted water (1½ tablespoons salt per gallon water) 30 minutes to remove insects. Wash well. Drain. If desired, greens can be chopped. Blanch as follows: Spinach—1½ minutes; beet, kale, chard, mustard, and turnip greens—2 minutes; collard greens—3 minutes. Drain well. Cool. Pack. Seal, label, date, freeze.

To Use: Cook in very small amount of salted water 2 to 3 minutes or longer as taste dictates.

Storage Time: Up to 6 months.

Mixed Vegetables Prepare each vegetable as directed, and mix together after blanching and cooling. Pack. Seal, label, date, freeze.

To Use: Cook longest length of time directed for vegetable in pack.

Storage Time: Shortest length of time for vegetable in pack.

Mushrooms 1½ pounds mushrooms is needed for 1 pint if packed whole; 2 pounds for each pint if sliced. Select fresh white mushrooms, approximately the same size. Choose size depending on ultimate use (large if to be served whole; smaller if to be combined with other foods). Wash and trim stems. Slice if desired. Soak in solution of 2 teaspoons lemon juice to 1 quart water for 5 minutes. Blanch by steaming over boiling water for 3½ minutes. Cool. Pack. Seal, label, date, freeze.

To Use: Use for fresh mushrooms. Brush whole mushrooms with butter or oil, and broil 2 to 3 minutes 3 inches from heat or until nicely browned.

Storage Time: Up to 6 months.

Okra   I pound makes 1 pint; ½ bushel (13 pounds) makes 14 to 15 pints. Select young tender pods. Remove stem end. (Do not cut or break pods.) Wash well. Sort for size if necessary. Blanch 2 to 3 minutes, depending on size. Cool. Pack. Seal, label, date, freeze.

To Use: Cook in salted water about 15 minutes or until tender.

Storage Time: Up to 6 months.

Onions, Whole   1 pound makes 1 pint. Select small white onions. Soak 5 minutes in very hot (not boiling) water. Drain, peel, and cut off stem and root end. Blanch 5 minutes. Cool. Pack. Seal, label, date, freeze.

To Use: Use as fresh onions in stews or other dishes. Or cook in salted water 8 to 10 minutes or until tender. Serve buttered or creamed.

Storage Time: Up to 6 months.

Onions, Chopped   3 pounds will make about 5 cups chopped onion. Choose yellow-skinned onions. Soak 5 minutes in very hot (not boiling) water. Remove yellow skin, and cut off stem and root ends. Chop medium fine. Blanch 1 minute. Drain well, and cool. Either freeze loose or pack in recipe-size units (½ cup, etc.). Seal, label, date, freeze.

To Use: Use as fresh onions in recipes.

Storage Time: Up to 4 months.

Peas: Black-Eyed, Fresh 2 to 2½ pounds makes 1 pint. Select firm pods with tender peas. Shell. Discard tough and immature peas. Wash. Blanch 2½ minutes. Cool. Pack. Seal, label, date, freeze.

To Use: Cover with boiling salted water, and cook about 25 minutes or until tender.

Storage Time: Up to 9 months.

Peas: Black-Eyed, Dried Cook dried black-eyed peas about 20 minutes less than directed on package. Cool and pack in family-size units with liquid in which they were cooked. Seal, label, date, freeze.

To Use: Reheat in a covered container over low heat, adding additional water if necessary. Break up block with fork as peas defrost. Season as desired with chopped onion, cooked bacon, salt, and pepper.

Storage Time: Up to 6 months.

Peas, Green 2 to 2½ pounds makes 1 pint; 1 bushel (30 pounds) makes 12 to 15 pints. (These figures are for peas in the pod.) Shell. Discard tough or immature peas. Wash. Blanch 1½ minutes. Cool. Pack. Seal, label, date, freeze.

To Use: Cook in small amount of salted water 10 to 12 minutes or until tender.

Storage Time: Up to 9 months.

Peppers, Green Sweet or Hot Choose fresh crisp peppers with no blemishes. Remove stem, seeds, and white inner membrane. Cut in halves or slices. Blanch halves 2 minutes, slices 1 minute. Cool. Pack in recipe-size units. Seal, label, date, freeze.

To Use: Use as fresh peppers in recipes in which they will be cooked.

Storage Time: Up to 4 months.

Green sweet peppers may also be frozen without blanching. Proceed as in above directions but omit the blanching step.

To Use: Use in recipes where peppers need not be cooked, such as salads and sandwich fillings.

Storage Time: Up to 4 months.

Potatoes, Sweet 3 pounds makes 2 pints. Select firm, medium-sized potatoes. Wash and cook until done. Peel and put through food mill or masher. Cool. Pack into containers. Seal, label, date, freeze.

To Use: Defrost at room temperature to use in any recipe calling for mashed sweet potatoes. Or defrost in top of double boiler, season with salt, pepper, and butter, and serve as mashed sweet potatoes.

Storage Time: Up to 9 months.

Potatoes, White 3 pounds makes 2 pints. Use potatoes that have a mealy quality when cooked. Peel and cook in a minimum amount of water until done, 20 to 40 minutes, depending on size. Drain. Put through a food mill or masher. Add milk to make a fluffy consistency. Cool. Pack. Seal, label, date, freeze.

To Use: Defrost at room temperature, and use in any recipe calling for mashed potatoes. Or defrost in top of double boiler. Season with salt, pepper, and butter, and add more milk if necessary for texture.

Storage Time: Up to 9 months.

Pumpkin or Winter Squash 3 pounds makes 2 pints. Select firm ripe pumpkin or squash. Wash well. Cut into quarters or smaller, depending on size. Remove seeds and membrane. Steam in a small amount of water until soft. Scoop pulp from shell, and put through food mill or masher. Cool. Pack into containers. Seal, label, date, freeze.

To Use: Defrost pumpkin at room temperature, and use in recipes that call for canned pumpkin. Defrost squash in top of double boiler. Season to taste with salt, pepper, and butter.

Storage Time: Up to 9 months.

Squash, Zucchini or Yellow Summer Neither of these squashes is particularly good frozen raw, but they can be prepared in simple recipes and frozen. About 2 pounds makes 2 pints. Scrub well, cut off tip ends, and slice thin. (Young squash need not be peeled; older squash may require peeling.) Rinse, leaving some water clinging to the squash in saucepan. Cover and simmer over moderate heat about 5 minutes or until wilted and partially cooked. Cool. Pack into containers. Seal, label, date, freeze.

To use: Place frozen squash in saucepan. Add 2 tablespoons water and 2 tablespoons butter or margarine. Cover and cook over low heat until defrosted, stirring occasionally. Season to taste with salt and pepper.

Storage Time: Up to 8 months.

Zucchini and Tomatoes: Sauté ½ cup chopped onion in 2 tablespoons oil until tender. Add 3 medium zucchini squash, scrubbed and sliced crosswise, 1 cup canned tomatoes, ¼ teaspoon oregano, ¾ teaspoon salt. Cover and cook 10 minutes. Cool. Pack into containers. Seal, label, date, freeze.

To Use: Place frozen squash in saucepan. Cover and cook over low heat until defrosted, stirring occasionally. Makes 4 servings.

Storage Time: Up to 4 months.

Tomato, Juice 3½ pounds of tomatoes makes 2 pints of juice. Wash. Remove stem ends and blemishes, and cut up tomatoes. Heat in kettle until juice boils. Strain to remove skin and seeds. Add salt to taste. Cool Pack in rigid containers, leaving ½ to 1½ inches of headspace, depending on size of container. Seal, label, date, freeze.

To Use: Defrost. Use as a beverage or in any recipe calling for tomato juice.

Storage Time: Up to 6 months.

Tomatoes, Sliced 1 pound makes 1½ pints. Choose hard, ripe tomatoes. Wash. Slice off both stem and bottom end and cut tomatoes crosswise into 1-inch-thick slices. Dip in flour and brown lightly on both sides in cooking oil. Cool. Stack slices in containers. Seal, label, date, and freeze.

To Use: Put rows of frozen tomato slices on side in flat, buttered casserole. Season lightly with salt, pepper, and about 1 teaspoon sugar per pint of tomato slices.

Sprinkle with buttered crumbs. Bake in a 350° F. oven until tomatoes are hot and tender, about 35 minutes.

Storage Time: Up to 4 months.

Tomatoes, Whole Whole tomatoes may be frozen for use only in cooked dishes. Because of their high water content when defrosted, they collapse too much to use in salads or similar uncooked dishes. However, they are excellent when used in cooking. Choose firm ripe tomatoes. Wash. Blanch 1 minute. Cool. Peel and remove stem end. Pack in rigid containers or plastic bags. Seal, label, date, freeze.

To Use: Partially defrost to chop and measure. Use in recipes where tomatoes will be cooked.

Storage Time: Up to 6 months.

Turnips, Yellow 3 pounds makes 2 pints. Select turnips that are medium-size and not too old or woody. Peel and cut into cubes. Cook in water to cover until tender. Drain. Put through a food mill or masher. Cool. Pack in rigid containers. Seal, label, date, freeze.

To Use: Reheat in saucepan over low heat, turning block over as turnips defrost. (Or defrost in top of double boiler.) Season to taste with salt, pepper, and butter.

Storage Time: Up to 6 months.

Turnips, Yellow or White 3 pounds diced makes 4 to 5 pints. Select young tender turnips. Peel and dice. Blanch 2 minutes. Cool, pack, seal, label, date, freeze.

To Use: Cook in salted water until tender. Drain and mash yellow turnips. Serve white turnips cubed. Season with pepper and butter.

Storage Time: Up to 6 months.

SUGGESTIONS FOR SERVING
FROZEN VEGETABLES

Ingenuity and inventiveness in the use of seasonings can be used in cooking vegetables to give them a little different taste from the same old green beans and corn. Here are simple but tasty suggestions.

For peas, carrots, beans, or spinach, sauté a little chopped onion in butter in the saucepan, and add the vegetable and a small amount of water. Cover and cook until the vegetable is tender. Season with salt and pepper, or add a pinch of an herb or a spice.

Sauté a few chopped mushrooms, and add to beans or peas.

Dress whole cooked cauliflower, broccoli, asparagus, or brussels sprouts with a tasty French dressing.

Grate a little hard-cooked egg yolk and white on top of vegetables at serving time. This is especially good with spinach or other greens, brussels sprouts, cauliflower, or broccoli.

Heat herb-seasoned croutons or crumbs in melted butter, and sprinkle over the cooked vegetable at serving time. This trick will add flavor to almost any vegetable except perhaps the squashes and turnips.

Make a quick sauce by gently combining 1 part lemon juice to 2 parts mayonnaise. This tangy combination is good with hot cooked cauliflower, broccoli, asparagus, brussels sprouts, and green or lima beans.

Vegetables can be served Polonaise style by browning ½ cup unseasoned dry bread crumbs in ¼ cup butter. Add ½ teaspoon paprika and 2 tablespoons lemon juice, and mix well. This is enough for 4 servings and is particularly good sprinkled over cooked cauliflower, asparagus, or green beans.

SAUCES

VINAIGRETTE SAUCE

1 teaspoon salt
¼ teaspoon paprika
Dash Tabasco sauce
1 tablespoon tarragon
    vinegar
2 tablespoons cider vinegar
6 tablespoons salad oil

1 tablespoon chopped green
    pepper
1 tablespoon chopped sweet
    gherkin pickle
1 tablespoon chopped parsley
1 tablespoon chopped chives
4 tablespoons capers, drained

Combine all ingredients, and mix well. Chill. Serve with cold cooked asparagus spears on crisp lettuce.

Makes about ⅔ cup sauce.

BLENDER HOLLANDAISE

3 egg yolks
2 tablespoons lemon juice
½ teaspoon salt

Dash Tabasco sauce
½ cup soft butter
½ cup boiling water

Combine egg yolks, lemon juice, salt, Tabasco sauce, and butter in blender container. Cover and blend until smooth, about 5 seconds. Remove cover, and gradually add boiling water while continuing to blend. Pour mixture into top of double boiler, and cook over hot water, stirring constantly, until sauce thickens. Remove from heat, and keep warm over hot water until serving time. Or sauce can be immediately refrigerated. Serve hot or cold over asparagus, broccoli, cauliflower, brussels sprouts, or spinach.

Makes 1 cup sauce.

SOUR CREAM AND CUCUMBER SAUCE

1 large cucumber
2 tablespoons lemon juice
½ teaspoon salt

Dash Tabasco sauce
1 cup dairy sour cream

Peel cucumber, and cut coarsely into blender container. Add lemon juice, salt, and Tabasco sauce. Cover and blend until cucumber is finely cut. Fold into sour cream. Serve with green beans, lima beans, asparagus, broccoli, cauliflower, or spinach.

Makes 1½ cups.

CHEESE SAUCE

1 egg, well beaten
4 tablespoons lemon juice
½ teaspoon salt

Dash Tabasco sauce
1 3-ounce package cream
  cheese, softened

Combine egg, lemon juice, salt, and Tabasco sauce, and mix well. Gradually beat into cream cheese until smooth and fluffy. Serve with hot cooked asparagus, broccoli, green beans, brussels sprouts, or cauliflower.

Makes about 1 cup sauce.

RECIPES

ARTICHOKES

ARTICHOKE OMELET

4 artichokes, defrosted   ½ cup chopped onion
¼ cup olive oil   6 eggs
1 clove garlic, minced   4 tablespoons water
3 tablespoons chopped   ½ teaspoon salt
    parsley   Dash freshly ground pepper

Cut artichokes in half, and remove the choke from the bottom of the artichoke. Slice lengthwise into thin slices. Heat the olive oil in an 8- or 9-inch skillet, and sauté the artichokes, garlic, and parsley for about 5 minutes. Add the onion, and continue cooking until onion is soft but not browned. Mix the eggs with water, salt, and pepper until blended, but do not beat. Pour over artichoke mixture, and cook until eggs are set, pulling egg mixture gently into center from edges as it cooks. Fold in half, and slide onto a platter.
Makes 4 servings.

CORN

CORN TREAT

2 tablespoons chopped   2 cups frozen whole-kernel
    canned pimiento   corn
2 tablespoons chopped green   2 tablespoons water
    pepper   ½ teaspoon salt
2 tablespoons butter   1 teaspoon chili powder

Sauté the pimiento and green pepper in butter for about 3 minutes. Add the corn and water, season with salt and chili powder, and stir well. Cover and cook 5 minutes.
Makes 4 servings.

EGGPLANT

EGGPLANT PASQUALINO

2 cups diced frozen eggplant
4 tablespoons butter
½ cup chopped onion
¾ cup chopped green pepper
3 tablespoons chopped
    parsley
3 tablespoons flour
2 cups strained canned
    tomatoes

2 teaspoons brown sugar
½ small bay leaf, crushed
1 clove, crushed
½ teaspoon salt
½ cup fine dry bread crumbs
3 tablespoons grated
    Parmesan cheese

Layer the diced eggplant in a buttered 1½-quart casserole. Heat the butter in a skillet, and sauté the onion, green pepper, and parsley until onion is tender but not browned. Mix in the flour. Add the tomatoes, brown sugar, bay leaf, clove, and salt. Cook and stir until mixture boils and is thickened. Spoon over eggplant in casserole. Mix together the bread crumbs and cheese. Sprinkle over tomatoes. Bake in a 350° F. oven for 30 minutes or until eggplant is tender when pierced with fork.
Makes 4 to 6 servings.

GREEN BEANS

GREEN BEANS MANCHU

¼ pound fresh pork
1 tablespoon peanut oil
½ teaspoon ginger root

2 cups frozen cut green beans
½ cup water
2 teaspoons soy sauce

Cut the pork into thin strips about 1½ inches long. Heat the oil in a skillet, and sauté the pork and ginger root until lightly browned. Add the green beans, water, and soy sauce. Cover and cook 7 to 8 minutes or until beans are beginning to "wilt."

Makes 4 servings.

LIMA BEANS

LIMA BEAN CASSEROLE

2½ cups cooked green lima
  beans
4 frankfurters, cut in fourths
2 tablespoons bacon fat
1 tablespoon flour
½ cup tomato juice
1 tablespoon brown sugar
½ teaspoon salt

⅛ teaspoon Tabasco sauce
2 teaspoons prepared
  mustard
½ cup grated American
  cheese
½ cup buttered bread
  crumbs

Mix lima beans and frankfurters together, and put into a buttered 1-quart casserole. Heat the bacon fat in a saucepan, and blend in the flour. Gradually stir in the tomato juice, brown sugar, salt, Tabasco sauce, and mustard. Cook and stir until thickened. Pour over beans in casserole. Mix together the cheese and bread crumbs, and sprinkle over casserole. Bake in a 375° F. oven 30 minutes or until browned and bubbly.

Makes 4 servings.

MIXED VEGETABLES

VEGETABLE MEDLEY

2 tablespoons olive oil
½ clove garlic, crushed
½ cup frozen chopped green
   pepper
½ cup frozen chopped onion
2 cups sliced yellow squash
1 cup frozen cut green beans

1 cup frozen whole-kernel
   corn
1 teaspoon salt
1 teaspoon chili powder
1 tablespoon lemon juice
Freshly ground pepper

Heat olive oil in 1½-quart saucepan. Add garlic, green pepper, and onion. Sauté 3 to 5 minutes. Add squash, green beans, and corn. Cover and cook over low heat about 20 minutes, stirring occasionally. Add salt, chili powder, lemon juice, and pepper, and mix.

Makes 4 servings.

MUSHROOMS

MUSHROOMS A LA LIMPET

¼ cup butter
2 cups sliced frozen
  mushrooms
1 cup frozen small onions
2 tablespoons chopped
  parsley

¼ teaspoon freshly grated
  nutmeg
½ teaspoon salt
2 tablespoons flour
1 cup Chicken Broth
  (page 167)
¼ cup sweet sherry wine

Heat the butter in a skillet, and sauté the mushrooms and onions for 5 minutes. Season with parsley, nutmeg, and salt. Cover and cook over low heat 5 minutes longer. Stir in the flour. Gradually add the Chicken Broth and sherry. Cook and stir until mixture boils and is thickened.
Makes 4 servings.

OKRA

SAUTÉED OKRA

2 cups frozen okra, partially
  defrosted
3 tablespoons butter

½ teaspoon salt
Dash freshly ground pepper

Cut okra pods in half lengthwise. Heat the butter in a skillet. Add the okra, and sauté 3 minutes. Season with salt and pepper. Cover and cook over low heat 10 minutes. If necessary, uncover and cook until okra is dry.
Makes 4 servings.

POTATOES

POTATO PATTIES

2 cups mashed potatoes,
  defrosted
1 egg, well beaten
2 tablespoons grated onion
½ teaspoon salt

Dash freshly ground pepper
Yellow or white cornmeal
  (about ½ cup)
Bacon fat or butter for frying

Mix together the potatoes, egg, onion, salt, and pepper. Shape into 6 or 8 flat patties. Coat well with cornmeal. Heat ¼ inch fat in skillet. Fry patties over moderately high heat, turning to brown both sides.

Makes 6 to 8 patties.

PUMPKIN

PUMPKIN GROG

2 eggs, separated
1 cup pumpkin, defrosted
½ cup firmly packed light
  brown sugar
1 cup milk
½ teaspoon cinnamon

2 tablespoons frozen orange-
  juice concentrate
½ cup light rum
1 cup softened vanilla
  ice cream
1–2 teaspoons freshly grated
  nutmeg

Beat the egg yolks until light. Mix in the pumpkin, brown sugar, milk, cinnamon, orange-juice concentrate, and rum. Beat the egg whites until stiff but not dry. Fold with vanilla ice cream into pumpkin mixture. Serve in low glasses or cups with a spoon. A grating of fresh nutmeg can be put on each serving.

Makes 6 servings.

SQUASH

SQUASH PUFF

2 cups mashed squash,
  defrosted
⅓ cup dark molasses
2 tablespoons flour
1 teaspoon salt

¼ teaspoon freshly grated or
  ground nutmeg
¼ teaspoon ground cloves
2 eggs, separated

Mix the squash with the molasses, flour, salt, nutmeg, and cloves. Fold in the egg yolks which have been beaten lightly. Beat the egg whites until stiff, and fold into squash mixture. Spoon into a buttered 1½-quart casserole. Bake in a 350° F. oven for 1 hour or until golden brown. Serve with ham or pork.

Makes 4 to 6 servings.

PART II
COURSES TO FREEZE

8 Appetizers

GENERAL RULES FOR FREEZING APPETIZERS

Because most appetizers take time, work, and special ingredients, it is very handy to have some ready in the freezer.

Remember that the flavors of highly spiced foods do not hold up as well under freezer storage as those of blander foods. For maximum flavor count on shorter storage period, or when possible, add spices after defrosting.

Mayonnaise breaks down in freezing. Substitute butter on small sandwiches made for freezing.

To freeze small canapé sandwiches, place unwrapped on baking sheet, and freeze through. Then package in containers or on cardboard to keep from being damaged. Seal. Label and date, and return to freezer.

Cooked egg whites become rubbery when frozen.
Cocktail-size unfilled cream puffs can be frozen. To use, recrisp in a 400° F. oven for 10 minutes. Fill and serve.

RECIPES

AVOCADO

AVOCADO DIP

2 ripe avocados
1 large ripe tomato, peeled
1 small clove garlic, peeled
1 teaspoon salt

1 teaspoon chili powder
1 tablespoon lemon juice
¼ teaspoon cumin

Peel and chop avocados. Discard seeds and juicy pulp of tomatoes, and chop fine. Press garlic with salt until thoroughly mashed. Combine avocado with tomatoes, garlic and salt, chili powder, lemon juice, and cumin. Chill.
Makes 2 cups.

To Freeze: Spoon into 1 2-cup or 2 1-cup containers, and cover tightly. Seal, label, and date. Freeze.

To Serve: Defrost, stir, and serve with corn chips.

Storage Time: About 1 month. If chili powder and cumin are omitted at freezing time and added when defrosting, the keeping time can be extended several weeks. If this is done, be sure to note amount of seasonings to be added on container.

CHEESE

CHEESE MOLD

1 tablespoon (1 envelope)
  unflavored gelatin
¼ cup cold water
1 cup chopped blanched
  almonds
⅔ cup prepared mayonnaise
½ teaspoon salt
1½ teaspoons dry mustard

Dash Tabasco sauce
2 cups grated sharp cheddar
  cheese
½ cup grated Parmesan
  cheese
¼ cup crumbled Danish blue
  cheese
1 cup heavy cream, whipped

After Freezing:

Parsley sprigs

Crackers

Soften gelatin in cold water. Dissolve over hot water. Stir in remaining ingredients. Blend well. Spoon into 1-quart ring mold. Freeze.

Makes 1 quart.

To Freeze: Cover mold with freezer wrap, and seal, label, and date. Return to freezer.

To Serve: Unmold on plate. Garnish center with parsley. Surround with assorted crackers. Have knife for spreading cheese on crackers.

Storage Time: Up to 6 weeks.

CHEESE PASTRIES

2 cups sifted all-purpose flour
1 teaspoon salt
½ cup shortening

½ cup grated sharp cheddar
   cheese
Ice water (about ⅓ cup)
Flour

After Freezing:

Paprika

Sift flour and salt into a bowl. Cut in shortening and cheese with a pastry blender or 2 knives until mixture is well blended. Gradually stir in water, mixing lightly with a fork until pastry mixture follows fork. Chill. On a lightly floured board form into 2 rolls about 1½ inches thick and 6 inches long.

Makes 2 rolls; each roll will make about 24 pastries.

To Freeze: Wrap each roll individually in freezer wrap. Seal, label, and date. Freeze.

To Bake: When ready to use, remove from freezer, and defrost slightly. Cut into ¼-inch-thick slices. Sprinkle with paprika. Bake in a 400° F. oven for 10 to 12 minutes or until lightly browned.

Storage Time: Up to 3 months.

Variation: Sprinkle unbaked slices with sesame seeds or onion salt before baking.

DANISH BLUE CHEESE ROLLS

1 cup Danish blue cheese,
   softened
1 8-ounce package cream
   cheese, softened
2 teaspoons Worcestershire
   sauce

2 to 4 tablespoons heavy
   cream
1 cup finely chopped toasted
   almonds or cashew nuts

Mix Danish blue cheese and cream cheese with Worcestershire sauce and enough cream to give a smooth consistency. Chill. When chilled, shape into 2 rolls, and coat outside with chopped nuts.

To Freeze: Wrap with freezer wrap. Seal, label, and date. Freeze.

To Serve: Defrost partially. Serve with crackers and knife for spreading.

Storage Time: Up to 2 months.

SNAPPY CHEESE ROLLS

4 cups shredded sharp
    cheddar cheese
½ pound Danish blue cheese
1 8-ounce package cream
    cheese
4 tablespoons sweet sherry or
    port wine

½ cup finely chopped
    walnuts
1 teaspoon grated onion
4 tablespoons finely chopped
    parsley

Blend cheddar, Danish blue, and cream cheeses together. Add sherry or port, walnuts, onion, and parsley, mix well. Chill until mixture is firm enough to shape into rolls. Make 4 rolls.

To Freeze: Wrap in freezer wrap. Seal, label, date, and freeze.

To Serve: Defrost. Serve with crackers and knife for spreading.

Storage Time: About 4 weeks.

CHEESE ROLLED SANDWICHES

1 loaf thinly sliced white
    sandwich bread
1 8-ounce package cream
    cheese, at room tempera-
    ture
¼ teaspoon salt
1 teaspoon prepared mustard
Dash Tabasco sauce

1 teaspoon prepared grated
    horseradish
2 to 4 tablespoons heavy
    cream or milk
24 stuffed medium olives,
    well drained
24 thin strips green pepper
24 thin strips pimiento

Get as fresh bread as possible. Trim off crusts, and wrap in dampened towel. Soften cream cheese, and mix with salt, mustard, Tabasco, and horseradish. Add enough cream, a small amount at a time, so that mixture will spread easily. Place 3 slices of bread on board. Spread filling on ends of center slice, and pinch all 3 slices together. Spread filling on top side of all three slices. Place olives across one end, alternating strips of green pepper and pimiento crosswise at about 2-inch intervals. Starting at olive end, roll sandwich carefully, pressing ends of center slice so slices do not separate. Repeat spreading and rolling process 8 times.

To Freeze: Wrap immediately in freezer wrap or transparent wrap. Label, date, and freeze.

To Serve: Defrost. Slice roll with a sharp knife into thin slices.
    Each roll should make about 6 sandwiches.

Storage Time: Up to 6 months.

CHICKEN

CHINESE CHICKEN WINGS

16 chicken wings ½ cup honey
½ cup soy sauce 2 cloves garlic, crushed
½ cup lemon juice 4 to 6 tablespoons peanut oil
After Freezing:
1 or 2 tablespoons peanut oil

Disjoint chicken wings, wash, and dry. Save tips for soup. Mix soy sauce with lemon juice, honey, and garlic in a large bowl. Add chicken wings to mixture. Cover and marinate in refrigerator several hours or overnight, turning occasionally so that all wings are coated. When ready to cook, put oil in a 9-inch skillet over medium heat. Drain chicken wings, and add to hot oil. Cook, turning often, for about 25 minutes or until chicken wings are browned and cooked throughout.
Makes 32 pieces.

To Freeze: Remove from skillet, and cool. Wrap each wing in transparent wrap, and pack in a container, or overwrap with freezer wrap. Seal, label, and date. Freeze.

To Use: Remove all wrappings. Put frozen wings in skillet with 1 or 2 tablespoons oil over low to medium heat. Cook, turning occasionally, until wings are hot. This takes 5 to 10 minutes. If desired, increase heat last few minutes to crisp the skin. Serve hot. Since these wings are precooked, however, they can be defrosted and eaten cold.

Storage Time: About 4 months.

MEATBALLS

COCKTAIL MEATBALLS SUPERB

1 egg, well beaten
1 teaspoon salt
1 tablespoon chili sauce
¼ cup water
1 slice bread
1½ pounds ground beef
    chuck
2 tablespoons vegetable or
    olive oil
¼ cup finely diced onion

1 clove garlic, crushed
1 tablespoon flour
1 teaspoon dry mustard
1 cup Beef Stock (page 163)
¼ teaspoon oregano
¼ cup rye or bourbon
    whiskey
¼ cup dry vermouth
¼ teaspoon Angostura bitters

Beat egg in a large bowl. Add salt, chili sauce, water, and bread, and mix well. Add ground beef, and blend thoroughly. Form into 50 small meatballs. Place on flat pan, and chill thoroughly. After meatballs have chilled, heat oil in a skillet, and brown meatballs on all sides, removing them from pan as browned. Add onion, and sauté until tender but not browned. Stir in garlic, flour, and mustard. Add Beef Stock and stir until mixture comes to a boil and is thickened. Add oregano, whiskey, vermouth, and bitters, and simmer a few minutes. Return meatballs to gravy, and cook 5 minutes.
Makes 50 tiny meatballs.

To Freeze: Cool meatballs and gravy. Pack into containers or plastic bags. Seal, label, and date. Freeze.

To Serve: Heat meatballs and gravy. Serve in chafing dish over hot water.

Storage Time: Up to 3 months.

PÂTÉ

PÂTÉ DE FOIE POULET

2 cups (14 or 16 pairs) chicken livers
½ cup chicken broth
½ teaspoon salt
½ teaspoon freshly grated nutmeg

2 teaspoons grated onion
Dash cloves
½ cup butter or rendered chicken fat

After Freezing:
2 tablespoons red wine or brandy

Wash chicken livers, and put in a small skillet or saucepan with chicken broth. Simmer over low heat about 5 minutes, turning chicken livers once or twice, until all pink is removed. While still hot, combine chicken livers and broth with salt, nutmeg, grated onion, cloves, and butter in blender, and blend until smooth. (If no blender is available, push chicken livers while still warm through a sieve, and mix with remaining ingredients.) Chill.
Makes about 2 cups.

To Freeze: Pack pâté into 2 containers. Cover. Label, date, and freeze.

To Serve: Defrost pâté, and stir. Blend with red wine or brandy before serving. Serve with crackers or melba toast.

Storage Time: Up to 2 months.

PORK AND VEAL PÂTÉ

2 pounds lean pork
2 pounds veal shank
1½ quarts water
2 teaspoons salt
8 peppercorns
6 whole allspice
2 bay leaves

4 whole cloves
1 onion, peeled
1 carrot, peeled
½ tablespoon (½ envelope)
  unflavored gelatin
2 tablespoons wine vinegar

After Freezing:

2 hard-boiled eggs, sliced

¼ cup freshly chopped
  parsley

Rinse pork and veal, and put in kettle with water. Bring to a boil, and skim off any foam. Add salt, peppercorns, allspice, bay leaves, cloves, onion, and carrot. Cover and simmer until meat is tender, 1½ to 2 hours. Remove meat from broth. When cooled, cut meat from bones. Return bones to broth, and cook 30 minutes longer. Strain. Measure. Cook until reduced to 4 cups. Soften gelatin in vinegar, and add to hot broth. Using coarse blade, put meat through grinder. Mix with broth. Cool until mixture begins to thicken. Then pack into a 5 x 8-inch loaf pan. Chill until firm.

Makes 6 servings.

To Freeze: Can be frozen in pan, or unmold on tray. If on tray, freeze, then wrap frozen loaf in freezer wrap. Seal, label, and date. Return to freezer. To freeze in pan, cover with freezer wrap, seal, label, and date.

To Serve: Defrost in refrigerator. Place on platter. Garnish with sliced hard-cooked eggs and parsley. Slice to serve.

Storage Time: Up to 3 months.

SALMON

SMOKED SALMON TIDBITS

1 3-ounce package cream
    cheese, softened
¼ teaspoon salt
1 tablespoon lemon juice
Dash Tabasco sauce

1 teaspoon grated horse-
    radish
1 teaspoon capers (optional)
½ pound smoked salmon,
    thinly sliced

Season cream cheese with salt, lemon juice, Tabasco, and horseradish. If desired, a few drained capers may be mixed into the cheese. Spread on slices of salmon, and roll. Makes about 36 tidbits.

To Freeze: Wrap chilled rolls in freezer wrap. Seal, label, and date.

To Serve: Cut frozen rolls crosswise into about 1-inch pieces. When defrosted sufficiently, spear with cocktail toothpicks.

Storage Time: Up to 3 months.

9 Stocks and Soups

GENERAL RULES FOR
FREEZING HOMEMADE STOCKS AND SOUPS

Homemade soups taste especially good when all you have to do is take them out of your freezer and reheat.

Concentrate the soups as much as needed, considering primarily the amount of freezer space available. Table-ready soups can be frozen, but many homemakers do not have space in the freezer for such additional storage.

The only special rules to remember when freezing soup are: Leave headspace in the containers to allow for expansion of the frozen liquid. Package the soups in as small quantities as is reasonable, since the larger the block of frozen soup, the longer it takes to reheat it. Thick soups can be reheated in a double boiler over boiling water, and you will not have to watch them so closely.

A good homemade soup is not particularly inexpensive, but one likes to think it is, so I save all my beef, chicken, pork, and lamb trimmings and freeze them in labeled containers or freezer bags until I accumulate enough to make stock. Pork, beef, and chicken can be combined to make a marvelous stock. I generally keep lamb separate until I have enough bones and trimmings to make a lamb stock for lamb-barley soup. Or you can buy soup bones, beef shank, or a bone cut of beef chuck, and start with that.

I never throw out vegetable juices but add them to a labeled freezer container and use them in making soup stock.

RECIPES

BEEF STOCK

2 to 4 pounds beef, pork, and/or chicken bones and trimmings
2 quarts water or vegetable juice (or to cover)
1 large whole onion, peeled
1 piece celery
1 carrot, peeled
1 bay leaf
8 peppercorns
1 teaspoon salt
4 sprigs fresh parsley
½ teaspoon thyme

Put bones and trimmings in a large saucepot. Cover with water and/or vegetable juice. Bring to a boil, separating bones as they defrost, if they were frozen. When liquid is boiling, skim off the foam that will accumulate on top. Reduce heat to a simmer, and add the onion, celery, carrot, bay leaf, peppercorns, salt, parsley, and thyme. Cover and simmer 3 to 4 hours. Cool. Strain broth into a bowl, and refrigerate overnight. Remove meat from bones and dice. Refrigerate.

Next day, skim fat off cold stock. Reheat and taste for strength and seasoning. If the stock is to be frozen, it can be boiled until it is concentrated to half its volume. The meat can be frozen for future use.

Makes about 2 quarts.

To Freeze: Chill concentrated stock, and pour into pint or quart containers. Leave 1-to-1½-inch space at top of container. Label, date, seal, and freeze. Be sure to indicate on label the concentration of stock (for example: Add equal parts water, add ½ amount of water).

To Serve: Place frozen stock in saucepan over medium heat with the required amount of water. Cover and cook until completely defrosted and hot.

Storage Time: Up to 3 months.

ONION SOUP

1 quart frozen concentrated
   Beef Stock (page 163)
2 cups water
10 to 12 medium-size red
   onions (if not available,
   Bermuda onions may be
   substituted)
2 tablespoons olive oil

2 tablespoons butter
Salt and freshly ground
   pepper to taste
1 tablespoon sugar
6 rounds French bread,
   toasted
Grated Parmesan cheese

Bring stock and water to boil. Peel onions, and slice slantwise so as not to make rings. Heat olive oil and butter in a skillet, and sauté onions until tender but *not browned.* Season with salt, pepper, and sugar. Divide between 6 heatproof casseroles. The traditional serving dish for onion soup is a ceramic casserole which holds about 1½ cups and has its own lid or can be covered. Pour Beef Stock over onions. Place toasted bread on soup, and sprinkle generously with

Parmesan cheese. Cover and heat in a 375° F. oven for 15 minutes.

Pass additional Parmesan cheese. Makes 6 servings.

TOMATO-VEGETABLE SOUP

1 quart frozen concentrated
   Beef Stock (page 163)
Diced meat from Beef Stock
1 cup diced carrots
½ cup diced onion
½ cup diced celery
2 cups canned tomatoes

½ teaspoon basil
3 tablespoons uncooked long-
   grain rice
Salt and freshly ground
   pepper
3 tablespoons chopped
   parsley

Put stock in a large saucepot. Bring to a boil. Add meat, carrots, onion, celery, tomatoes, and basil. Simmer, covered, for about 1 hour. Add rice, and cook 20 minutes longer. Season to taste with salt and pepper. Sprinkle with chopped parsley.

Makes 4 to 6 servings.

To Freeze: Tomato-Vegetable Soup can be frozen. If made to be frozen, it is not necessary to freeze Beef Stock; make the stock and continue with the recipe. Chill soup, and pour into pint or quart containers. Leave 1-to-1½-inch space at top of container. Label, date, seal, and freeze.

To Serve: Heat to boiling.

Storage Time: Up to 3 months.

LAMB-BARLEY SOUP

Prepare 1 quart of lamb stock as directed for Beef Stock (page 163). I like to add ½ teaspoon thyme with the seasonings to lamb bones and trimmings.

¼ cup pearl barley
1 quart frozen concentrated
    lamb stock
2 cups water
1 cup diced carrots

½ cup diced onion
½ cup diced celery
Diced meat from lamb
Salt and pepper to taste

Soak barley with 2 cups water overnight. Add to lamb stock and 2 cups water. Simmer, covered, 1 hour. Add carrots, onion, celery, and meat, and simmer 30 to 40 minutes longer. Add salt and pepper to taste.

Makes 4 to 6 servings.

To Freeze: If Lamb-Barley Soup is to be frozen, omit 2 cups of liquid, and do not freeze the lamb broth. Make lamb broth as directed, and continue with soup. Chill soup, and pour into pint or quart containers. Leave 1-to-1½-inch space at top of container. Label, date, seal, and freeze.

To Serve: Heat to boiling.

Storage Time: Up to 2 months.

MISSION LENTIL SOUP

3 tablespoons butter
1 cup chopped onion
1 carrot, chopped
¾ pound dried lentils
6 cups Beef Stock (page 163)
    or water

1 marrow bone, cracked
1 teaspoon salt
⅛ teaspoon freshly ground
    pepper

After Freezing:

2 tablespoons lemon juice   ½ teaspoon ground cumin

Heat butter in a large saucepot. Add onion and carrot, and cook 5 minutes, stirring. Wash lentils in hot water. Drain and add to vegetables with stock, marrow bone, salt, and pepper. Cover and simmer over low heat until lentils are soft, about 1 hour. Remove bone, and puree soup either through a sieve or in a blender.

Makes 2 quarts, or 8 servings.

To Freeze: Chill. Spoon into 2 containers. Cover, label, date, and freeze. Note on label that lemon juice and cumin are to be added to heated soup.

To Serve: Defrost and heat. Add lemon juice and cumin powder to hot soup.

Each container makes 1 quart, or 4 servings.

Storage Time: Up to 3 months.

CHICKEN BROTH

3 to 4 pounds chicken necks, backs, etc., or a 4-pound plump hen
2 quarts water
1 teaspoons salt
6 peppercorns
1 onion, peeled
1 carrot, sliced
2 stalks celery
Several sprigs parsley
1 bay leaf
½ teaspoon thyme

Wash chicken well, and put in large saucepot. Cover with water, and bring to a boil. Skim off any foam that forms. Add salt, peppercorns, onion, carrot, celery, parsley, bay leaf, and thyme, and simmer slowly, covered, for 1½ hours. Cool. Strain broth into a bowl, and refrigerate overnight. Remove chicken meat from bones. Finely dice.

Next day, skim fat off cold broth. Reheat and taste for strength and seasoning. If the broth is to be frozen, it can be boiled until it is concentrated to half its volume.

Makes about 2 quarts.

To Freeze: Chill concentrated broth, and pour into pint or quart containers. Leave 1-to-1½-inch space at top of container. Label, date, and freeze. Be sure to indicate on label the concentration of stock (for example: Add equal parts water, add ½ amount of water).

To Serve: Place frozen broth in saucepan with the required amount of water. Cover and cook until completely defrosted and hot.

Storage Time: Up to 3 months.

CHICKEN-RICE SOUP

3 cups Chicken Broth   ¼ cup uncooked long-grain
   (page 167)   rice

To Chicken Broth, add ¼ cup white rice. Cook for approximately 20 to 25 minutes or until rice is tender.
Makes 4 to 6 servings.

CHICKEN-VEGETABLE SOUP

1 quart frozen concentrated   1 cup diced celery
   Chicken Broth (page 167)   ½ cup diced onion
2 cups water   Salt and pepper to taste
1 cup diced carrots   2 tablespoons chopped
1 cup diced green beans   parsley

Bring broth and water to a boil. Add carrots, green beans, celery, and onion. Season with salt and pepper. Simmer, covered, for 1 hour. Add chopped parsley, and serve.
Makes 4 to 6 servings.

To Freeze: If Chicken-Vegetable Soup is to be frozen, it is not necessary to freeze Chicken Broth. Make broth, and continue with recipe. Chill soup, and pour into pint or quart containers. Leave 1-to-1½-inch space at top of container. Label, date, seal, and freeze.

To Serve: Heat to boiling.

Storage Time: Up to 3 months.

FRESH MUSHROOM SOUP

1 pound fresh mushrooms	½ cup flour
¼ cup minced onion	½ teaspoon nutmeg
½ cup butter	

After Freezing (for 1 container):

2 cups light cream or milk	Salt and pepper to taste
or 1 cup light cream and	
1 cup Chicken Broth	
(page 167)	

Chop mushrooms, and sauté with onion in butter for 5 minutes. Blend in flour, and season with nutmeg.

To Freeze: Chill. Pack into 4 1-cup containers. Label, date, and freeze. Note on label that 2 cups light cream or milk or 1 cup light cream and 1 cup Chicken Broth are to be added.

To Serve: Defrost 1 container. Add the light cream (or half light cream, half Chicken Broth), and cook and stir until mixture is slightly thickened. Season with salt and pepper.
Each container makes 4 servings.

Storage Time: Up to 3 months.

TURKEY BROTH

No soup section would be complete without talking about the place of the roast-turkey carcass in soup! After turkey has seen better days, I strip off all the meat, and package and freeze it for future use. If there is any stuffing left inside, I take that out also. If enough, it can be packaged and frozen.

To Freeze: Depending on the size of the turkey, either break or saw the bones into manageable pieces, and compress them into as neat a package as possible. If there are sharp bone ends, cover them with several thicknesses of foil. Wrap with freezer wrap, and seal. Label and date. Freeze.

Storage Time: Frozen turkey carcass will keep up to 6 months.

To Make Turkey Broth: Follow substantially the same recipe as for Beef Stock (page 163). You may have to start with more water, depending on the size of the carcass, in which case you will probably have to boil the broth a little longer to concentrate.

Turkey Broth can be used in the same recipes as Chicken Broth.

MIDWEST CHILI WITH BEANS

2½ cups dried red beans
2 tablespoons bacon fat
2 cups coarsely diced onion

2 green peppers, chopped
2 pounds ground beef chuck
3 teaspoons salt

After Freezing:

5 cups canned tomatoes
¼ teaspoon cayenne pepper

4 tablespoons chili powder

Soak beans overnight. Cook until tender in water to cover. Drain. Heat bacon fat in skillet, and sauté onion and green pepper until tender. Add beef, and cook until lightly browned. Add salt and beans.

To Freeze: Cool. Spoon into 2 freezer containers (about

1 quart). Label, date, and freeze. Note on label that 2½ cups canned tomatoes, ⅛ teaspoon cayenne pepper, and 2 table-spoons chili powder are to be added to *each* container when chili is heated.

To Serve: Put chili in a saucepan. Add tomatoes, cayenne pepper, and chili powder. Cover and simmer, stirring occa-sionally. Makes 8 to 12 servings.

Storage Time: Up to 4 months.

APPLE SOUP

A European food custom that has never caught on much in the States is the fruit soup. This Apple Soup makes a delightful start to a luncheon or dinner on a hot summer day.

12 tart apples	Rind of 2 lemons, finely
1 cup water	grated
2 3-inch sticks cinnamon	6 tablespoons sugar
4 cloves	Dash salt

After Freezing:

4 tablespoons lemon juice	¼ cup sour cream
4 cups claret wine	

Wash and cut apples into quarters. Remove stems, and cut out any bruised spots. Put into a 5-quart saucepan. (Apples should fill saucepan to about ⅔ of its capacity.) Add water, cinnamon, cloves, and lemon rind. Bring mixture to a boil over high heat, cover, and reduce heat to medium, and cook 5 to 10 minutes or until apples are soft, stirring apples once. While still hot, remove spices, and push pulp through a sieve or food mill. Stir in sugar and salt.

To Freeze: Chill. Spoon into 2 freezer containers. Cover,

label, date, and freeze. Note on label to add 2 tablespoons lemon juice and 2 cups claret wine to each container.

To Serve: Defrost. Mix with lemon juice and chilled claret wine. Serve very cold with a dollop of sour cream. Makes about 1 quart ready-to-serve, or 6 servings.

Storage Time: Up to 3 months.

10 Breads

GENERAL RULES FOR FREEZING BREADS

Breads, both yeast and quick, really take to the freezer. Once you've sampled the products of a day spent baking and freezing your own breads, you'll have another hard choice to make on what to freeze when the freezer starts to get full!

There are a *few* rules:

Don't overbake products so that they dry out before they get to the freezer.

Frost coffee breads or any product that needs frosting *after* it comes from the freezer.

Reheat breads quickly so they won't dry out.

Bread slices more easily if sliced while still partially frozen.

One of the rules of the game when making your own

bread is that you buy a *good* bread knife for slicing. My own preference is a knife with a finely serrated edge.

NOTES ON MAKING BREAD

To Knead: Form the bread into a ball on a floured board, pick up a side of the ball, and with the part of the palm nearest the wrist push the dough into the center. Next, give the ball a quarter turn, and repeat. Continue this procedure until the bread is smooth and elastic. It will be necessary to add flour while kneading, but don't be too heavy-handed. You'll be surprised how long you can knead before the dough begins to stick.

To get a good nest in which to incubate the bread, put the bread dough in a bowl in a cold oven. Then fill a bowl with boiling water, and set it in beside the bread. You may have to empty the bowl and refill it with boiling water once more during the rising time, but this is a simple way to assure a cozy place for the bread to rise.

All the bread recipes are developed so they can be either cut in half or multiplied, as your refrigerator space and other needs dictate.

For storage times we have given you the shortest times. It is possible to store most of the baked goods longer. For two reasons we suggest you make it not much longer:

1. The quality starts to deteriorate.

2. We just don't believe in keeping things forever in the freezer. It's poor economy because the food starts to look like it's been there too long and no one will eat it.

FREEZING UNBAKED DOUGH

As all of you know, it is possible to buy unbaked or partially baked breads from the store freezer. It is also *possible* to freeze unbaked yeast products that are made at home, but this is not recommended. Commercially prepared unbaked or partially baked frozen bread products are made under highly scientifically controlled conditions so that each time they are prepared they are the same. This is not as true at home. However, some recipes have recently been developed for home freezing of unbaked dough. Several of these are included at the end of this chapter. For complete success follow the recipe and directions carefully.

RECIPES

YEAST BREADS

WHITE BREAD

1 quart milk, scalded
6 tablespoons shortening
¼ cup granulated sugar
2 tablespoons salt

2 packages active dry yeast
¼ cup lukewarm water
12 cups sifted all-purpose
    flour

Combine milk with shortening, sugar, and salt. Cool to lukewarm. Soften yeast in water, and mix with milk mixture. Add enough flour (about 12 cups) to make a stiff dough, and mix thoroughly. Turn out on a floured board, and knead for 10 minutes until smooth and satiny.

Grease a large bowl with soft shortening. Put in the dough, and grease it. Cover first with waxed paper, then with a towel. Set in a warm place (about 80° F.) away from drafts. Let rise until doubled in bulk. This takes from 1½ to 2 hours, depending on warmth of place where bread is. Punch dough down, and let stand 30 minutes. Then turn out on lightly floured board, and shape into 4 balls. Cover and let rest 10 minutes. Then shape into loaves by flattening balls into rectangles about 9 inches long. Roll from long side into tight roll, and place in 4 greased 9½ x 5½-inch loaf pans. Grease tops of loaves with soft shortening. Cover as before, and let rise in warm place until doubled in bulk —about 1½ to 2 hours.

Bake in a 400° F. oven for 40 minutes. Remove immediately from pans onto rack. Brush with butter while warm.

Makes 4 loaves.

To Freeze: Cool. Wrap bread tightly in freezer wrap or plastic bags, excluding all air if bags are used. Seal. Label, date, and freeze.

To Use: Defrost. Wrap in foil, and heat at 425° F. for 15 minutes.

Storage Time: Up to 1 year.

WHOLE WHEAT BREAD

1 quart milk, scalded
6 tablespoons shortening
4 tablespoons molasses
2 tablespoons brown sugar
2 tablespoons salt
2 packages active dry yeast

¼ cup lukewarm water
8 cups unsifted whole wheat
   flour (if available, use
   stone-ground whole
   wheat flour)
4 cups sifted all-purpose flour

Combine milk with shortening, molasses, brown sugar, and salt. Cool to lukewarm. Soften yeast in water, and mix with milk mixture. Add whole wheat flour and enough of the white flour (about 4 cups) to make a stiff dough, and mix thoroughly. Turn onto a floured board, and knead for 10 minutes until smooth and satiny.

Grease a large bowl with soft shortening. Put in the dough, and grease it. Cover first with waxed paper, then with a towel. Set in a warm place (about 80° F.) away from drafts. Let rise until doubled in bulk. This takes about 2 hours, depending on warmth of place where bread is. Punch dough down, and let stand 30 minutes. Then turn out on lightly floured board, and shape into 4 balls. Cover and let rest 10 minutes. Shape into loaves by flattening balls into rectangles about 9 inches long. Roll from long side into tight rolls and place in 4 greased 9½ x 5½-inch loaf pans. Grease loaves with soft butter. Cover as before, and let rise in warm place until doubled in bulk, about 1½–2 hours.

Bake in a 400° F. oven for 40 minutes. Remove immediately from pans onto rack. Brush with butter while warm.

Makes 4 loaves.

To Freeze: Cool. Wrap bread tightly in freezer wrap or plastic bags, excluding all air if bags are used. Seal. Label, date, and freeze.

To Use: Defrost. Wrap in foil, and heat at 425° F. for 15 minutes.

Storage Time: 3 months to 1 year.

POTATO BREAD

4 cups lukewarm potato
    water
1 package active dry yeast
2 cups mashed potatoes
4 tablespoons granulated
    sugar

6 tablespoons shortening,
    melted
2 tablespoons salt
12 cups sifted all-purpose
    flour

Combine potato water with yeast, and let stand about 30 minutes. Stir in potatoes and 1 tablespoon sugar. Let stand 1 hour. Stir. Cover and let stand in a warm place overnight.

Next morning, add shortening, 3 tablespoons sugar, salt,

and half the flour to the potato mixture. Beat until smooth. Stir in remaining flour to make a stiff dough. Turn out on a floured board, and knead 10 minutes until smooth and satiny.

Grease a large bowl with soft shortening. Put in the dough, and grease it. Cover first with waxed paper, then with a towel. Set in a warm place (about 80° F.) away from drafts. Let rise until doubled in bulk. This takes from 1½ to 2 hours, depending on warmth of place where bread is. Punch dough down, and let stand 30 minutes. Then turn out on lightly floured board, and shape into 4 balls. Cover and let rest 10 minutes. Then shape into loaves by flattening balls into rectangles about 9 inches long. Roll from long side into tight rolls, and place in 4 greased 9½ x 5½-inch loaf pans. Grease loaves with soft shortening. Cover as before, and let rise in warm place until doubled in bulk, 1½ to 2 hours.

Bake in a 400° F. oven for 40 minutes. Remove immediately from pan onto rack. Brush with butter while warm.

Makes 4 loaves.

To Freeze: Cool. Wrap bread tightly in freezer wrap or plastic bags, excluding all air if bags are used. Seal. Label, date, and freeze.

To Use: Defrost. Wrap in foil, and heat at 425° F. for 15 minutes.

Storage Time: 3 months to 1 year.

FRENCH BREAD

1 package active dry yeast
1½ cups warm water
1 tablespoon granulated
    sugar

1½ teaspoons salt
2 tablespoons butter
4 cups sifted all-purpose flour

Combine yeast and warm water in a large bowl. Add sugar, salt, and butter. Stir in flour, mixing well. Put bowl in a warm place, away from drafts, and stir through dough with a spoon every 10 minutes for 5 times. Keep dough covered with a towel. Turn dough out on a lightly floured board. Divide in half, and shape into 2 balls. Let rest 10 minutes, covered.

Roll each ball into a rectangle 10 x 8 inches. Roll up from long side, and seal edge. Place on greased baking sheet. Slash diagonally 4 or 5 times. Cover and let rise until doubled in bulk (about 1 to 1½ hours). Bake in a 400° F. oven for 30 to 35 minutes. Brush with butter while warm.

Makes 2 loaves.

To Freeze: Cool. Wrap loaves in freezer wrap. Seal. Label, date, and freeze.

To Use: *Plain:* Defrost. Wrap in foil, and heat in a 425° F. oven for 10 to 12 minutes. *Garlic Bread:* Defrost. Crush ½ clove garlic in garlic press or mince finely. Mix garlic with 4 to 6 tablespoons butter. While bread is partially frozen cut into 1-inch slices. Spread with garlic butter, and rearrange into loaf on a long piece of aluminum foil. Fold foil around bread, and heat in a 425° F. oven for about 15 minutes. Serve at once.

Storage Time: 3 months to 1 year.

DUTCH HOLIDAY BREAD

1 cup milk
¾ cup granulated sugar
1 cup butter, melted
1 teaspoon salt
2 packages active dry yeast
½ cup lukewarm water
8 cups sifted all-purpose flour

4 eggs, well beaten
1 cup light raisins
1 cup finely chopped candied
    lemon peel
1 cup blanched almonds,
    finely chopped

Scald milk. Add sugar, butter, and salt to milk. Cool to lukewarm. Soften yeast in water. Combine with milk mixture. Add about half the flour. Add beaten eggs, and beat well. Add enough of remaining flour to make a smooth dough. Mix in raisins, lemon peel, and almonds.

Turn dough into 2 greased and floured 9-inch cake tins. Cover with towel, and let rise in warm place (1 to 2 hours) until doubled in bulk. Place in a moderate oven (375° F.), and bake about 40 minutes until nicely browned. Remove from pan, and cool on rack.

Makes 2 loaves.

To Freeze: Wrap bread tightly in freezer wrap or plastic bags, excluding all air if bags are used. Seal. Label, date, and freeze.

To Use: Defrost. Serve plain or toasted.

Storage Time: Up to 3 months.

ORANGE-CINNAMON BREAD

1 envelope active dry yeast
2 cups orange juice
6 tablespoons granulated
    sugar
2 teaspoons salt

2 teaspoons grated orange
    rind
¾ cup melted butter
6 cups sifted all-purpose flour
1 cup granulated sugar
3 teaspoons cinnamon

Mix together yeast, orange juice, 6 tablespoons sugar, salt, and orange rind, stirring until yeast is softened. Stir in ¼ cup of the melted butter and enough flour (approximately 6 cups) to make a stiff dough. Mix thoroughly. Turn out on a floured board, and knead for 10 minutes until smooth and satiny.

Grease a large bowl with soft shortening. Put in dough, and grease it. Cover first with waxed paper, then with a towel. Set in a warm place (about 80° F.) away from drafts.

Let rise until doubled in bulk. This takes from 1 to 2 hours, depending on warmth of place where bread is. Punch dough down, and let stand 30 minutes. Turn out on lightly floured board, and shape into 2 balls. Cover and let rest 10 minutes. Roll each ball into a rectangle about 9 x 6 inches. Spread each with ¼ cup melted butter, and sprinkle each half with the 1 cup sugar and the cinnamon, which have been mixed together. Roll from short side, and pinch edges together. Place in greased 9½ x 5½-inch pans. Grease with soft butter. Cover and let rise until doubled in bulk.

Bake in a 375° F. oven about 45 minutes. Remove immediately from pans onto rack. Brush with butter while warm.

Makes 2 loaves.

To Freeze: Cool. Wrap bread tightly in freezer wrap or plastic bags, excluding all air if bags are used. Seal, label, date, and freeze.

To Use: Defrost. Serve plain or toasted.

Storage Time: 3 months to 1 year.

OATMEAL-RAISIN BREAD

1 cup uncooked oatmeal
   (quick or old-fashioned)
1 tablespoon butter
2 teaspoons salt
1 cup raisins
1½ cups boiling water

1 package active dry yeast
½ cup lukewarm water
¼ cup molasses
¼ cup firmly packed brown
   sugar
5 cups sifted all-purpose flour

Combine oatmeal, butter, salt, and raisins with boiling water. Cool to lukewarm. Soften yeast in lukewarm water. Add yeast with molasses and brown sugar to oatmeal mixture, and stir to mix. Add flour, stirring well, until a stiff dough is formed. Turn onto a floured board, and knead for 10 minutes until smooth and satiny.

Grease a large bowl with soft butter. Grease dough with butter, and add to bowl. Cover dough first with waxed paper, then with a towel. Set in a warm place (about 80° F.) away from drafts. Let rise until doubled in bulk. This takes about 2 hours, depending on warmth of place where bread is. Punch dough down, and let stand 30 minutes. Then turn out on lightly floured board, and shape into 2 balls. Cover and let rest 10 minutes. Shape into rectangles about 9 inches by 4 inches long. Roll from long side into tight rolls, and place in 2 greased 9½ x 5½-inch loaf pans. Grease loaves with soft butter. Cover as before, and let rise in warm place until doubled in bulk, about 2 hours.

Bake in a 375° F. oven for 45 minutes. Remove immediately from pans onto rack. Brush with butter while warm. Makes 2 loaves.

To Freeze: Cool. Wrap bread tightly in freezer wrap or plastic bags, excluding all air if bags are used. Seal, label, date, and freeze.

To Use: Defrost. Serve plain or toasted.

Storage Time: Up to 3 months.

CHEESE BREAD RING

2 packages active dry yeast
½ cup lukewarm water
½ cup milk, scalded and
   cooled
1⅓ cups mashed potatoes
⅔ cup melted butter

4 eggs
2 cups shredded Swiss cheese
6 cups sifted all-purpose flour
2 teaspoons salt
2 teaspoons granulated sugar

Soften yeast in water in a large bowl. Add cooled milk, and let stand 5 minutes. Add mashed potatoes, butter, and eggs. Mix and beat until well blended. Stir in cheese. Sift flour with salt and sugar, and blend into yeast mixture, mixing thoroughly. Turn out onto a lightly floured board, and knead for 8 to 10 minutes until smooth and satiny.

Grease a large bowl with soft butter. Put in the dough, and grease it. Cover first with waxed paper, then with a towel. Set in a warm place (about 80° F.) away from drafts. Let rise until double in bulk. This takes about 1 hour, depending on warmth of place where bread is. Punch dough down. Let stand 10 minutes. Turn out onto floured board, and shape into 2 long rolls, and fit into 2 well-greased 9-inch ring molds. Pinch ends together. Cover and let rise in a warm place until doubled in bulk, about 45 minutes. Bake in a 375° F. oven for 30 to 35 minutes. Turn immediately onto rack.

Makes 2 loaves.

To Freeze: Cool. Wrap bread tightly in heavy-duty foil. Seal. Label, date, and freeze.

To Use: Unwrap loaf, and put into ring mold in which it was originally baked. Cover top with foil, and bake in a 425° F. oven 20 minutes or until hot through. Serve warm with a light meal or lunch, or cut bread in thin slices, and serve with cocktails.

Storage Time: Up to 3 months.

FOLDOVERS

These rich pastries are a favorite with morning coffee.

8 cups sifted all-purpose flour
6 tablespoons granulated
    sugar
2 teaspoons salt
2 cups shortening or butter
2 packages active dry yeast
½ cup lukewarm water
6 eggs, separated

2 cups milk, scalded and
    cooled
1 cup firmly packed brown
    sugar
½ cup seedless raisins
½ cup chopped pecans or
    walnuts

After Freezing:

1 cup confectioners' sugar

1 or 2 tablespoons milk

Sift flour with granulated sugar and salt. Cut in butter with 2 knives or a pastry blender until texture of cornmeal. Soften yeast in water. Beat egg yolks, mix with milk and softened yeast, and stir into flour mixture, blending well. Cover and store in refrigerator overnight.

Next morning, knead dough on a lightly floured surface until it is smooth and satiny. Divide into 8 pieces. Roll each piece about 14 inches long and 8 inches wide. Beat egg whites, and spread on dough. Sprinkle all with brown sugar and half with raisins, the other half with nuts. Bring sides over filling. Seal edges together. Place on greased baking sheet. Let rise until double in bulk, 1½ to 2 hours.

Bake in 375° F. oven for about 35 minutes. Put on rack and cool.

Will make about 8 Foldovers.

To Freeze: Wrap each Foldover separately with freezer wrap. Seal, label, and date. When frozen, store together in box or plastic bag.

To Use: Defrost and heat in a 400° oven for about 5 minutes. Spread with icing made by mixing confectioners' sugar with milk. Cut crosswise into any width strips to serve.

Storage Time: Up to 4 months.

MRS. MARSHALL'S REFRIGERATOR ROLLS

2 packages active dry yeast
¼ cup lukewarm water
¾ cup milk
½ cup shortening or butter
¼ cup granulated sugar
½ teaspoon salt

2 eggs, well beaten
4 cups sifted all-purpose flour
1 tablespoon melted
    shortening
¼ cup melted butter

Mix yeast and water to soften yeast. Combine milk, ½ cup shortening, sugar, and salt in a saucepan. Heat until shortening is just melted. Cool to lukewarm. Combine with yeast and eggs, and mix well. Stir in flour gradually until a soft dough is formed. Store covered in the refrigerator 24 hours.

To bake, divide dough into fourths. On a floured bread board roll each fourth into a circle ¼ inch thick. Cut each circle into 8 pie-shaped wedges. Starting at wide end, roll into crescents. Dip in melted shortening mixed with butter, and place on a baking pan. Cover and let rise at room temperature until doubled in bulk. Bake in a 450° F. oven for 10 to 12 minutes.

Makes 32 rolls.

To Freeze: Cool on rack. Put whatever number of rolls you will need at one time together in a plastic bag. Seal, label, date, and freeze.

To Use: Defrost. Remove rolls from plastic bag. Wrap in a piece of foil. Heat in a 400° F. oven for 10 minutes. Serve hot.

Storage Time: 3 months to 1 year.

MARJORIE'S BUTTERMILK BISCUITS

This is an old-fashioned biscuit. Use it as bread or for shortcake.

8 cups sifted all-purpose flour
4 tablespoons granulated
    sugar
2 teaspoons salt
1 teaspoon baking powder
½ teaspoon baking soda

3 tablespoons shortening
3 tablespoons butter
2 packages active dry yeast
1 quart buttermilk
3 tablespoons melted butter
    or shortening

Sift flour with sugar, salt, baking powder, and baking soda into a bowl. Cut in shortening and butter with 2 knives or a pastry blender. Soften yeast in a small amount of buttermilk. Mix with remaining buttermilk into flour mixture, and beat vigorously. Turn dough onto a well-floured surface, and knead (adding extra flour as needed) until dough sticks together and not on the board. Roll out ¾ inch thick, and cut with a 2-inch-round biscuit cutter. Dip top into melted butter or shortening, and place biscuits side by side in pans. Cover and let rise 1 hour or until light. Bake in a 400° F. oven for 12 to 15 minutes until nicely browned.

Makes about 60 rolls.

To Freeze: Cool on rack. Do not separate rolls, but freeze 6 or 12 in 1 package. Wrap with freezer wrap, or put in plastic bags. Seal, label, date, and freeze.

To Use: Remove rolls from package. Wrap in aluminum foil. Heat in 400° F. oven for 10 minutes. Serve hot.

Storage Time: 3 months to 1 year.

APPLE ROLLS

1¾ cups milk, scalded
1 cup granulated sugar
½ cup butter or shortening
2 teaspoons salt
2 packages active dry yeast
¼ cup lukewarm water
2 eggs, beaten
7 cups sifted all-purpose flour

1 teaspoon nutmeg
1 cup thick applesauce
2 tablespoons brown sugar
½ cup raisins
2 tablespoons melted butter
2 tablespoons sugar
½ teaspoon nutmeg

Combine scalded milk with ½ cup sugar, butter or shortening, and salt, and cool to lukewarm. Soften yeast in water, and beat with eggs into milk mixture. Add 2 cups of flour. Cover and let rise in warm place until bubbly (about 45 minutes). Then add remaining ½ cup sugar, remaining

5 cups flour, and nutmeg, and mix well. Cover and let rise until doubled, 1½ to 2 hours.

Turn out onto lightly floured board, and roll ¼ inch thick. Cut into 4-inch squares. Combine applesauce with brown sugar and raisins. Put a spoonful in the center of each square. Bring corners up to center, and pinch edges together to seal. Place on greased baking pan. Brush with melted butter, and sprinkle with sugar, which has been mixed with nutmeg. Let rise until double in bulk.

Bake in a 375° F. oven for 25 minutes.

Makes 2½ dozen rolls.

To Freeze: Cool on rack. Rolls may be wrapped individually in freezer wrap and stored together in box or plastic bag. Seal, label, and date each roll. Or wrap them in suitable numbers in freezer wrap or in a plastic bag. Seal, label, and date. Freeze.

To Use: Place frozen rolls on baking sheet, and heat in a 400° F. oven until hot, about 12 to 15 minutes. Individually wrapped frozen rolls can be put in lunch boxes. They will defrost in time for lunch.

Storage Time. Up to 3 months.

BRIOCHE

1 cup melted butter	¼ cup lukewarm water
½ cup granulated sugar	6 eggs, beaten
½ teaspoon salt	4½ cups sifted all-purpose
¼ cup milk, scalded	flour
2 packages active dry yeast	1 egg yolk, beaten

Add butter, sugar, and salt to scalded milk. Cool to lukewarm. Soften yeast in lukewarm water, and stir into cooled milk mixture. Add beaten eggs. Stir in 3 cups flour, and beat 4 minutes with an electric mixer. Add remaining flour, and beat until smooth. Cover and let rise in a warm place (about 80° F.) until doubled in bulk, about 1 hour. Stir. Cover and refrigerate overnight.

Next day, roll dough into balls about half the size of the brioche pans or muffin tins, in which they will be baked, and press into the greased pans. With scissors, cut a little cross on top of the dough. Make another ball about half the size of the first, and place it on top of the dough in the pan. Let rise until double in bulk. Lightly brush with beaten egg yolk.

Bake in a 400° F. oven for 12 to 15 minutes until nicely browned.

Makes 30 brioches.

To Freeze: Cool on rack. Wrap brioches individually in aluminum foil, and store together in box or plastic bag. Seal. Label, date, and freeze.

To Use: Defrost and heat in brioche or muffin pans in a 400° F. oven for 10 minutes.

Storage Time: Up to 3 months.

SQUASH BREAD

This recipe was adapted from a cookbook published in 1908. It tastes great and is a marvelous color—the squash makes it yellow.

2 cups milk, scalded
¼ cup granulated sugar
3 teaspoons salt
2 tablespoons butter
2 cups mashed cooked squash
    (butternut or acorn)

1 envelope active dry yeast
¼ cup lukewarm water
8 cups sifted all-purpose flour
    (amount of flour de-
    pends on dryness of
    squash)

Combine the scalded milk with the sugar, salt, butter, and squash. Cool to lukewarm. Soften the yeast in warm water, and add to the milk mixture. Add enough flour to make a stiff dough, and mix thoroughly. Turn out on floured board, and knead for 10 minutes until smooth and satiny.

Grease a large bowl with soft shortening. Put the dough in, and grease it. Cover first with waxed paper, then with a towel. Set in a warm place (about 80° F.) away from drafts. Let rise until doubled in bulk (1½ to 2 hours). Punch dough down, and let stand 30 minutes. Turn out on lightly floured board, and cut into 3 pieces. Cover and let rest 10 minutes. Shape into 3 loaves by flattening dough into rectangles about 9 inches by 4 inches. Roll from long side into tight roll, and place in 3 greased 9½ x 5½-inch loaf pans. Grease loaves, cover as before, and let rise in a warm place until doubled in bulk, about 2 hours. Bake in a 400° F. oven for 40 minutes. Remove immediately from pan onto rack. Brush with butter while warm.

Makes 3 loaves.

To Freeze: Wrap cooled bread tightly in freezer wrap or plastic bags, excluding all air if bags are used. Seal. Label, date, and freeze.

To Use: Defrost. Wrap in foil, and heat at 425° F. for 15 minutes.

Storage Time: Up to 6 months.

QUICK BREADS

FRUIT BREAD

6 cups sifted all-purpose flour
1 teaspoon salt
9 teaspoons baking powder
2 cups granulated sugar
1½ cups chopped raisins

1½ cups diced mixed candied fruit
1½ cups chopped nuts
6 eggs, beaten
3 cups milk
⅔ cup melted shortening

Sift flour with salt, baking powder, and sugar into a bowl. Stir in raisins, fruits, and nuts. Combine eggs with milk and shortening. Add to flour mixture, stirring just to blend. Line 2 9½ x 5½-inch loaf pans with waxed paper, and grease. Spoon batter into pans, and let stand at room temperature 30 minutes. Then bake in a 350° F. oven for 1 hour or until done. Let stand in pans on rack for 10 minutes. Remove from pans, and remove waxed paper. Cool on rack.

Makes 2 loaves.

To Freeze: Wrap each loaf tightly with freezer wrap. Seal, label, date, and freeze.

To Use: Defrost. Bread can be sliced more easily while still slightly frozen.

Storage Time: Up to 2 months.

DATE AND NUT BRAN BREAD

2 cups chopped dates
3 cups boiling water
4 cups sifted all-purpose flour
4 teaspoons baking soda
1 teaspoon cinnamon
½ teaspoon nutmeg
¼ teaspoon ground cloves

2 teaspoons salt
3 cups all-bran
1½ cups chopped walnuts
4 cups firmly packed light
    brown sugar
6 tablespoons melted butter
2 eggs, slightly beaten

Combine dates with boiling water, and cool. Sift flour with baking soda, cinnamon, nutmeg, cloves, and salt. Mix in bran and walnuts. Mix dates and water with brown sugar, butter, and egg. Add to flour mixture, and stir just enough to moisten all flour. Spoon into 2 9½ x 5½-inch greased loaf pans. Bake in a 350° F. oven about 60 minutes. Cool in pans on rack 10 minutes. Remove from pan, and cool loaves on rack.

Makes 2 loaves.

To Freeze: Wrap each loaf tightly in freezer wrap. Seal. Label, date, and freeze.

To Use: Defrost. Bread can be sliced more easily while still slightly frozen. Date and Nut Bran Bread is especially good served as sandwiches, at tea, or toasted for breakfast.

Storage Time: Up to 2 months.

SPICED BANANA TEA LOAF

4 cups sifted all-purpose flour
2 teaspoons baking soda
1 teaspoon salt
1 teaspoon cinnamon
½ teaspoon nutmeg
¼ teaspoon ground cloves

1 cup butter
2 cups granulated sugar
4 eggs
2 cups mashed banana
1 cup finely chopped walnuts
    or pecans

Sift flour with baking soda, salt, cinnamon, nutmeg, and cloves. Cream butter and sugar until light and fluffy. Beat in eggs, one at a time. Add sifted dry ingredients alternately with mashed banana, stirring only to blend. Fold in walnuts. Spoon into 2 greased 9½ x 5½-inch loaf pans. Bake in a 350° F. oven for about 1 hour. Cool 10 minutes in pans on rack. Remove from pans, and cool on rack.

Makes 2 loaves.

To Freeze: Wrap each loaf tightly in freezer wrap. Seal. Label, date, and freeze.

To Use: Defrost. Bread can be sliced more easily while still slightly frozen.

Storage Time: Up to 2 months.

RICH COFFEE CAKE

5 cups sifted all-purpose flour
8 teaspoons baking powder
½ teaspoon salt
1 teaspoon cinnamon
1 cup butter
1½ cups granulated sugar
2 eggs

2 teaspoons grated orange
  rind
2 cups milk
1 cup chopped raisins
1 cup chopped pecans
½ cup sugar
2 teaspoons cinnamon

Sift the flour with the baking powder, salt, and 1 teaspoon cinnamon. Soften the butter in a bowl, and gradually beat in 1½ cups sugar until light and fluffy. Add the eggs and orange rind, and beat well. Alternately add flour mixture and milk, stirring just to moisten. Fold in the raisins and pecans. Spoon batter into 2 greased and floured 9 x 9 x 2-inch pans. Mix ½ cup sugar with 2 teaspoons cinnamon, and sprinkle on top of batter. Bake in a 350° F. oven for 30 minutes.

Makes 2 cakes.

To Freeze: Cool in pans on rack. Remove coffee cake from pans, and wrap tightly in freezer wrap. Seal. Label, date, and freeze.

To Use: Defrost. To heat, cut into squares, wrap in aluminum foil, and heat in a 400° oven for 10 to 15 minutes.

Storage Time: Up to 3 months.

HAWAIIAN MUFFINS

4 cups sifted all-purpose flour
8 teaspoons baking powder
1 teaspoon salt
½ cup butter
1 cup granulated sugar

2 eggs
2 cups undrained crushed
    pineapple
½ cup chopped macadamia
    nuts or pecans

Sift flour with baking powder and salt. Cream butter and sugar until light and fluffy. Beat in eggs. Add flour alternately with pineapple, stirring only to blend. Fold in macadamia nuts or pecans. Fill paper-lined muffin pans ⅔ full, and bake at 400° F. for 20 to 25 minutes.
Makes 2½ dozen muffins.

To Freeze: Cool. Freeze muffins, and pack into a plastic bag in a number that will be practical for use. Seal. Label, date, and return to freezer.

To Use: Defrost muffins. Wrap in foil package, and heat in a 400° F. oven about 10 minutes.

Storage Time: Up to 3 months.

QUICK BRUNCH BREAD

4 cups sifted all-purpose flour
4 teaspoons baking powder
½ teaspoon salt
1 teaspoon cinnamon
¼ teaspoon ground cloves
½ teaspoon nutmeg

½ cup butter
1 cup granulated sugar
1 egg
¾ cup milk
2 cups chopped fresh
    cranberries

Sift flour with baking powder, salt, cinnamon, cloves, and nutmeg. Soften butter, and gradually add sugar to butter, beating until light and fluffy. Beat in egg. Add milk alternately with flour mixture, stirring only enough to moisten flour. Fold in cranberries. Divide batter between 2 greased and floured 8 x 8 x 2-inch pans. Bake in a 350° F. oven 45 minutes.
Makes 2 cakes.

To Freeze: Cool on rack in pans. Remove bread from pan, and wrap tightly in freezer wrap. Seal. Label, date, and freeze.

To Use: Defrost. Cut into squares. Wrap in aluminum foil, and heat in a 400° F. oven for 10 to 15 minutes.

Storage Time: Up to 3 months.

CRANBERRY BREAD

4 cups sifted all-purpose flour
1⅓ cups granulated sugar
1 teaspoon salt
3 teaspoons baking powder
2 medium oranges

4 tablespoons butter
Hot water
2 eggs, beaten
2 cups cranberries, chopped
1 cup chopped pecans

Sift the flour with the sugar, salt, and baking powder into a bowl. Grate the rind of the oranges. Remove juice from oranges, and strain into a measuring cup. Add butter and enough hot water to orange juice to make 1½ cups. Add orange-juice mixture and eggs to flour mixture in bowl. Stir just to moisten. Fold in cranberries and pecans. Spoon batter into 2 greased and floured 8 x 8 x 2-inch pans. Bake in a 350° F. oven for 30 to 40 minutes or until a cake tester

comes out clean. Allow bread to stand in pans on rack 10 minutes. Remove from pans. Cool on rack.
Makes 2 loaves.

To Freeze: Wrap cooled bread in freezer wrap. Seal, label, and date. Freeze.

To Use: Defrost.

Storage Time: 3 to 4 months.

BRAN-RAISIN MUFFINS

3 cups 40% Bran Flakes
1½ cups milk
2 eggs
½ cup butter or shortening, softened

2¼ cups sifted all-purpose flour
¾ cup granulated sugar
4½ teaspoons baking powder
1½ teaspoons salt
½ cup raisins

Combine the bran flakes with the milk, and let stand several minutes or until all liquid is absorbed. Beat in the eggs and butter or shortening. Sift flour with the sugar, baking powder, and salt. Fold with the raisins into the bran mixture, stirring just to moisten flour. Fill greased 2½-inch muffin pans ¾ full. Bake in a 400° F. oven about 25 minutes. Remove at once from pans.
Makes 18 muffins.

To Freeze: Pack cooled muffins into plastic bag according to the number needed at one time. Seal, label, and date. Freeze.

To Serve: May be defrosted and served cold, or wrap

in aluminum foil, and heat in 400° F. oven for 15 to 20 minutes or until hot.

Storage Time: 6 months.

RECIPES FOR FREEZING UNBAKED DOUGH

FROZEN DINNER ROLLS

5½ to 6½ cups unsifted all-purpose flour
½ cup granulated sugar
1½ teaspoons salt
2 packages active dry yeast

1¼ cups water
½ cup milk
⅓ cup margarine
2 eggs (at room temperature)

In a large bowl thoroughly mix 2 cups of the flour with the sugar, salt, and undissolved active dry yeast. Combine the water, milk, and margarine in a saucepan. Stir over low heat until the liquids are very warm. (The margarine does not have to be melted.) Liquids should be 120° to 130° F., which is below boiling, but above the lukewarm temperature generally called for in yeast doughs. Gradually add warm liquids to dry ingredients, and beat 2 minutes at medium speed of electric mixer, scraping bowl occasionally. Add eggs and ½ cup flour. Beat at high speed 2 minutes, scraping bowl. Stir in enough additional flour to make a soft dough. Turn out onto lightly floured board, and knead until smooth and satiny, about 8 to 10 minutes. Cover with plastic wrap and then a towel, and let rest 20 minutes. Punch down dough. Shape into desired shapes for freezing.

To Freeze: Place on greased baking sheets. Cover with plastic wrap and foil, and seal well. Freeze until firm. Transfer to plastic or nylon bags in amounts to serve family use. Seal, label, date, and return to freezer.

To Use: Remove from freezer bags, and place on greased baking sheets. Cover. Let rise in warm place, free from drafts, until doubled in bulk, about 1½ hours. Bake at 350° F. for 15 minutes or until golden brown. Serve hot.

Makes about 4 dozen rolls.

Storage Time: Up to 4 weeks.

To Shape:
Cloverleaf Rolls:
Shape dough into tiny balls. Dip in melted margarine and place 3 together. To bake, place 3 balls in greased muffin tins, and let rise and bake as directed.

Biscuit Rolls:
Roll dough ½ inch thick, and cut into 2-inch circles with a biscuit cutter. Place circles on greased cookie sheet and bake as directed.

Parkerhouse Rolls:
Roll dough a little less than ½ inch thick, and cut in circles with 2-inch biscuit cutter. Lightly brush top with melted margarine. Crease across the center with the back edge of a dinner knife. Fold over, and lightly pinch edges together.

FREEZER RYE LOAVES

3½ to 4½ cups unsifted all-purpose flour
2 cups unsifted rye flour
1 tablespoon salt
1 tablespoon caraway seeds

2 packages active dry yeast
¼ cup softened margarine
2 cups very warm tap water
   (120° to 130° F.)
⅓ cup molasses

Combine flours. In a large bowl thoroughly mix 2 cups of the flour mixture with the salt, caraway seeds, and un-dissolved active dry yeast. Add margarine. Gradually add tap water and molasses to dry ingredients, and beat 2 minutes at medium speed of electric mixer, scraping bowl occasionally. Add ¾ cup flour mixture. Beat at high speed 2 minutes, scraping bowl. Stir in enough additional flour mixture to make a stiff dough. Turn onto lightly floured board, and knead until smooth and satiny, about 8 to 10 minutes. Divide dough in half, and form each half into a smooth round ball. Flatten each ball into a mound 7 inches in diameter.

Makes 2 loaves of dough.

To Freeze: Place dough on greased baking sheets. Cover with plastic wrap. Freeze until firm. Transfer to plastic bags. Seal. Label, date, and return to freezer.

To Use: Remove from freezer bag, and place on ungreased baking sheet. Cover and let stand at room temperature until fully thawed, about 2 hours. Let rise in warm place, free from drafts, until doubled in bulk, about 2 hours. Bake at 350° F. about 35 minutes or until done. Remove from baking sheets, and cool on wire rack.

Storage Time: Up to 4 weeks.

FREEZER STICKY PECAN BUNS

½ cup margarine
1 cup firmly packed dark
    brown sugar
½ cup light corn syrup
1 cup broken pecan meats
5½ to 6½ cups unsifted all-
    purpose flour
¾ cup granulated sugar
1 teaspoon salt

3 packages active dry yeast
½ cup softened margarine
1 cup very warm tap water
    (120° to 130° F.)
3 eggs (at room temperature)
¼ cup melted margarine
½ cup firmly packed dark
    brown sugar

Heat ½ cup margarine, 1 cup brown sugar, and corn syrup together, stirring until sugar is dissolved. Divide between 2 greased 9-inch-square pans. Sprinkle each pan with ½ cup broken pecan meats.

In a large bowl thoroughly mix 1¼ cups flour, granulated sugar, salt, and undissolved active dry yeast. Add the softened margarine. Gradually add tap water to dry ingredients, and beat 2 minutes at medium speed of electric mixer, scraping bowl occasionally. Add eggs and ¼ cup flour, and beat at high speed 2 minutes, scraping bowl. Stir in enough additional flour to make a soft dough. Turn onto lightly floured board, and knead until smooth and satiny, about 8 to 10 minutes. Divide dough in half. Roll into rectangle 14 x 9 inches. Brush with half margarine, and sprinkle on ¼ cup brown sugar. Roll up from short end to form a roll 9 inches long. Pinch seam to seal. Cut into 9 1-inch slices, and place, cut side down, in one of the prepared pans. Repeat with remaining half of dough, using remaining margarine and brown sugar.

Makes 1½ dozen buns.

To Freeze: Cover pans tightly with plastic wrap and then with aluminum foil. Seal, label, date, and freeze.

To Use: Remove pan from freezer and let stand, covered with plastic wrap, until fully thawed, about 3 hours. Let rise in a warm place, free from draft, until more than doubled in bulk, about 1 hour and 15 minutes. Bake at 375° F. for 20 to 25 minutes or until done. Cool 10 minutes in pan. Invert rolls onto plate to cool.

Storage Time: Up to 4 weeks.

11 Main Dishes and Leftovers

GENERAL RULES FOR FREEZING MAIN DISHES

Freezing main dishes can save time and money if done with discretion. Almost any main dish can be frozen with success, so the big problem is not to get carried away and freeze too many. It's easy to get too much food budget tied up in the freezer.

DOS AND DON'TS

Don't let the freezer fill up with main dishes you're always going to use tomorrow. Use them today!

Rotate dishes as they are stored, and use the earliest-stored dishes first.

Do watch for food bargains, and make double batches: one to eat right away, one to freeze for future use.

Don't overcook main dishes to be frozen. Remember that they will have additional cooking when reheated.

Don't forget to label main dishes with number of servings in container.

Don't plan to keep combination main dishes longer than 3 months, particularly those with spices and herbs, which begin flavor deterioration if kept longer. In many cases herbs or spices can be added when the dish is being reheated. This should be marked on the label.

Don't freeze dishes that take longer to defrost and cook than when started from scratch.

Don't forget to allow room at the top of containers for expansion. Allow ½ inch in pints and 1 inch in quarts with wide tops; ¾ inch in pints and 1½ inches in quarts with narrow tops.

POINTERS

Main dishes to be frozen should be cooled quickly to retard further cooking. Set hot pan of food in ice and water or in a cold place.

If packaging cooked dish in rigid container, fill container about ⅓ full, put in a layer of freezer wrapper (foil or cellophane), spoon in another ⅓, put in another layer of freezer wrapper, and fill container, leaving headspace. Cover and freeze. When food is taken from the container, it can be separated into 3 blocks and will reheat more quickly.

To freeze a casserole dish in the casserole and not tie up the casserole in the freezer, line the dish with heavy-duty foil, leaving enough up over sides to cover top. Fill and bake as directed. Chill. Cover and freeze. When frozen, remove from casserole. If necessary, overwrap with another layer of foil to be sure the seal is tight. Label and date, and return to freezer. To serve, reheat in same dish.

Fat, including butter and oil, in sauces and main dishes is not a very good keeper, so use recipes with a minimum of fat.

Cook macaroni and vegetables *al dente* in dishes to be frozen so that they won't overcook when reheated.

Sauces and gravies have a tendency to separate when reheated. Stir while reheating. Do not plan to store frozen sauces or gravies longer than 2 to 3 months.

Frozen unbaked pastry crusts are preferable to frozen prebaked.

Converted rice freezes better than other varieties.

PROCEDURES FOR REHEATING FROZEN MAIN DISHES

While it is preferable to reheat frozen main dishes without defrosting, sometimes it is necessary to thaw the food at least partially. Quick defrosting can be done by setting the container in warm water long enough to allow easy removal from the containers, or defrost in the refrigerator.

Frozen main dishes can be reheated in the oven or on top of the range. Oven heating takes longer and, of course, should be used for casserole dishes that were originally baked in the oven. Foods reheated in the oven need less stirring so are likely to retain better quality.

Creamed and sauced dishes should be reheated in a double boiler when possible. If dish is reheated over direct heat, keep the heat low, and stir often while the food defrosts.

When several frozen blocks of food are reheated at once, use a wider pan to prevent blocks from stacking against each other and taking longer to refrost.

FREEZING LEFTOVERS

Leftovers can be frozen to serve another day. Do not plan to keep them more than 3 or 4 weeks, and unless you have unlimited freezer space, don't allow them to clutter up the freezer just because you think you're being thrifty.

When you save a leftover, plan how you are going to use it when it goes into the freezer. For example, a cup of spaghetti meat sauce can be layered with cooked noodles and sour cream for a casserole. Or several cups of cooked rice can be made into fried rice. Or a few pieces of cooked chicken can be saved for a chicken and apple salad.

RECIPES

BAKED BEANS

BOSTON BAKED BEANS

"Real" baked beans take 5 to 6 hours to bake. When they come from the freezer, it takes only 40 minutes to defrost and reheat. Make several batches at once.

2 pounds pea beans	2 teaspoons dry mustard
1 teaspoon baking soda	4 teaspoons salt
1 pound salt pork	½ teaspoon freshly ground
1 medium-size onion	pepper
8 tablespoons brown sugar	4 cups boiling water
⅔ cup molasses	

Pick over and wash beans. Soak overnight in water. In the morning parboil the beans for 10 minutes with baking soda. (Use a large kettle, as the soda foams.) Drain the beans in a colander, and rinse with cold water. Cut piece of salt pork in half through its rind, and dice the rind into 1-inch squares. Put the onion and ½ of the salt pork in bottom of 2½-quart bean pot. Spoon in beans. Mix sugar, molasses, mustard, salt, and pepper with boiling water. Pour over beans in pot. Press the remaining diced salt pork into beans. If necessary, add additional boiling water to make liquid come up just to top of beans. Bake in a 300° F. oven for 5 hours, adding water as necessary.

Makes 2 quarts beans.

To Freeze: Chill. Discard the onion. Set salt pork aside. Spoon beans into 4 pint freezer containers, leaving room for piece of salt pork. Put a piece of salt pork into each container. Cover, label, date, and freeze.

To Serve: Defrost sufficiently, either in refrigerator or in warm water, to remove from cartons. Place in casserole. Cover and heat in 375° F. oven for 40 minutes or until defrosted, stirring several times.

Storage Time: Up to 3 months.

HAM-BEAN BAKE

2 pounds dry pea beans
2 quarts water
⅓ cup ham fat
1 cup finely chopped onion
6 tablespoons all-purpose
    flour
1½ teaspoons dry mustard

1 teaspoon salt
1½ tablespoons Worcester-
    shire sauce
5½ cups milk
3 cups diced cooked ham
2 cups grated American
    cheese

After Freezing:

Buttered dry bread crumbs
    (if casserole is used)

Pick over and wash beans. Soak overnight in water. Next morning, cook in same water about 1½ hours or until slightly underdone. Drain. Heat ham fat in large saucepan, and cook onion until lightly browned. Add flour, mustard, and salt, and mix well. Stir in Worcestershire sauce and milk, and cook and stir until mixture comes to a boil and is thickened. Stir in ham, beans, and cheese carefully. Cool.

Makes 16 1-cup servings.

To Freeze: Pack in freezer containers or oven-proof dishes. Wrap. Seal, label, date, and freeze.

To Serve: If frozen in container, transfer contents to top of double boiler, and reheat, stirring occasionally. If in casserole, sprinkle top with buttered dry bread crumbs, and heat in a 400° F. oven for about 60 minutes for quart size.

Storage Time: Up to 2 months.

CASSEROLES

BEEF, CHEESE, AND NOODLE COMBO

4 tablespoons vegetable or olive oil
1 cup chopped onion
4 tablespoons minced parsley
1 pound ground beef
4 cups canned tomatoes
2 cups tomato juice
⅔ cup freshly grated Parmesan cheese
1 teaspoon garlic salt

2 teaspoons Worcestershire sauce
4 teaspoons salt
¼ teaspoon freshly ground pepper
2 8-ounce packages medium noodles
1 pound American cheese, sliced

Heat oil, and cook onion, parsley, and beef until lightly browned. Add tomatoes, tomato juice, and Parmesan cheese, and season with garlic salt, Worcestershire sauce, salt, and pepper. Simmer 30 minutes. Cook noodles in boiling salted water until almost tender, approximately 10 minutes. Drain. Layer noodles, meat sauce, and sliced cheese into 2 buttered 2-quart casseroles which have been lined with foil, ending with noodles. Cool.
Makes 12 servings.

To Freeze: Freeze both dishes. Remove from casseroles. Overwrap. Seal, label, date, and return to freezer.

To Use: Remove freezer wrappings. Place food in original casserole, buttered. Cover and bake in a 400° F. oven for 30 minutes. Remove cover, stir slightly, and continue baking 30 minutes longer until hot and bubbly.

Each casserole makes 6 servings.

Storage Time: Up to 3 months.

PORK SUEY CASSEROLE

1 cup chopped green pepper
2 cups chopped onion
1½ cups chopped celery
3½ cups canned tomatoes
2 tablespoons butter
1½ pounds ground lean pork

1 8-ounce package medium-
    size noodles, cooked
    and drained
1 cup grated American cheese
1½ teaspoons salt
¼ teaspoon freshly ground
    pepper

After Freezing:

½ cup grated American
   cheese

½ cup dry bread crumbs

Mix green pepper, onion, celery, and tomatoes. Cook for 10 minutes, covered. Heat butter in skillet, and brown pork lightly. Mix cooked vegetables together with pork, noodles, cheese, salt, and pepper. Chill.

Makes 6 servings.

To Freeze: Pack into containers. Cover, label, date, and freeze.

To Serve: Defrost in refrigerator, and put into a buttered 2-quart casserole. Cover and bake at 400° F. for 30 minutes. Separate with fork. Sprinkle top with grated cheese mixed with dry bread crumbs. Continue baking until mixture is hot and bubbly, approximately 10 more minutes.

Storage Time: Up to 3 months.

LUNCHEON SAUSAGE

2 cups cooked chopped
   spinach
1 cup chopped celery
¼ cup chopped onion
1 cup soft bread crumbs

½ pound bulk sausage
1 egg
1 teaspoon salt
¼ teaspoon nutmeg

After Freezing:

½ cup grated American cheese

Lightly mix spinach, celery, onion, bread crumbs, sausage, and egg. Season with salt and nutmeg. Line a 1½-quart casserole with heavy-duty foil and butter. Spoon in mixture. Bake in a 350° F. oven for 30 minutes. Chill.

Makes 4 servings.

To Freeze: Cover chilled casserole with extra foil, using drugstore fold to seal (double over twice). Label and date. Freeze. When thoroughly frozen, remove from casserole, and store in freezer.

To Serve: Remove wrappings, and put food in buttered casserole. Bake at 400° F. for 40 minutes or until hot. Last 10 minutes sprinkle with grated cheese.

Storage Time: Up to 2 months.

RUTH'S SAUERKRAUT

2 pounds sauerkraut
2 cups diced ham
½ cup diced salami
4 slices bacon, cut up
1 cup diced carrot

1 cup cubed peeled apples
1 cup minced onion
1½ cups finely diced potato
1 cup Beef Stock (page 163)
1 cup dry white wine

Line a 2-quart casserole with aluminum foil. Arrange sauerkraut, ham, salami, bacon, carrot, apple, onion, and potato in layers in casserole. Pour Beef Stock and wine over all. Cover and bake in a 350° oven 1½ hours. Cool.

To Freeze: Freeze until contents of dish are frozen. Remove from casserole. Overwrap. Seal, label, date, and return to freezer.

To Use: Remove freezer wrappings. Place food in original casserole, buttered. Bake covered in a 400° F. oven for 45 minutes, stirring gently several times. Uncover and bake 15 minutes longer or until hot and bubbly. If necessary, add a little more dry white wine.
Makes 8 to 10 servings.

Storage Time: Up to 2 months.

POTATO PASTA

GNOCCHI

6 medium-size potatoes, pared	1 cup all-purpose flour
1 teaspoon salt	1 egg
	olive oil

Boil the potatoes with salt in water to cover until tender. Drain. Put through ricer or sieve. Put flour on board. Spoon potatoes onto flour, making a well in center. Let cool long enough to handle easily (but not cold). Break egg in well. Lightly knead egg and potato mixture in the flour until mixture is not sticky. Add additional flour if necessary, and knead about 10 minutes. Shape into a rope about ½ inch in diameter, and cut into 1-inch pieces. Flatten in the middle. When all are shaped, drop in boiling water a few at a time.

As they rise to the top, remove with a slotted spoon, and drain in a strainer. Mix with a small amount of olive oil.
Makes 6 servings.

To Freeze: Cool. Spoon into containers. Seal, label, and date. Freeze.

To Serve: Defrost, and heat in boiling water. Drain, and serve with melted butter.

Storage Time: Up to 3 months.

RICE PANCAKES

PANCAKES ALOHA

3 cups cooked long-grain rice
1 teaspoon salt
2 cups milk
2 cups sifted all-purpose flour
8 teaspoons baking powder
4 tablespoons granulated
    sugar
½ teaspoon nutmeg
2 eggs, well beaten
4 tablespoons melted butter
1 cup drained crushed
    pineapple

Combine all the ingredients, and mix thoroughly. Bake to a golden brown on a hot, greased griddle, making the pancakes about 5 inches in diameter.
Makes 2½ to 3 dozen pancakes.

To Freeze: Cool pancakes on cake rack. Separate with foil or freezer wrap dividers, and overwrap with freezer wrap in family-size units. Seal, label, date, and freeze.

To Use: Place pancakes on greased baking sheet, and heat in a 425° F. oven for 6 to 8 minutes. Serve with butter and syrup.

Storage Time: Up to 3 months.

VEGETABLE PIE

ONION TART

Pastry to Freeze (page 251)
    for 2 9-inch pies
6 cups finely chopped
    Spanish onions
½ cup butter
4 tablespoons flour

4 eggs, beaten
2 cups heavy cream
1 teaspoon salt
⅛ teaspoon freshly ground
    pepper
1 cup grated Swiss cheese

Line 2 9-inch pie plates with pastry. Flute edges. Sauté onions in butter until tender but not browned. Stir in flour, and cook 5 minutes. Remove from heat. Combine eggs, cream, salt, and pepper. Mix well. Stir in cheese and onion. Pour into 2 pastry shells.
Makes 2 pies.

To Freeze: Cool. Put unwrapped pies in freezer until frozen. Wrap with freezer wrap. Seal, label, date, and return to freezer.

To Serve: Defrost pie, and bake in a 375° F. oven for 30 to 35 minutes or until nicely browned. Cut into wedges, and serve hot.

Storage Time: Up to 2 months.

Variations: 6 cups of your favorite vegetable may be substituted for the onion, such as spinach, tomatoes, zucchini, or mushrooms, or any combination of them.

12 Salads

GENERAL RULES FOR FREEZING SALADS

Although greens, cucumbers, and tomatoes for salads cannot be frozen successfully, there are a number of types of salads which can be frozen. A rich frozen fruit salad served with rolls or tiny sandwiches is ideal for a luncheon. It can also double for salad or dessert.

Molded salads can be frozen in the mold, then unmolded, wrapped securely, and kept in the freezer. They are less likely to become damaged if kept in a pan or mold, however. Aluminum freezer pans are ideal for salads, as they come in a variety of shapes and are inexpensive enough so that they can be used for freezer storage.

When freezing gelatin salads, reduce liquid by ¼ to keep the salad from "weeping" when defrosted.

Use commercial mayonnaise in frozen salads, as it has a stabilizer that prevents separation of oil.

RECIPES

FRUIT SALADS

FROZEN CRANBERRY SALAD

2 1-pound cans whole
    cranberry sauce
2 cups dairy sour cream

2 9-ounce cans drained,
    crushed pineapple
1 cup finely chopped walnuts

After Freezing:

1 small head Boston or Bibb
    lettuce

½ cup mayonnaise
    (optional)

Blend cranberry sauce with sour cream. Fold in pineapple and nuts. Spoon into 2 4 x 8-inch pans. Freeze. Makes 12 servings.

To Freeze: Cover pans with freezer wrap. Seal. Label, date, and return to freezer.

To Serve: Cut frozen salad into squares. Serve on lettuce leaves with mayonnaise dressing if desired.

Storage Time: Up to 6 months.

FROZEN FRUIT MEDLEY

1 8-ounce package cream
    cheese
⅓ cup prepared mayonnaise
¼ teaspoon salt
2 cups heavy cream, whipped
½ cup chopped canned
    kumquats
½ cup chopped seeded fresh
    dates

¼ cup chopped maraschino
    cherries
½ cup drained crushed
    pineapple
2 tablespoons finely chopped
    preserved ginger
½ cup chopped blanched
    almonds

After Freezing:

1 small head Boston or Bibb
    lettuce

½ cup mayonnaise

Soften cream cheese at room temperature. Blend in mayonnaise and salt. Fold in whipped cream, kumquats, dates, cherries, pineapples, ginger, and almonds. Spoon into an 8 x 8 x 2-inch pan. Freeze.
Makes 8 servings.

To Freeze: Cover pan with freezer wrap, and seal. Label, date, and freeze.

To Serve: Cut frozen fruit medley into squares. Serve on lettuce leaves with additional mayonnaise.

Storage Time: Up to 6 weeks.

FROZEN FRUIT SALAD

1 8-ounce package cream cheese	1 cup crushed pineapple, drained
1 cup prepared mayonnaise	1 cup Royal Anne cherries, pitted
2 cups heavy cream, whipped	
½ cup mashed bananas	1 tablespoon lemon juice
1 cup seeded white grapes	¼ teaspoon salt

After Freezing:

1 small head Boston or Bibb lettuce	½ cup mayonnaise

Soften cream cheese at room temperature. Blend in mayonnaise. Fold in whipped cream, bananas, grapes, pineapple, cherries, lemon juice, and salt. Spoon into an 8 x 8 x 2-inch pan. Freeze.
Makes 6 to 8 servings.

To Freeze: Cover pan with freezer wrap, and seal. Label, date, and freeze.

To Serve: Cut frozen fruit salad into squares. Serve on lettuce leaves with additional mayonnaise.

Storage Time: 4 to 6 weeks.

FROZEN DRESSING FOR FRUIT SALAD

4 teaspoons cornstarch
¼ cup sugar
¼ teaspoon salt
2 tablespoons lemon juice
¼ cup orange juice

1 cup unsweetened pineapple
   juice
2 eggs, beaten
1 8-ounce package cream
   cheese, softened

In a saucepan mix cornstarch with sugar and salt. Add lemon, orange, and pineapple juices, and blend. Cook and stir until mixture comes to a boil and is thickened. Stir a little of the hot mixture into the eggs, and return to pan. Stir over very low heat for 2 to 3 minutes. Cool slightly. Blend into softened cream cheese, mixing until smooth. Chill.
Makes 2 cups dressing.

To Freeze: Pack into containers that will be suitable for use at one time. Label, date, and freeze.

To Use: Defrost and beat with a fork. Use for fruit salads.

Storage Time: Up to 6 weeks.

FROZEN CHEESE BALLS

1 8-ounce package cream
   cheese
4 tablespoons finely chopped
   green pepper
½ cup chopped toasted
   almonds

½ cup heavy cream, whipped
½ teaspoon salt
¼ teaspoon paprika
⅛ teaspoon Tabasco sauce
1 tablespoon lemon juice

Soften cream cheese at room temperature. Add green pepper, almonds, and whipped cream, and season with salt, paprika, Tabasco sauce, and lemon juice. Mix well. Shape into balls, and place on baking pan or other flat surface. Freeze.

Makes 48 cheese balls.

To Freeze: Pack frozen cheese balls in a container or plastic bag in a quantity that will be suitable for each use. Seal, label, date, and return to freezer.

To Use: Remove number needed, and partially defrost. Use as a garnish for fruit or vegetable salads.

Storage Time: 4 to 6 weeks.

SEAFOOD SALADS

FROZEN LOBSTER SALAD

1 8-ounce package cream cheese
1 10½-ounce can condensed tomato soup
2 tablespoons (2 envelopes) unflavored gelatin
½ cup cold water
2 tablespoons sherry wine

1 teaspoon onion salt
1 cup commercial mayonnaise
¾ cup finely diced celery
¾ cup finely diced green pepper
¾ pound lobster meat

After Freezing:

1 small head Boston or Bibb lettuce

½ cup mayonnaise (optional)

Soften cream cheese, and blend with tomato soup in top of double boiler. Stir over boiling water until mixture is hot. Meanwhile, soften gelatin in cold water. Add to cream-cheese–soup mixture, and stir until gelatin is dissolved. Stir in sherry wine and onion salt. Cool. Fold in mayonnaise,

celery, and green pepper. Dice lobster and remove spines, and fold into mixture. Spoon into 6-to-8-cup mold.
Makes 6 servings.

To Freeze: Freeze. Cover mold with freezer wrap, and seal. Label and date. Return to freezer.

To Serve: Serve partially or completely defrosted on lettuce leaves with additional mayonnaise if desired.

Storage Time: Up to 8 weeks.

TUNA MOUSSE

2 tablespoons (2 envelopes) unflavored gelatin	2 7-ounce cans tuna fish, drained and flaked
¼ cup cold water	1½ cups chopped celery
1¼ cups hot water	½ cup chopped stuffed olives
6 tablespoons vinegar	2 tablespoons horseradish
½ teaspoon salt	½ cup heavy cream, whipped
½ teaspoon dry mustard	

After Freezing:

1 small head Boston or Bibb lettuce	½ cup mayonnaise

Soften gelatin in cold water. Dissolve in hot water. Stir in vinegar, salt, and mustard. Chill until mixture begins to thicken. Then fold in tuna fish, celery, olives, horseradish, and whipped cream. Spoon into a 6-to-8-cup mold.
Makes 8 servings.

To Freeze: Freeze. Either cover mold tightly, label, date, and freeze until ready to use, or dip mold quickly in hot water, unmold on freezer wrap, wrap, and label, date, and freeze.

To Use: Put salad mold on a serving platter. Defrost

at room temperature or in refrigerator. Garnish with lettuce leaves and mayonnaise.

Storage Time: Up to 1 month.

RELISH SALAD

RELISH SALAD

1 tablespoon (1 envelope) unflavored gelatin
¼ cup cold water
1 cup prepared chili sauce
1 cup cottage cheese

¼ cup pickle relish, drained
½ cup prepared mayonnaise
¼ teaspoon salt
¾ cup heavy cream, whipped

After Freezing:

1 small head Boston or Bibb lettuce

1 large tomato, cut in wedges
1 cup mayonnaise

Soften gelatin in cold water. Dissolve over hot water. Mix together with the chili sauce, cottage cheese, pickle relish, mayonnaise, salt, and whipped cream. Spoon into an 8 x 8 x 2-inch pan.
Makes 8 or 9 servings.

To Freeze: Cover relish salad with freezer wrap. Seal, label, date, and freeze.

To Use: Defrost enough to cut into squares. Serve on lettuce leaves with garnish of tomato wedge and mayonnaise.

Storage Time: 4 to 6 weeks.

13 Sandwiches

GENERAL RULES FOR FREEZING SANDWICHES

Most sandwiches freeze very well. Don't plan to keep them longer than a month. If you make sandwiches to freeze for lunch boxes, rotate them so that the oldest get used first.

Lunch-box sandwiches can go directly from the freezer to the lunch box and will be defrosted in time for lunch and at the same time will keep other things in the box cold.

Lettuce and tomato slices, since they cannot be frozen, should be added when the sandwich is partially or wholly defrosted. For lunch-box sandwiches wrap 1 or 2 crisp lettuce leaves in waxed paper or transparent wrap, and tuck the package into the box. The lettuce can be added to the sandwich before it is eaten.

Mayonnaise has a tendency to separate when frozen, but

if commercial mayonnaise is used in fillings and salads, it separates less than homemade.

Spread the bread with butter. It forms a more solid lining on the bread so the fillings don't soak into the bread during freezing or defrosting. Always butter both pieces of bread.

Wrap all sandwiches tightly, and seal, label, and date. Store them together in a plastic bag or box. Defrost before serving.

Sandwiches can also be made for grilling or broiling.

FLAVORED BUTTERS FOR SANDWICHES

To ½ pound whipped butter add any of the following flavors, increasing or decreasing the amounts to suit personal tastes.

Chili Sauce Butter: 3 to 4 tablespoons chili sauce and about 1 teaspoon lemon juice. Use as a spread for roast beef, corned beef, cheese, or sliced chicken sandwiches.

Tabasco Butter: ½ to ¾ teaspoon Tabasco sauce. Use as a spread for meat, fish, or poultry sandwiches.

Chive Butter: 3 tablespoons finely chopped fresh or freeze-dried chives and 1 tablespoon lemon juice. Good with any type sandwich.

Horseradish Butter: Drain ¼ cup horseradish, and mix with butter. Good with fish, meat, or poultry sandwiches.

Pickle Relish Butter: Drain ¼ cup pickle relish, and mix with butter. Good with cheese, meat, poultry, or fish.

Maple Butter: 3 tablespoons maple syrup and ¼ teaspoon vanilla. Use with breads such as banana, date, or cranberry.

Honey Butter: 3 tablespoons honey and ⅛ teaspoon grated orange rind. Use with breads such as banana or date.

These butters are suggested for spreading on the bread

to be used for frozen sandwiches. They can also be frozen in covered containers for future use.

To Freeze: Package in a container suitable for your needs. Label, date, and freeze.

To Use: Defrost.

Storage Time: Up to 1 month.

SANDWICH COMBINATIONS AND COLD FILLINGS THAT FREEZE WELL

COMBINATIONS

Jelly and peanut butter
Marshmallow fluff and peanut butter
Sliced ham with mustard
Roast beef and chopped chutney
Corned beef with horseradish mustard
Sliced chicken or turkey and orange marmalade
Cream cheese, jelly, and nuts
Cream cheese, crumbled cooked bacon, and strawberry jam
Sliced ham, Swiss cheese, provolone cheese, and drained
    whole pimiento on a hard roll
American cheese and ham or bologna
Minced ham and cream cheese

FILLINGS

CORNED BEEF SALAD

1 cup ground cooked corned beef	1 teaspoon prepared mustard
¼ cup ground dill pickle	2 teaspoons prepared horseradish
¼ teaspoon Tabasco sauce	3 tablespoons softened butter

Blend corned beef with dill pickle, Tabasco, mustard, horseradish, and butter.

Makes enough for about 4 sandwiches.

DEVILED HAM SALAD

2 4½-ounce cans deviled ham ½ cup stuffed olives, chopped
1 cup diced celery ¼ cup softened butter

Blend deviled ham with celery, olives, and butter.
Makes enough for about 4 sandwiches.

CHICKEN SALAD

1 cup ground cooked chicken ¼ teaspoon salt
½ cup diced celery 2 tablespoons butter,
1 tablespoon prepared softened
   mayonnaise

Blend chicken with celery, mayonnaise, salt, and butter.
Makes enough for about 4 sandwiches.

RECIPES

BEEF

BARBECUED BEEF

1 cup catsup 4 teaspoons Dijon mustard
4 tablespoons vinegar 16 thin slices cold cooked
2½ tablespoons brown sugar beef
After Freezing:
16 slices toasted bread

Mix catsup with vinegar, brown sugar, and mustard. Arrange 2 slices of beef on a strip of freezer foil, and spread ¼ of the sauce on the beef. Repeat until all sauce and beef are used.

Makes enough for 8 sandwiches.

To Freeze: Seal. Label, date, and freeze.

To Serve: Put on baking sheet, and bake in a 425° F. oven for 20 to 25 minutes or until heated through. Serve on toasted bread.

Storage Time: Up to 4 weeks.

SANDWICH BAKE

1 tablespoon butter	1 egg, beaten
1 pound ground beef	¼ teaspoon Tabasco sauce
½ cup chopped onion	1 teaspoon salt
¼ cup grated Parmesan cheese	8 squares Biscuit Dough (page 223), buttered
½ cup grated Swiss cheese	

After Freezing:

1 ½ cups Mushroom Sauce
    (page 223)

Heat butter in skillet, and sauté the meat and onion until the meat is no longer red but not browned. If a great deal of fat cooks out of the meat, pour off all but about 2 tablespoons. Cool. Mix with cheeses, egg, Tabasco, and salt. Spread 4 squares of buttered Biscuit Dough with meat mixture, and top with a plain square, butter side up. Carefully transfer to a greased baking sheet, and bake in a 400° F. oven 30 minutes or until lightly browned.

Makes 4 servings.

To Freeze: Cool. Wrap individually in aluminum foil, and seal. Label, date, and freeze.

To Serve: Place foil-wrapped sandwiches on baking sheet, and bake 20 to 30 minutes in a 425° F. oven. Serve with Mushroom Sauce.

Storage Time: Up to 4 weeks.

Biscuit Dough

2 cups sifted all-purpose flour	½ cup shortening
3 teaspoons baking powder	1 egg, slightly beaten
1 teaspoon salt	½ cup milk
½ teaspoon oregano	Softened butter
½ teaspoon thyme	

Sift the flour with the baking powder and salt. Mix in oregano and thyme. Cut in shortening with 2 knives or a pastry blender until well blended. Mix the egg with the milk, and stir in with a fork until just blended. Pat out on a lightly floured board into a rectangle about ¼ inch thick. Spread with softened butter, and cut into squares.
Makes 8 squares.

Mushroom Sauce

1 cup sliced mushrooms	1 cup Beef Stock (page 163)
1 tablespoon butter	Salt and freshly ground
2 tablespoons flour	pepper

Sauté mushrooms in butter. Stir in flour. Add Beef Stock. Season to taste with salt and pepper.
Makes 1½ cups sauce.

SAVORY SANDWICH LOAF

2 loaves French or Italian
    bread
1 cup tomato juice
½ cup grated onion
2 eggs
1½ pounds ground beef

1½ teaspoons salt
½ teaspoon freshly ground
    pepper
2 teaspoons Worcestershire
    sauce

Cut a V-shaped piece lengthwise from the top of each loaf of bread. Remove pieces, and with a fork remove crumbs from inside of loaves, leaving about a 1-inch shell of bread and crust. Measure 3 cups of bread crumbs, and mix with the tomato juice, onion, eggs, and ground beef. Season with salt, pepper, and Worcestershire sauce. Fill bread shells with mixture, and replace V strips.

Each loaf makes about 10 servings.

To Freeze: Wrap tightly with freezer foil. Seal, label, date. Freeze.

To Serve: Place frozen loaf on baking sheet. Bake in a 425° F. oven for 50 to 60 minutes. Cut crosswise into slices.

Storage Time: Up to 4 weeks.

CHICKEN

CHICKBURGERS

1 pound boneless raw
    chicken meat *
1 egg
½ cup soft bread crumbs
1 tablespoon chopped fresh
    parsley

1 tablespoon chopped onion
1 teaspoon salt
⅛ teaspoon freshly ground
    pepper
Dash Tabasco sauce
1 or 2 tablespoons milk

After Freezing:

2 tablespoons butter

8 buttered hamburger buns

* Raw turkey meat may be substituted.

Put chicken through finest blade of grinder, grinding twice if necessary to get finely ground. Mix lightly with the egg, bread crumbs, parsley, and onion. Season with salt, pepper, and Tabasco. Then add enough milk to make a mixture that can be shaped into patties. Form into 8 flat patties.

Makes 8 Chickburgers.

To Freeze: Wrap each pattie in freezer wrap. Seal, label, and date. Freeze. When frozen, store together in box or plastic bag.

To Use: Defrost and sauté over medium heat in a small amount of butter for 15 minutes, turning to brown both sides. Serve on buttered buns or bread.

Storage Time: Up to 4 weeks.

CRAB

HOT CRAB-WICHES

2 cups flaked crab meat	1 cup grated cheddar cheese
½ cup finely diced celery	¾ cup prepared mayonnaise
2 tablespoons grated onion	8 hamburger buns
¼ teaspoon salt	Softened butter

Combine crab meat with celery, onion, salt, cheese, and mayonnaise. Mix lightly. Spread split hamburger buns with softened butter. Spread crab-meat mixture on 8 halves. Top with remaining bun halves.

Makes 8 sandwiches.

To Freeze: Wrap each filled bun in freezer foil. Seal, label, and date. Freeze. When frozen, store together in box or plastic bag.

To Serve: Put frozen buns in foil on baking sheet. Bake in a 425° F. oven for 25 minutes or until hot through.

Storage Time: Up to 4 weeks.

14 Cookies

GENERAL RULES FOR FREEZING COOKIES

Both cookie dough and baked cookies can be frozen successfully. I prefer to freeze the dough, since freshly baked cookies are more appealing. However, if you are making many cookies for some special occasion, bake and freeze. Package baked cookies in boxes or containers so that they do not get broken if they get pushed around in the freezer. Baked or unbaked, most cookies will store a long time —6 to 8 months.

"Ice-box"-type cookies (rolls) are particularly successful because they can be sliced and baked with very little defrosting. All frozen dough should be baked as soon as it begins to defrost.

Cookie dough such as ice-box rolls can be wrapped in freezer wrap. Other dough can be packed into containers.

Be sure to put the baking directions on the label when freezing unbaked dough!

RECIPES

CHOCOLATE COOKIES

BEST CHOCOLATE COOKIES

1⅔ cups sifted all-purpose
    flour
2 teaspoons baking powder
¼ teaspoon salt
⅛ teaspoon baking soda
½ cup shortening
1 cup firmly packed light
    brown sugar

2 eggs, separated
2 1-ounce squares unsweet-
    ened chocolate, melted
1 teaspoon vanilla extract
½ cup milk
1 cup finely chopped walnuts
Chocolate Frosting (page 228)

Sift flour with baking powder, salt, and baking soda. Cream shortening with the brown sugar until light and fluffy. Beat in egg yolks, chocolate, and vanilla. Alternately add sifted flour mixture and milk. Add the walnuts. Beat egg whites until stiff but not dry, and fold into batter. Drop by teaspoonfuls 1 inch apart on a greased baking sheet. Bake in a 350° F. oven for 10 to 12 minutes. Cool. Frost with Chocolate Frosting.

Makes 4 dozen cookies.

To Freeze: Freeze cookies unwrapped in freezer. When frozen, wrap in a plastic bag. Store in a box to keep from being damaged in freezer. Seal, label, date, and return to freezer.

To Use: Defrost.

Storage Time: Up to 6 months.

Chocolate Frosting

⅔ cup milk
2 cups granulated sugar
2 1-ounce squares unsweetened chocolate

¼ cup butter
1 teaspoon vanilla extract

Combine milk with sugar, chocolate, and butter in a saucepan, and cook, stirring, until chocolate is melted and mixture forms a soft ball. Add the vanilla, and beat until mixture is stiff enough to spread. If necessary, keep over hot water so that frosting remains soft while being spread.

Makes enough frosting for 4 dozen cookies.

CHOCO-ORANGE REFRIGERATOR COOKIES

2½ cups sifted all-purpose
flour
½ teaspoon baking soda
½ teaspoon salt
½ cup shortening
1 cup firmly packed light-
brown sugar

2 eggs
2 tablespoons orange juice
2 tablespoons grated orange
rind
½ cup chopped walnuts
1 8-ounce package chocolate
chips

Sift the flour with the baking soda and salt. Cream the shortening and brown sugar until light and fluffy. Beat in the eggs, orange juice, and grated orange rind. Add the flour, walnuts, and chocolate chips. Form into 2 rolls.

Makes enough dough for 6 dozen cookies.

To Freeze: Wrap rolls in waxed paper and then in freezer wrap. Seal, label, date. Freeze.

To Bake: Defrost enough to cut in thin slices. Place on an ungreased baking sheet, and bake in a 375° F. oven for 8 to 10 minutes.

Storage Time: Up to 6 months.

FRUIT COOKIES

CRANBERRY COOKIES

3 cups sifted all-purpose flour
1 teaspoon baking powder
¼ teaspoon baking soda
½ teaspoon salt
½ cup butter
1 cup granulated sugar
¼ cup firmly packed light-
    brown sugar

4 tablespoons orange juice
1 egg
1 cup chopped blanched
    almonds
2½ cups fresh cranberries,
    coarsely chopped

After Freezing:
½ cup granulated sugar

Sift flour with baking powder, soda, and salt. Cream butter with granulated sugar and brown sugar until light and fluffy. Beat in orange juice and egg. Stir in flour mixture. Add almonds and cranberries.
Makes enough dough for 10 dozen cookies.

To Freeze: Pack batter into freezer containers. Seal, label, date, and freeze.

To Bake: Partially defrost. Drop by teaspoonfuls on a

greased baking sheet. Sprinkle tops with granulated sugar. Bake in a 375° F. oven for 12 to 15 minutes.

Storage Time: Up to 6 months.

DATE WHIRLS

½ pound fresh dates, pitted
¼ cup granulated sugar
¼ cup water
1 teaspoon lemon juice
1 tablespoon butter
¼ cup chopped pecans or walnuts

½ cup butter
1 ¼ cups firmly packed light brown sugar
1 egg
2 cups sifted all-purpose flour
½ teaspoon baking soda
¼ teaspoon salt

Combine dates with granulated sugar and water, and simmer 5 minutes. Stir in lemon juice and 1 tablespoon butter. Cool. Add pecans. Cream ½ cup butter with brown sugar until light and fluffy. Beat in egg. Sift flour with baking soda and salt, and mix into creamed butter-sugar. Chill in refrigerator about 30 minutes. Divide dough into 2 parts, and pat into 2 rectangles on a piece of lightly floured waxed paper about 12 inches long. Spread half of date mixture on each piece of dough. Starting on the long side, roll dough to form 2 12-inch rolls. Wrap in waxed paper.
Makes enough dough for about 6 dozen whirls.

To Freeze: Overwrap waxed paper–covered rolls with freezer wrap. Seal, label, and date.

To Bake: Unwrap rolls and let dough partially defrost. Cut crosswise into thin slices. Place on a greased baking sheet, and bake in a 400° F. oven about 10 minutes.

Storage Time: Up to 6 months.

HOLIDAY FRUIT COOKIES

2¾ cups sifted all-purpose
 flour
3 teaspoons baking powder
¼ teaspoon salt
½ teaspoon ground cloves
1 teaspoon cinnamon
½ teaspoon nutmeg
1 cup shortening
2 cups granulated sugar

2 eggs
⅔ cup milk
1 cup raisins, chopped
1 cup candied cherries,
 chopped
½ cup candied chopped
 pineapple
1 cup chopped pecans or
 walnuts

Sift the flour with baking powder, salt, cloves, cinnamon, and nutmeg. Cream the shortening and sugar until fluffy. Beat in the eggs. Add the flour mixture alternately with the milk. Mix in the raisins, cherries, pineapple, and pecans. Makes enough dough for 6 dozen cookies.

To Freeze: Pack dough in containers. Seal. Label, date, and freeze.

To Bake: Defrost enough to drop by teaspoonfuls on a greased baking sheet. Bake at 350° F. for 15 minutes.

Storage Time: Up to 4 months.

SOFT RAISIN COOKIES

2 cups raisins
1 cup water
2½ teaspoons baking soda
4 cups sifted all-purpose flour
1 teaspoon salt
1 teaspoon baking powder
1½ teaspoons cinnamon
¼ teaspoon nutmeg

¼ teaspoon allspice
1 cup shortening
2 cups granulated sugar
3 eggs
1 teaspoon vanilla extract
1 cup chopped toasted
 almonds

Wash raisins. Combine with 1 cup water, and boil 5 minutes. Drain, and measure liquid. Should be ½ cup (if not, add water to make ½ cup). Return to raisins, and cool. When cool, add baking soda. Sift flour with salt, baking powder, cinnamon, nutmeg, and allspice. Cream shortening with sugar until fluffy. Beat in eggs 1 at a time. Add vanilla and cooled raisin-soda mixture. Stir in flour mixture and almonds, and mix until flour is just moistened.

Makes enough dough for 6 dozen cookies.

To Freeze: Pack into containers. Label, date, and freeze.

To Bake: Defrost dough just enough to form spoonfuls. Drop by spoonfuls on a greased baking sheet, and bake at 400° F. for 12 to 15 minutes.

Storage Time: Up to 6 months.

OATMEAL COOKIES

OATMEAL SLICES

1 ½ cups sifted all-purpose
    flour
1 teaspoon salt
1 teaspoon baking soda
1 cup shortening
1 cup firmly packed light
    brown sugar

1 cup granulated sugar
2 eggs
1 teaspoon vanilla extract
3 cups uncooked quick-
    cooking oatmeal
½ cup chopped walnuts

Sift flour with salt and soda. Cream shortening with sugars until light and fluffy. Add eggs and vanilla, and beat well. Fold in flour, oatmeal, and walnuts. Shape into 3 rolls.

Makes enough dough for 6 dozen slices.

To Freeze: Wrap in freezer wrap. Label, date, and freeze.

To Use: Partially defrost. Slice into thin slices, and place on an ungreased baking sheet. Bake in a 350° F. oven for 10 minutes or until lightly browned.

Storage Time: Up to 6 months.

OLD-FASHIONED RANGER COOKIES

2 cups sifted all-purpose flour
1 teaspoon baking soda
½ teaspoon baking powder
½ teaspoon salt
1 cup shortening
1 cup granulated sugar
1 cup firmly packed light
    brown sugar
2 eggs
1 teaspoon vanilla extract
2 cups uncooked quick-
    cooking oatmeal
2 cups crisp rice cereal
1 cup shredded coconut

Sift the flour with the baking soda, baking powder, and salt. Cream the shortening with the granulated and light brown sugars until light and fluffy. Beat in the eggs and vanilla. Add the oatmeal, rice cereal, coconut, and flour mixture. (The mixture will be slightly crumbly.)
Makes enough dough for 4 dozen cookies.

To Freeze: Pack into cartons. Seal, label, date. Freeze.

To Bake: Defrost dough enough so that it can be shaped into small balls. Flatten balls on an ungreased baking sheet. Bake in a 350° F. oven for 10 to 12 minutes.

Storage Time: Up to 6 months.

SPICE COOKIES

MOLASSES-CREAM COOKIES

1 cup granulated sugar
1 cup molasses
1 cup dairy sour cream
2 teaspoons baking soda
2 egg yolks, beaten

½ teaspoon ground cloves
½ teaspoon ginger
1 teaspoon cinnamon
¼ teaspoon salt
6 cups sifted all-purpose flour

After Freezing:
½ cup granulated sugar

Mix sugar and molasses in large bowl. Mix the sour cream with the baking soda. Add the eggs, cloves, ginger, cinnamon, and salt to the molasses and sugar mixture, and beat well. Add the sour cream alternately with flour, mixing well.

Makes enough dough for 5 dozen cookies.

To Freeze: Pack dough in cartons. Seal, label, and date. Freeze.

To Bake: Defrost dough just enough to roll into small balls. Dip in water, and roll in ½ cup sugar (or more if needed). Place on a greased baking sheet, and bake in a 350° F. oven for 12 minutes.

Storage Time: 3 to 4 months.

CHEWY PUMPKIN COOKIES

1 ¼ cups sifted all-purpose
    flour
1 ½ teaspoons salt
1 teaspoon baking powder
¼ teaspoon baking soda
1 teaspoon cinnamon
½ teaspoon nutmeg
¾ cup uncooked quick-
    cooking oatmeal
1 cup firmly packed light-
    brown sugar
¾ cup granulated sugar
½ cup shortening
1 egg
1 cup canned pumpkin
1 6-ounce package chocolate
    chips
1 cup raisins
1 cup chopped walnuts

Sift flour with salt, baking powder, baking soda, cinnamon, and nutmeg. Mix in oatmeal. Cream light brown and granulated sugars with the shortening until well blended. Beat in the egg. Add flour mixture alternately with the pumpkin. Stir in the chocolate chips, raisins, and walnuts. Makes enough dough for 3 dozen cookies.

To Freeze: Pack into containers. Seal, label, date, and freeze.

To Bake: Partially defrost, and drop by rounded teaspoonfuls on a greased baking sheet. Bake in a 375° F. oven for 15 minutes.

Storage Time: Up to 6 months.

SPICE BOX COOKIES

3 cups sifted all-purpose flour
¼ teaspoon salt
½ teaspoon cinnamon
½ teaspoon nutmeg
½ teaspoon baking soda
1 cup butter
½ cup granulated sugar
1 cup firmly packed light-
    brown sugar
2 eggs
1 teaspoon vanilla extract
1 cup finely chopped walnuts

Sift flour with salt, cinnamon, nutmeg, and baking soda. Cream butter with the granulated and light brown sugars until light and fluffy. Beat in the eggs and vanilla. Add sifted dry ingredients and nuts. Form into 3 rolls. Wrap in waxed paper.

Makes enough dough for 6 dozen cookies.

To Freeze: Wrap waxed-paper–wrapped rolls in freezer wrap. Seal, label, and date. Freeze.

To Bake: Slightly defrost cookie rolls, and slice into thin slices. Bake on an ungreased baking sheet in a 375° F. oven for 10 to 15 minutes.

Storage Time: Up to 6 months.

15 Desserts

GENERAL RULES FOR FREEZING DESSERTS

Many desserts can be fully or partially prepared and frozen. Desserts such as ice-cream pies or ice-cream cakes need not be defrosted and are an easy way to make a simple meal have a glamorous finish. Desserts that have fragile edges, such as ice-cream pie, should be wrapped and then stored in a box to protect them. Most desserts should not be stored longer than 4 months.

If the frozen dessert requires additional cooking, be sure to include that information on the label.

RECIPES

COLD DESSERTS

BAKED ALASKA

1 layer of cake (pound cake or a relatively firm butter cake), 1 inch thick	3 egg whites
1 quart brick of vanilla ice cream	⅛ teaspoon cream of tartar
	1 teaspoon vanilla extract
	½ cup granulated sugar

The layer of cake should be cut to have a margin about 1 inch larger on each side than the brick of ice cream. It does not necessarily have to be all one piece, but it should fit to make a solid cake base. Place cake on a platter that can go into the oven. Have ice cream frozen as hard as possible. Whip the egg whites until foamy with cream of tartar. Add the vanilla extract and then gradually add the sugar, beating after each addition until whites are very stiff and shiny. Remove the wrapper from the ice cream, and place it in the center of the cake. Working very rapidly, cover ice cream with meringue, sealing it to cake at base. Bake in a 425° F. oven until lightly browned (5 minutes). Serve at once cut in slices.

Makes about 6 slices.

To Freeze: Freeze ice cream and cake without the meringue. Wrap in freezer wrap, and seal, label, and date. Store in freezer in a box.

To Serve: Cover with meringue. Bake at 425° F. for 5 minutes.

Storage Time: Up to 4 weeks.

CRANBERRY SHERBET

1 pound cranberries
2 cups boiling water
1 teaspoon unflavored gelatin

¼ cup cold water
2 cups granulated sugar
1 pint bitter-lemon soda

Wash cranberries, and cook in boiling water until skins pop. Strain, pressing pulp through strainer. Soften gelatin in cold water, and add along with the sugar to the strained cranberries. Stir to dissolve. Cool. Add bitter lemon, and freeze until mushy. Put into chilled mixing bowl, and beat with rotary beater until fluffy. Return to freezer and freeze until firm.

Makes about 1 quart.

To Freeze: Pack frozen sherbet into freezer containers. Seal. Label, date, and freeze.

To Serve: Serve frozen.

Storage Time: Up to 2 months.

EASY ELEGANT DATE ROLL

32 graham crackers (single)
40 large marshmallows
1 pound fresh dates, pitted

2 cups cut-up walnuts
⅔ to 1 cup cream

Roll crackers to make very fine crumbs. Reserve 6 to 8 tablespoons. Cut marshmallows into eighths. Cut each date into 3 or 4 pieces. Mix crumbs, marshmallows, dates, and walnuts. Add enough cream to moisten. Form into 2 rolls about 3 inches in diameter. Place on freezer wrap, and sprinkle with reserved crumbs.

Each roll will make 6 servings.

To Freeze: Wrap and seal rolls. Label, date, and freeze.

To Serve: Partially defrost rolls, and cut into slices. Serve with whipped cream if desired.

Storage Time: Up to 6 months.

ICE-CREAM ROLL

¾ cup sifted cake flour
1 teaspoon baking powder
¼ teaspoon salt
4 eggs, separated
¾ cup granulated sugar

1 teaspoon vanilla extract
2 tablespoons water
Confectioners' sugar
1 quart ice cream, softened

After Freezing:

Favorite Chocolate Sauce
    (page 242)
or Strawberry Sauce
    (page 243)

Sift flour with baking powder and salt. Beat egg whites until stiff but not dry. Gradually beat half the sugar into the egg whites, adding about 2 tablespoons at a time. Beat egg yolks until thick and lemon-colored. Beat in remaining sugar and vanilla, beating until very thick. Slowly add water, stirring constantly. Gently fold in beaten whites. Add flour mixture, sifting about ¼ cup over surface each time. Spoon into a shallow 8 x 16-inch pan which has been lined with waxed paper. Bake in a 375° F. oven 15 to 20 minutes. Sprinkle confectioners' sugar on a clean towel, which is slightly larger than the cake. Turn warm cake out on towel. Peel off paper, and trim off edges. Roll cake in cloth. Work quickly and gently. Cool in cloth.
Makes 8 to 10 servings.

To Freeze: When cool, unroll cake, and spread with softened ice cream. Quickly reroll. Wrap in freezer wrap and seal. Label, date, and freeze.

To Serve: Slice frozen cake crosswise into serving pieces. Serve at once with Favorite Chocolate Sauce or Strawberry Sauce.

Storage Time: Up to 4 months.

PUMPKIN ICE CREAM

1¼ cups firmly packed light brown sugar
1 tablespoon cornstarch
¼ teaspoon salt

2 teaspoons pumpkin pie spice
3 cups half-and-half
1½ cups canned pumpkin
4 egg yolks, slightly beaten

Mix the brown sugar with the cornstarch, salt, and pumpkin pie spice in a saucepan. Stir in 1 cup of the half-and-half, and cook and stir until mixture thickens. Mix the pumpkin with the egg yolks, and add to the hot sugar mixture. Cook, below boiling, for about 2 minutes, stirring constantly. Chill. Add remaining half-and-half. Pour mixture into freezer trays, and freeze until firm. Break into pieces, put into a chilled bowl, and beat with electric mixer until mixture is free from lumps and fluffy. Return to freezer, and freeze until firm.
Makes about 1¼ quarts.

To Freeze: Pack into containers, and cover. Label, date, and return to freezer.

Storage Time: Up to 4 weeks.

STRAWBERRY MOUSSE

1 pint fresh strawberries
¾ cup granulated sugar
1 pint heavy cream

1 teaspoon vanilla extract
Dash salt
2 egg whites, stiffly beaten

Wash and hull the strawberries. Crush berries with sugar, and heat just until sugar is dissolved. Chill. Beat cream until stiff, and fold in berries, vanilla, and salt. Fold in stiffly beaten egg whites. Pour into 6-cup mold, and freeze until firm.

Makes 6 to 8 servings.

To Freeze: Overwrap and seal. Label, date, and return to freezer.

To Serve: Slice crosswise.

Storage Time: Up to 6 weeks.

ICE-CREAM SAUCES

FAVORITE CHOCOLATE SAUCE

½ cup light corn syrup
1 cup granulated sugar
1 cup water
3 1-ounce squares un-
    sweetened chocolate

1 teaspoon vanilla extract
Dash salt
2 tablespoons butter
1 cup evaporated milk

Combine syrup, sugar, and water. Bring to a boil, and cook, stirring occasionally, over low heat for 5 minutes. Remove from heat, and stir in chocolate, vanilla, salt, and butter. Stir until chocolate is melted and blended. Slowly stir in the evaporated milk, blending thoroughly. Store in refrigerator. To serve hot, heat over boiling water.

Makes 3½ cups sauce.

STRAWBERRY SAUCE

½ cup water
½ cup sugar

2 cups frozen whole or sliced
  strawberries

Mix water and sugar, and boil 5 minutes. Add strawberries. Cool.
Makes 2½ cups sauce.

BUTTERSCOTCH ALMOND SAUCE

1½ cups firmly packed light-
  brown sugar
¾ cup light corn syrup
4 tablespoons butter

¾ cup light cream
½ cup toasted chopped
  almonds

Combine the brown sugar with the corn syrup and butter. Bring to a boil, and cook to 235° F. or when a soft ball forms when a small amount is dropped in cold water. Add the cream, mixing well. Cool. Add the almonds. Store in refrigerator.
Makes 3½ cups sauce.

PIES

Pies may be frozen before baking or after baking, or the filling may be frozen and added to the crust at the time of baking. Directions for freezing are given in each recipe.

BLUEBERRY PIE

¾ cup granulated sugar
¼ cup all-purpose flour
¼ teaspoon salt
4 cups fresh or frozen blueberries, washed and
drained
Pastry for 2 9-inch pie crusts
1 teaspoon lemon juice
2 tablespoons softened butter

In a large bowl mix the sugar, flour, and salt. Carefully stir in the blueberries. Line the pie plate with 1 pastry crust. Spoon in blueberry-sugar-flour mixture. Sprinkle with lemon juice, and dot with butter. Add the top crust. Seal and flute edges. Freeze.

To Freeze: If desired, frozen pie may be removed from pie plate. Wrap tightly in freezer wrap, and seal. Label, date, and return to freezer. Store in box to prevent damage. Otherwise, pie may be stored in pie plate. Overwrap with freezer wrap.

To Serve: Defrost pie. Return pie to pie plate. Cut several slits in top. Bake in a 425° F. oven for 30 to 40 minutes or until pie juices bubble up through slits.

Pie may be baked from a frozen state. When pie is warm enough, cut several slits in top. Add another 30 minutes to baking time. If edges begin to get too brown, cover with aluminum foil.

Storage Time: Up to 6 months.

JIFFY CHEESE PIE

1 ½ cups vanilla-wafer
crumbs
⅓ cup melted butter
2 tablespoons granulated
sugar
1 8-ounce package cream
cheese
⅔ cup sweetened condensed
milk
1 teaspoon grated lemon peel
3 tablespoons lemon juice
1 cup frozen whipped top-
ping, defrosted

Mix the vanilla-wafer crumbs with the butter and sugar. Press into the bottom and sides of a 9-inch pie plate. Chill well. Soften the cream cheese at room temperature. Stir in the condensed milk, grated lemon peel, and lemon juice, and blend well. Fold in the whipped topping. Spoon into chilled pie shell. Chill and freeze.

To Freeze: Overwrap frozen pie with freezer wrap, and seal. Label, date, and return to freezer.

To Serve: Defrost.

Storage Time: Up to 2 months.

CHOCOLATE PECAN PIE

2 1-ounce squares un-sweetened chocolate	½ cup granulated sugar
	Dash salt
2 tablespoons butter	¾ cup dark corn syrup
1 teaspoon vanilla extract	¾ cup pecan halves
3 eggs	1 unbaked 9-inch pie shell

Melt the chocolate and butter over very low heat. With a rotary beater combine the chocolate mixture, vanilla, eggs, sugar, salt, and corn syrup. Stir in the pecans. Spoon into an unbaked pie shell. Bake in a 375° F. oven 45 minutes or until just set. Cool on rack.

To Freeze: Freeze. If desired, frozen pie may be removed from pie plate. Wrap tightly in freezer wrap, and seal. Label, date, and return to freezer. Store in box to prevent damage. Otherwise, pie may be stored in pie plate. Overwrap with freezer wrap.

To Serve: Defrost. If desired, serve with unsweetened whipped cream.

Storage Time: Up to 1 month.

ICE-CREAM-SUNDAE PIE

1¼ cups chocolate-cookie
    crumbs
⅓ cup melted butter

2 tablespoons granulated
    sugar
1 quart vanilla ice cream

After Freezing:

1 recipe All-American Sauce
    (below)

Mix the chocolate-cookie crumbs with the butter and sugar. Pack into bottom and sides of a 9-inch pie plate. Chill well. Fill with the vanilla ice cream.

To Freeze: Freeze. Overwrap frozen ice-cream pie with freezer wrap, and seal. Label, date, and return to freezer.

To Serve: Cut pie into wedges. Serve frozen pie with All-American Sauce.

Storage Time: Up to 4 weeks.

All-American Sauce

1 cup thin chocolate sauce
1 cup marshmallow fluff

½ cup pecans

Mix chocolate sauce with marshmallow fluff and pecans. Makes 1¾ cups sauce.

FROZEN ORANGE PIE

2 egg whites
¼ teaspoon salt
1 cup granulated sugar
½ cup cooked sieved prune
    pulp

1 orange rind, grated
¼ cup orange juice
4 tablespoons lemon juice
2 cups heavy cream, whipped
2 baked 9-inch pie shells

After Freezing:

1 orange, separated into
    sections

Beat the egg whites with the salt and sugar until stiff. Fold in the prune pulp. Add the grated orange rind and orange and lemon juice. Fold in the whipped cream. Freeze for 1 to 1½ hours. Spoon into pie shells, and return to freezer.

Makes 2 pies.

To Freeze: If desired, frozen pies may be removed from pie plates. Wrap tightly in freezer wrap, and seal. Label, date, and return to freezer. Store in box to prevent damage. Otherwise, pies may be stored in pie plates. Overwrap with freezer wrap.

To Serve: Decorate tops with orange sections.

Storage Time: Up to 3 months.

BUTTERSCOTCH-PEACH PIE

1 cup firmly packed light
    brown sugar
4 tablespoons flour
¼ teaspoon salt
1 teaspoon nutmeg

8 tablespoons butter
Pastry to Freeze (page 251)
    for 2 9-inch pies
7 cups sliced peaches
2 tablespoons lemon juice

Combine the brown sugar, flour, salt, nutmeg, and butter in a small saucepan. Cook and stir until the mixture boils and thickens. Line 2 9-inch pie plates with pastry. Spoon in the sliced peaches. Sprinkle with lemon juice. Spread the brown-sugar mixture over the peaches. Top with crust. Seal and flute edges. Freeze.

Makes 2 pies.

To Freeze: If desired, frozen pies may be removed from pie plates. Wrap tightly in freezer wrap, and seal. Label, date, and return to freezer. Store in box to avoid damage. Otherwise, pies may be stored in pie plates. Overwrap with freezer wrap.

To Serve: Return pie to pie plate. Defrost. Cut several slits in top. Bake in a 425° F. oven for 30 to 40 minutes or until juices bubble up through slits.

Pie may be baked from frozen state. When pie is warm enough, cut several slits in top, and add another 30 minutes to baking time. If edges begin to get too brown, cover with aluminum foil.

Storage Time: Up to 6 months.

PEPPERMINT PINK PIE

1 cup crushed peppermint stick candy	½ teaspoon salt
1 cup granulated sugar	6 egg yolks, slightly beaten
2 tablespoons (2 envelopes) unflavored gelatin	8 or 9 drops red food coloring
2½ cups milk	6 egg whites
	1 cup heavy cream, whipped
	2 baked 9-inch pie shells

Combine peppermint candy, ½ cup of the sugar, and the gelatin, milk, salt, and egg yolks in saucepan. Cook and stir over low heat until the candy and gelatin are melted and mixture is slightly thickened. Tint with food coloring. Chill until the mixture begins to thicken. Beat the egg whites until foamy. Gradually beat in the remaining sugar until it is stiff enough to stand in peaks. Fold the egg whites and cream into the peppermint mixture. Spoon into baked pie shells. Chill until firm. Freeze.

Makes 2 pies.

To Freeze: Wrap frozen pies in freezer wrap, and seal. Label and date. Store in freezer in box.

To Serve: Partially defrost.

Storage Time: Up to 1 month.

STRAWBERRY PIE

1 cup port wine	4 tablespoons lemon juice
2 cups water	2 3-ounce packages cream cheese
2 3-ounce packages straw-berry-flavored gelatin	2 tablespoons milk
4 cups sliced fresh straw-berries	2 baked 9-inch pie shells
½ cup granulated sugar	1 cup heavy cream, whipped

Heat the wine and water until it boils, and add the gelatin. Stir until the gelatin dissolves. Add the sliced strawberries, sugar, and lemon juice. Chill in the refrigerator until the mixture begins to thicken. Meanwhile, mix the cream cheese with the milk, and spread over the inside bottoms of 2 baked pie shells. Spoon in thickened strawberry mixture. Chill until set. Top with whipped cream. Freeze.

Makes 2 pies.

To Freeze: Overwrap frozen pies with freezer wrap, and seal. Label and date. Store in freezer in box.

To Serve: Partially defrost.

Storage Time: Up to 1 month.

STRAWBERRY AND RHUBARB PIE

2½ cups granulated sugar
6 tablespoons cornstarch
¼ teaspoon salt
4 cups strawberries, cut in
    half

3 cups diced rhubarb
Pastry to Freeze (page 251)
    for 2 9-inch pies
2 tablespoons lemon juice
4 tablespoons butter

Mix the sugar with the cornstarch and salt. Sprinkle this mixture over the strawberries and rhubarb, and mix lightly. Line 2 9-inch pie plates with pastry. Spoon in the fruit. Sprinkle with lemon juice, and dot with butter. Top with crust. Seal and flute edges. Freeze.

Makes 2 pies.

To Freeze: If desired, frozen pies may be removed from pie plates. Wrap tightly in freezer wrap, and seal. Label, date, and return to freezer. Store in box to avoid damage. Otherwise, pies may be stored in pie plates. Overwrap with freezer wrap.

To Serve: Return pie to pie plate. Defrost. Cut several slits in top. Bake in a 425° F. oven for 30 to 40 minutes or until juices bubble up through slits.

Pie may be baked from frozen state. When pie is warm enough, cut several slits in top. Add another 30 minutes to baking time. If edges begin to get too brown, cover with aluminum foil.

Storage Time: Up to 6 months.

PASTRY TO FREEZE

This recipe eliminates a lot of measuring.

1 2-pound bag all-purpose flour (8 cups sifted all-purpose flour)
1 tablespoon salt
1 1-pound can vegetable shortening (3⅔ cups)
1⅓ cups ice water

Sift flour and salt into a very large bowl. Add shortening, and blend into flour with pastry blender or 2 knives until mixture is well-blended and the texture of coarse meal. Lift mixture up from bottom of bowl to be sure all flour is blended with shortening. Sprinkle water over flour mixture gradually, and blend in with a fork until all mixture is moistened.

Divide pastry into 8 parts. Roll out each part on a square of waxed paper with a lightly floured rolling pin to form a 10-inch circle. When circle is rolled and trimmed (use trimmings in next pastry circle), cut waxed paper into a circle about ½-inch larger around than pastry. Continue until 8 pastry circles are rolled. Stack one on top of another as they are rolled. Cover loosely and freeze.

Makes pastry for 8 piecrusts.

To Freeze: Overwrap frozen pastry with freezer wrap, and seal. Label and date. Store in a box in freezer to avoid damage.

To Use: Remove 1 or 2 pastry circles from package, depending on whether you wish to make a single- or a double-crust pie, and defrost enough to fit into an 8- or 9-inch pie plate.

For a single baked crust, flute edge of pastry, and prick all over with fork. Bake in a 450° F. oven 10 to 15 minutes.

For a single unbaked crust, flute edge of pastry. Add filling, and bake as directed.

For a double crust, use second circle for top. Add filling to bottom crust, moisten pastry around edge of pie plate, add top crust, seal, and flute edge. Cut several slits in top crust. Bake as directed in recipe.

Storage Time: Up to 2 months.

CAKES

Almost all kinds of cakes are satisfactory for freezing. Unfrosted layers are more versatile, since they can be frosted any way one wishes at serving time or served unfrosted with berries, sauce, or ice cream.

If cakes are to be frosted, a butter-cream type is the most satisfactory for freezing. Freeze the cake before wrapping so the frosting won't get messed up.

Since spices have a tendency to get stronger in freezer storage, they can be reduced slightly in spice cakes if one wishes.

Unbaked cake batter is not particularly satisfactory to freeze, as there tends to be a loss in volume when baked.

VERY GOOD BANANA-NUT CAKE

2¼ cups sifted cake flour
2 teaspoons baking powder
¾ teaspoon baking soda
¾ teaspoon salt
1½ cups granulated sugar
¾ cup soft shortening
½ cup firmly packed light-
   brown sugar
6 tablespoons buttermilk
1½ cups mashed ripe
   bananas
3 eggs
1½ teaspoons vanilla extract
¾ cup chopped walnuts
6 tablespoons flour

In a large bowl sift together the cake flour, baking powder, baking soda, salt, and granulated sugar. Add the shortening, brown sugar, buttermilk, and bananas. Mix enough to dampen flour. Beat 2 minutes on low speed of electric mixer, scraping sides of bowl. If by hand, count beating time only. Add the eggs and vanilla, and beat 1 minute longer. Fold in nuts, which have been dusted with flour. To bake, spoon into greased and paper-lined 9-inch layer-cake pans. Bake in a 375° F. oven about 30 minutes or until top springs back when gently tapped with finger. Let stand in pan on rack for 5 minutes. Then carefully loosen around outside edge with a knife, and turn out on rack. Remove paper. Cool right side up on rack.

Makes 2 9-inch layers.

To Freeze: Wrap cooled layers in freezer wrap. Seal, label, date, and freeze.

To Use: Defrost and frost as desired.

Storage Time: Up to 6 months.

BUTTERSCOTCH CHIFFON CAKE

2¼ cups sifted cake flour
3 teaspoons baking powder
1 teaspoon salt
2 cups firmly packed light
    brown sugar
½ cup vegetable oil

5 medium egg yolks
¾ cup cold water
2 teaspoons vanilla extract
1 cup egg whites (7 or 8)
½ teaspoon cream of tartar

Into a medium-size bowl sift together the flour, baking powder, and salt. Mix in the brown sugar. Form a well in the center, and add the oil, egg yolks, water, and vanilla. Beat with a spoon until smooth. In a large second bowl put egg whites and cream of tartar. Whip until whites form *very stiff* peaks. Do not underbeat. Pour the egg-yolk mixture gradually over the beaten egg whites, and gently fold into the egg whites. Do *not* stir. Pour at once into an ungreased 10-inch tube pan, 4 inches deep. Bake 65 to 70 minutes at 325° F. or until top springs back when lightly touched. Invert until cool. If pan does not have "legs" to hold it off counter top, set center hole over soft-drink bottle to cool. Carefully loosen outer edge and around center of cake, and remove from pan.

To Freeze: Wrap cake carefully in freezer wrap, and seal. Label, date, and freeze.

To Serve: Defrost.

Storage Time: Up to 6 months.

BROWN SUGAR CHOCOLATE CAKE

2 cups sifted all-purpose flour
1 teaspoon baking soda
¾ teaspoon salt
2 cups firmly packed light-brown sugar
½ cup soft shortening
1 cup buttermilk
1 teaspoon vanilla extract
3 medium eggs
2 2-ounce squares unsweetened chocolate, melted
Flour to dust pans

After Freezing:
Sea Foam Frosting (below)

Sift the flour with baking soda and salt into a large bowl. Mix in the brown sugar. Add the shortening, buttermilk, and vanilla. Beat with mixer 2 minutes at medium speed. Add the eggs and chocolate. Beat 2 minutes longer. Scrape sides and bottom of bowl during beating. Spoon batter into 2 greased and floured 9-inch round layer-cake pans. Bake in a 350° F. oven for 30 to 35 minutes or until top springs back when lightly touched with fingertip. Cool in pans on rack for 10 minutes. Remove from pans, and cool on rack.
Makes 2 9-inch layers.

To Freeze: Wrap cooled layers in freezer wrap, and seal. Label, date, and freeze.

To Serve: Defrost and frost with Sea Foam Frosting.

Storage Time: Up to 3 months.

Sea Foam Frosting

2 egg whites
1½ cups firmly packed light-
    brown sugar

⅓ cup water
1 teaspoon vanilla extract
Dash salt

In the top of a double boiler combine egg whites, brown sugar, water, vanilla, and a dash of salt. Place over boiling water, and beat with rotary egg beater until mixture is light and fluffy and will hold its shape. Remove from heat, and continue beating until stiff peaks are formed.

Frosts tops and sides of 2 9-inch layers or 2 dozen cupcakes.

DESSERT LOAF CAKE

2 cups sifted all-purpose flour
2½ teaspoons baking powder
½ teaspoon salt
½ cup shortening, softened
1 cup granulated sugar
1 teaspoon vanilla extract

3 eggs
¾ cup milk
½ cup white raisins or ½ cup
    cut-up candied cherries
    (optional)
Flour to dust pan

Sift flour with baking powder and salt. Cream shortening and sugar together until light and fluffy. Add vanilla and eggs, and beat thoroughly. Add dry ingredients alternately with milk. Mix after each addition just until smooth. Stir in white raisins or candied cherries if desired. Spoon batter into a greased and floured 9½ x 5¼-inch loaf pan. Bake in a 350° F. oven for 45 minutes or until top springs back when lightly touched with finger. Cool in pan on rack 10 minutes. Loosen around outside edge of pan, and cool on rack.

To Freeze: Wrap cooled cake in freezer wrap, and seal. Label, date, and freeze.

To Serve: Defrost. Serve sliced with ice cream or sauce or frost as desired.

Storage Time: Up to 6 months.

FRUIT CAKE

1 pound candied cherries
½ pound candied citron
½ pound candied lemon peel
2 pounds mixed candied fruits
    (prunes, apricots,
    peaches)
1 pound raisins
¾ cup pineapple juice
3¾ cups sifted all-purpose
    flour
2 teaspoons salt

2 teaspoons baking powder
2 teaspoons allspice
2 teaspoons ground cloves
2 cups butter
1 cup granulated sugar
10 eggs
1 cup honey
½ pound pecans
½ pound toasted filberts
½ cup all-purpose flour
½ cup brandy

Slice the candied cherries crosswise into thin slices, and cut the candied citron and lemon peel into dice. Cut mixed candied fruits into dice. Mix the candied cherries, citron, lemon peel, and mixed fruit with the raisins and pineapple juice, and let stand overnight. Sift the 3¾ cups flour with the salt, baking powder, allspice, and cloves. Cream the butter until soft. Add the sugar, and beat until light. Beat in the eggs, 1 at a time, beating well after each addition. Stir in the sifted dry ingredients alternately with the honey. Fold in the pecans and filberts. Dredge the fruit with the ½ cup flour, and stir into batter.

Line 3 9 x 5½-inch loaf pans with 2 layers of buttered brown paper cut to fit bottom and sides. Fill pans ¾ full. Bake in a 275° F. oven for 5 hours. Remove from pan, and peel off paper. Soak clean cheesecloth in brandy, and wrap each cake in soaked cloth. Pour any leftover brandy carefully onto top of cakes. Wrap in aluminum foil. Let stand overnight (or 24 hours).

Makes 3 2-pound cakes.

To Freeze: Remove cheesecloth. Wrap cakes in freezer wrap, and seal. Label and date. Freeze.

To Use: Defrost. *Note:* Cake can be easily sliced into thin slices before being completely defrosted.

Storage Time: Up to 6 months.

CALIFORNIA FRUIT CAKE

1½ cups seedless raisins
1½ cups diced pitted fresh
   dates
2 cups granulated sugar
1½ cups boiling water
½ cup dry sherry
⅓ cup shortening

3 cups sifted all-purpose flour
1 teaspoon baking soda
2 teaspoons cinnamon
1 teaspoon ground cloves
1 teaspoon salt
1 cup chopped walnuts

Combine the raisins, dates, sugar, boiling water, sherry, and shortening in a saucepan, and simmer for 20 minutes. Cool. Sift the flour with baking soda, cinnamon, cloves, and salt. Mix into fruit mixture. Stir in nuts. Spoon batter into 2 greased and floured 8½ x 4½-inch loaf pans. Bake in a 325° F. oven for 1½ to 1¾ hours or until cake springs back when lightly touched with fingertip. Cool in pan on rack 10 minutes. Loosen cakes carefully around outside edges, and remove from pan. Cool on rack.
Makes 2 cakes.

To Freeze: Wrap cooled cakes in freezer wrap, and seal. Label, date, and freeze.

To Serve: Defrost. Cut in thin slices while still partially frozen.

Storage Time: Up to 4 months.

SOUTHERN PECAN LOAF

5¼ cups sifted all-purpose
   flour
3 teaspoons baking powder
1½ teaspoons baking soda
1½ teaspoons salt
6 tablespoons melted butter
2¼ cups orange juice

6 tablespoons grated orange
   peel
1½ cups finely cut, pitted
   fresh dates
3 cups granulated sugar
3 eggs
1½ cups chopped pecans

Sift flour with baking powder, baking soda, and salt. Mix together the butter, orange juice, grated orange peel, dates, sugar, eggs, and pecans well with a spoon. Stir in sifted flour mixture, and mix thoroughly. Pour into 2 well-greased and floured 9½ x 5¼-inch loaf pans. Bake in a 350° F. oven for 1 hour and 30 minutes. If top begins to get too brown, at end of hour place a piece of foil loosely over top of cake. Cake is done when top springs back when lightly touched with fingertip. Cool in pan on rack 10 minutes. Remove from pan. Cool on rack.

Makes 2 loaves.

To Freeze: Wrap cooled cake in freezer wrap, and seal. Label, date, and freeze.

To Serve: Defrost. Serve plain or with ice cream or sauce. May be frosted if desired.

Storage Time: Up to 6 months.

OLD-FASHIONED YELLOW SPONGE CAKE

1 cup sifted cake flour
5 eggs, separated
¼ teaspoon salt
¼ teaspoon cream of tartar
1 cup granulated sugar

1½ teaspoons grated lemon
   rind
2 tablespoons water
1½ tablespoons lemon juice

Sift flour once, and measure. Sift again 3 times. Put the egg whites into a large bowl, add salt, and beat with mixer at medium speed until foamy. Add cream of tartar, and continue beating until the egg whites are stiff but not dry. Continue beating, adding ½ cup of the sugar, 1 tablespoon at a time, beating only until sugar is blended.

Place the egg yolks, remaining ½ cup sugar, lemon rind, and water in small bowl of mixer. Beat at medium speed until thick and light. Add lemon juice gradually during last part of beating. Fold in the flour, stirring just to blend. Fold into egg-white mixture with a whisk or spatula. Bake in an ungreased 9-inch tube pan in a 325° F. oven for 60 minutes or until cake springs back when lightly tapped with the finger. Invert until cool. If pan does not have "legs" to hold it off counter top, set center hole over a soft-drink bottle to cool. Carefully loosen outer edge and around center of cake, and remove from pan.

To Freeze: Wrap cake carefully in freezer wrap, and seal. Label, date, and freeze.

To Serve: Defrost.

Storage Time: Up to 4 months.

TOPPER CAKE

1 ⅓ cups sifted all-purpose
    flour
1 cup granulated sugar
2 teaspoons baking powder
½ teaspoon salt
⅓ cup shortening
⅔ cup milk
1 teaspoon vanilla extract
1 large egg

¼ cup butter
⅓ cup brown sugar
⅓ cup honey
2 teaspoons grated orange
    rind
¼ teaspoon cinnamon
¼ cup diced toasted almonds
Flour to dust pan

Sift the flour with granulated sugar, baking powder, and salt in a bowl. Add the shortening, milk, and vanilla, and beat on medium speed of mixer for 2 minutes. Add the egg, and beat 2 minutes longer. Spoon batter into a greased and floured 9 x 9 x 2-inch aluminum freezer pan. Bake in a 350° F. oven for 30 to 35 minutes or until top springs back when touched lightly with the finger. Cool on rack in pan. Cream butter with brown sugar and honey. Add the grated orange rind, cinnamon, and almonds, and mix. Spread on cooled cake.

To Freeze: Freeze cake. Then overwrap with freezer wrap, and seal. Label, date, and return to freezer.

To Serve: Defrost cake. Place about 3 inches below broiler. Heat and broil 3 to 5 minutes or until brown and bubbly. To serve, cut into squares.

Storage Time: Up to 6 months.

PUDDING-CAKES

APPLE PAN DOWDY

2 cups sifted all-purpose flour
2 tablespoons granulated
    sugar
3 teaspoons baking powder
1 teaspoon salt
6 tablespoons shortening
⅔ cup milk

6 cooking apples, pared and
    cored (Jonathan, Rome
    Beauty, Winesap,
    Baldwin)
2 tablespoons water
½ cup granulated sugar
1 teaspoon cinnamon
2 tablespoons butter
1 tablespoon lemon juice

Sift the flour with 2 tablespoons sugar, the baking powder, and the salt into a bowl. Cut in the shortening with 2 knives or a pastry blender until well blended. With a fork stir in milk just to moisten. On a lightly floured board, pat dough to fit an 8 x 8-inch aluminum freezer pan. Slice apples into pan. Sprinkle with water. Mix ½ cup sugar and the cinnamon, and sprinkle over apples. Dot with butter, and sprinkle with lemon juice. Cover with dough. Bake in a 400° F. oven about 30 minutes. Cool.

To Freeze: Freeze Apple Pan Dowdy in pan. Overwrap with freezer wrap, and seal. Label, date, and freeze.

To Serve: Remove overwrap. Partially defrost. Bake in a 400° F. oven for 15 to 30 minutes or until hot and bubbly. Serve hot.
Makes 6 servings.

Storage Time: Up to 6 months.

CHEESE-APPLE PUDDING

3 cups soft bread crumbs
3 cups sliced apples,
    unpeeled
1⅓ cups grated American
    cheese
¾ cup granulated sugar

½ teaspoon cinnamon
½ teaspoon nutmeg
⅛ teaspoon salt
3 tablespoons butter
1½ cups unsweetened pine-
    apple juice

In a buttered deep aluminum freezer casserole place ⅓ of the bread crumbs, ½ the apples, ½ the cheese, and repeat, topping with remaining crumbs. Mix the sugar with the cinnamon, nutmeg, and salt, and sprinkle on crumbs. Dot with butter, and pour juice over all. Bake in a 350° F. oven for 50 minutes. Cool.
Makes 6 servings.

To Freeze: Overwrap casserole with freezer wrap. Seal. Label, date, and freeze.

To Serve: Defrost. To serve warm, bake in a 400° F. oven approximately 20 minutes. Serve with whipped cream if desired.

Storage Time: Up to 3 months.

CRANBERRY DESSERT

2 cups uncooked quick-cook-
   ing oatmeal
1 cup flour
2 cups firmly packed light
   brown sugar

½ teaspoon salt
1 cup butter
2 1-pound cans cranberry
   sauce

Mix the oatmeal with flour, brown sugar, and salt. Cut in the butter with 2 knives or a pastry blender until mixture is crumbly. Place ½ of the mixture in the bottom of 2 greased 8-inch-square aluminum-foil freezing pans. Spread cranberry sauce over the mixture in each pan. Top with the remaining oatmeal mixture. Bake in a 350° F. oven for 30 to 35 minutes. Cool on rack.

Each pan makes 6 to 8 servings.

To Freeze: Rewrap dessert in pan, and seal. Label, date, and freeze.

To Serve: Remove outer wrap, and defrost. Reheat in pan in 350° F. oven for 15 to 20 minutes. Serve cut in squares with scoop of vanilla ice cream.

Storage Time: Up to 6 months.

Appendix: Freezing Bits and Pieces

Consolidate many small packages into a single bag or carton so they don't get lost in the freezer.

Remove and discard any pulp left in orange rind or lemon rind. Wash and dry rind. Wrap in freezer wrap, and freeze. Grate while still frozen.

Wash celery, parsley, or herb leaves, and dry on paper towels. Freeze, uncovered, 8 to 12 hours. Remove from freezer, and let air-dry on paper towels. Crumble and store in airtight container. Herbs and other seasoning leaves dried in this way have a much livelier flavor than when air-dried without first freezing or oven-dried. They also air-dry much more quickly after being frozen.

If chives are frozen uncovered in freezer, they are much easier to cut up for freezing and can be measured to freeze in measured amounts or frozen loose in 1 package. Work quickly after they are taken from freezer.

Nuts may be stored in plastic bags or containers in freezer. They keep fresh several times longer than when stored in the cupboard. (This is after they have been opened. It is not necessary to store those in closed vacuum-pack cans in freezer.)

Freeze roux ready for sauces and gravy. Cream equal amounts of flour and butter together, and store in plastic bags or containers. Mark amount so you will know how much flour and butter you are getting—for example, 3 tablespoons butter plus 3 tablespoons flour.

Dairy products can be frozen for longer storage. Butter made from fresh (sweet) pasteurized cream stores best. Wrap in freezer wrap, seal, label, and date. Will keep up to 6 months if salted; unsalted butter up to 10 months.

Freeze cheese in small portions which will be used promptly after thawing. Packed in freezer wrap, cheese will keep several months in freezer, though some kinds may become crumbly on thawing. (Uncreamed-style cottage cheese is one.)

Forty percent butterfat cream can be frozen in airtight containers. Leave ½-inch headspace. Stores well 2 to 4 months. Defrost in refrigerator. Use for whipping. Solids and water separate, so it is not satisfactory for table use.

Freeze milk in container in which purchased. Will keep approximately 4 weeks. A pinch of ascorbic acid added to each quart aids flavor retention. Defrost in refrigerator.

Freeze eggs when price is right. Proceed as follows: Select fresh eggs. Wash shells before breaking eggs.
Whole eggs: Mix yolk and white together gently with a fork. Add 1 tablespoon sugar or light corn syrup per 2

cups eggs if eggs are to be used for sweet products, and 1 teaspoon salt for 2 cups eggs if used for products not sweetened. Label number of eggs and addition of sweetening or salt. Whole eggs should be used at once after defrosting.

Yolks only: Mix 3 tablespoons sugar or corn syrup with 2 cups yolks or 2 teaspoons salt for 2 cups yolks. Label for future reference. Yolks should be used at once after defrosting.

Whites only: Freeze in airtight containers. Label with number of whites for future reference. When defrosted, they will keep several days in refrigerator.

Eggs can be frozen in measured amounts in ice-cube trays. When frozen, put in plastic bags to remove as needed.

> 3 tablespoons = 1 whole egg
> 1½ tablespoons = 1 yolk
> 2 tablespoons = 1 white

When freezing eggs, label, date, and seal before freezing. Eggs will store up to 6 months. They should be used the same as fresh eggs.

Having a party? Put whipped cream or frozen topping (defrosted) through a pastry bag on metal baking sheet. Freeze, ready to adorn ice cream, pie, or meringue.

Going away? Put crackers, pretzels, or any other products that might be attractive to bugs in cans, and store them in the freezer.

Bait for fishing can be frozen. Label plainly!

Index

All-American Sauce, 246
Almond Sauce, Butterscotch, 243
Aluminum
   containers, 5
   -foil wraps, 5, 6
Anchovy Sauce, Fish Rolls with, 59
Appetizers, 151–161
   Avocado Dip, 152
   Cheese, 153–156
      Mold, 153
      Pastries, 154
      Rolled Sandwiches, 156
      Rolls, Danish Blue, 154–155
      Rolls, Snappy, 155
   Chinese Chicken Wings, 157
   Cocktail Meatballs Superb, 158
   freezing rules, 151–152
   Pâté, 159–160
      de Foie Poulet, 159
      Pork and Veal, 160
   Smoked Salmon Tidbits, 161
Apple(s)
   Crestwick, 119–120
   freezing instructions, 109–110
   Pan Dowdy, 260–261
   Pudding, Cheese-, 261
   Rolls, 186–187
   -sauce, 110
   season for, 109
   Soup, 171–172
Apple Pan Dowdy, 260–261
Apple Rolls, 186–187
Apple Soup, 171–172
Apples Crestwick, 119–120
Apricot(s)
   freezing instructions, 110–111
   Sauce for Game, 106
   season for, 109
   serving suggestions, 119
Apricot Sauce for Game, 106
Artichoke(s)
   freezing instructions, 127
   Omelet, 142
   season for, 126
Artichoke Omelet, 142
Ascorbic acid, use of, 108–109
Asparagus
   freezing instructions, 127
   season for, 126
   serving suggestions, 139, 140
Avocado Dip, 152

Bait, fishing, 265
Baked Alaska, 238
Baked Bass with Shrimp Stuffing, 63
Baked Fish Steaks with Creole Sauce,
   64–65
Baked Stuffed Whole Fish, 62–63
Baked Swordfish, 65–66
Baked Texas Chicken, 41
Banana(s)
   freezing instructions, 111–112
   -Nut Cake, Very Good, 252–253
   season for, 109
   Tea Loaf, Spiced, 191–192
Barbecued Beef, 221–222
Barbecued Meat Loaves, Individual,
   23–24
Barbecued Spareribs, 27–28
Barley Soup, Lamb-, 165–166
Basic Stuffing, 38
Bass with Shrimp Stuffing, Baked, 63–
   64
Bean(s)
   Bake, Ham-, 204–205
   Boston Baked, 203–204
   Casserole, Lima, 144–145
   freezing instructions, 128
   Manchu, Green, 144
   Midwest Chili with, 170–171
   season for, 126
   serving suggestions, 139
      green, 139, 140
      lima, 139
Béarnaise Sauce, 15–16
Beef
   Barbecued, 221–222
   Birds, Savory, 17
   Cheese, and Noodle Combo, 205–206
   Fillet Greté with Béarnaise Sauce,
      15–16
   freezing instructions, 10 ff.
   ground, 13, 19–20
      recipes, 20–25
   Pot Roast, 18
   recipes, 15–25
   Salad, Corned, 220–221
   -Steak Venezuela, 19
   Stock, 163–164
   storage time, 12–13
   See also Meat, Loaf(-ves); Meatballs
Beef, Cheese, and Noodle Combo, 205–
   206

266

Beef Fillet Greté with Béarnaise Sauce, 15–16
Beef Pot Roast, 18
Beef Stock, 163–164
Beefsteak Venezuela, 19
Beer Shrimp, 68
Beets
  freezing instructions, 128
  Harvard, 128–129
  season for, 126
Best Chocolate Cookies, 227–228
Biscuit(s)
  Dough, 223
  Marjorie's Buttermilk, 185–186
Bisque, Lobster, 87–88
Blackberries
  freezing instructions, 112
  season for, 109
Blanching, 125
Blender Hollandaise, 140–141
Blender Mayonnaise, 89–90
Blueberry(-ies), 107
  freezing instructions, 113
  Pie, 244
  season for, 109
Blueberry Pie, 244
Boston Baked Beans, 203–204
Boysenberries
  freezing instructions, 112
  season for, 109
Braccioli, 16–17
Bran Bread, Date and Nut, 190–191
Bran-Raisin Muffins, 195–196
Bread, 173–199
  Banana Tea Loaf, Spiced, 191–192
  Brioche, 187–188
  Buns, Freezer Sticky Pecan, 198–199
  Cranberry, 194–195
  Date and Nut Bran, 190–191
  Dutch Holiday, 179–180
  Foldovers, 183–184
  freezing, 173–175
  French, 178–179
  Fruit, 189–190
  Garlic, 179
  making, 174
  Oatmeal-Raisin, 181–182
  Orange-Cinnamon, 180–181
  Potato, 177–178
  Quick, 189–196
    Brunch, 193–194
  recipes, 175–199
  Ring, Cheese, 182–183
  Rye Loaves, Freezer, 197–198
  Squash, 188–189
  White, 175–176
  Whole Wheat, 176–177
  yeast, 175–189

Bread (cont.)
  See also Biscuit(s); Muffins; Rolls; Sandwiches
Breast of Duck Elaine, 52
Brioche, 187–188
Broccoli
  freezing instructions, 129
  season for, 126
  serving suggestions, 139
Broiled Scallops, 73
Broth
  Chicken, 167–168
  Turkey, 169–170
Brother Girard Scallops, 74
Brown Sugar Chocolate Cake, 254–255
Brunswick Stew, 102–103
Brussels sprouts
  freezing instructions, 129
  season for, 126
  serving suggestions, 139
Buns, Freezer Sticky Pecan, 198–199
Butter, 264
  Chili Sauce, 219
  Chive, 219
  flavored, 219–220
  Honey, 219
  Horseradish, 219
  Maple, 219
  Pickle Relish, 219
  on sandwiches, 151, 219
  Tabasco, 219
Buttermilk Biscuits, Marjorie's, 185–186
Butterscotch Almond Sauce, 243
Butterscotch Chiffon Cake, 253–254
Butterscotch-Peach Pie, 247–248
Butterscotch Peaches, 121–122

Cabbage
  freezing instructions, 129–130
  Rolls, Swedish, 24–25
  season for, 126
Cake, 252–260
  Banana-Nut, Very Good, 252–253
  Butterscotch Chiffon, 253–254
  Chocolate, Brown Sugar, 254–255
  Dessert Loaf, 255–256
  Fruit, 256–257
    California, 257
  Pecan Loaf, Southern, 258
  Sponge, Old-Fashioned Yellow, 258–259
  Topper, 260
California Fruit Cake, 257
Canapés, 151
  Lobster, 87
Carrots
  freezing instructions, 130

Carrots (*cont.*)
  season for, 126
  serving suggestions, 139
Catfish, Pan-Fried Trout, Perch, or, 62
Cauliflower
  freezing instructions, 130
  season for, 126
  serving suggestions, 139, 140
Celery
  freezing instructions, 130–131
  leaves, 263
  season for, 126
Cellophane wraps, 5, 6, 7
Cheese, 264
  appetizers, 153–156
  -Apple Pudding, 261
  Balls, Frozen, 214–215
  Bread Ring, 182–183
  Mold, 153
  and Noodle Combo, Beef, 205–206
  Pastries, 154
  Pie, Jiffy, 244–245
  Rolled Sandwiches, 156
  Rolls
    Danish Blue, 154–155
    Snappy, 155
  Sauce, 141
Cheese-Apple Pudding, 261
Cheese Bread Ring, 182–183
Cheese Mold, 153
Cheese Pastries, 154
Cheese Rolled Sandwiches, 156
Cheese Sauce, 141
Cherry(-ies)
  Delight, Quick, 120
  freezing instructions, 113–114
  season for, 109
Chestnut Stuffing, 38
Chewy Pumpkin Cookies, 235
Chickburgers, 224–225
Chicken
  Bahai, 51
  Baked Texas, 41
  Breasts
    Elsie, 42
    Parvenu, 50
    Sherried, 42
  broiling suggestions, 39
  Broth, 167–168
  freezing instructions
    cooked, 43
    uncooked, 32–37
  Fried, 43–44
    Rice, 45
  Golden, 44
  Hong Kong Baked, 41
  Kiev, 46
  Lotus, 49–50
  Marguerite, Cold, 48–49

Chicken (*cont.*)
  Marinade
    Herbed, 40
    Monterey, 40
    Rockport, 39–40
  Pie, Homemade, 47–48
  recipes, 39–51
  -Rice Soup, 168
  roasting suggestions, 37
  Salad, 221
  stuffing for, 38
  timetable for thawing in refrigerator, 33
  -Vegetable Soup, 168–169
  Wings, Chinese, 157
Chicken Bahai, 51
Chicken Breasts Elsie, 42
Chicken Breasts Parvenu, 50
Chicken Broth, 167–168
Chicken Fried Rice, 45
Chicken Kiev, 46
Chicken Lotus, 49–50
Chicken-Rice Soup, 168
Chicken Salad, 221
Chicken-Vegetable Soup, 168–169
Chili Sauce Butter, 219
Chili with Beans, Midwest, 170–171
Chinese Chicken Wings, 157
Chives, 263–264
Chive Butter, 219
Choco-Orange Refrigerator Cookies, 228–229
Chocolate
  Cake, Brown Sugar, 254–255
  Cookies, Best, 227–228
  Frosting, 228
  Pecan Pie, 245
  Sauce, Favorite, 242
Chowder
  Clam
    Base, Classic, 78–79
    Manhattan, 80
    New England, 79
  Scallop, 74–75
Cinnamon Bread, Orange-, 180–181
Clam(s), 75–82
  Chowder, 78–80
    Base, Classic, 78–79
    Manhattan, 80
    New England, 79
  Cocktail, 76
    Sauce, 76
  freezing raw, 76
  Fried, 80–81
    Fritters, 81
  Pie, 77
  Sauce for Spaghetti, White, 82
  Stuffed Baked, 78
Clam Cocktail, 76

Clam Cocktail Sauce, 76
Clam Pie, 77
Classic Clam Chowder Base, 78–79
Cloverleaf Rolls, 197
Cocktail
    Clam, 76
    Oyster, 83
    Shrimp, 68–69
Cocktail Meatballs Superb, 158
Coffee Cake, Rich, 192
Cold Chicken Marguerite, 48–49
Cookies, 226–236
    Choco-Orange Refrigerator, 228–229
    Chocolate, Best, 227–228
    Cranberry, 229–230
    Date Whirls, 230
    freezing rules, 226–227
    Holiday Fruit, 231
    Molasses-Cream, 234
    Oatmeal Slices, 232–233
    Old-Fashioned Ranger, 233
    Pumpkin, Chewy, 235
    Raisin, Soft, 231–232
    recipes, 227–236
    Spice Box, 236
Corn
    freezing instructions, 131
    season for, 126
    Treat, 142–143
Corn Treat, 142–143
Corned Beef Salad, 220–221
Crab, 90–93
    Deviled, 91–92
    freezing and cooking methods, 90–91
    -Meat
        Puff, 91
        Salad, 92
        Sandwiches, Hot, 93
    -wiches, 225
Crab-Meat Puff, 91
Crab-Meat Salad, 92
Crackers, 265
Cranberry(-ies), 107
    Bread, 194–195
    Cookies, 229–230
    Dessert, 262
    freezing instructions, 114
    Salad, Frozen, 212
    Sauce, 120–121
    season for, 109
    Sherbet, 239
Cream, 264
    puffs, 152
    whipped, 265
Cream-Braised Pheasant a la Mrs. Deeds, 98–99
Cream-Braised Rabbit, 100–101
Creole Sauce, Baked Fish Steaks with, 64–65

Cucumber Sauce, Sour Cream and, 141
Cured meats, instructions for storing uncooked, 13

Dairy products, 264
Danish Blue Cheese Rolls, 154–155
Date
    and Nut Bran Bread, 190–191
    Roll, Easy Elegant, 239–240
    Whirls, 230
Date Whirls, 230
Dessert Loaf Cake, 255–256
Desserts, 237–262
    Cake(s), 252–260
        Brown Sugar Chocolate, 254–255
        Butterscotch Chiffon, 253–254
        California Fruit, 257
        Dessert Loaf, 255–256
        Fruit, 256–257
        Old-Fashioned Yellow Sponge, 258–259
        Southern Pecan Loaf, 258
        Topper, 259–260
        Very Good Banana-Nut, 252–253
    cold, 238–242
        Baked Alaska, 238
        Cranberry Sherbet, 239
        Easy Elegant Date Roll, 239–240
        Ice-Cream Roll, 240–241
        ice-cream sauces, 242–243
        Pumpkin Ice Cream, 241
        Strawberry Mousse, 241–242
    freezing rules, 237
    Pie(s), 243–252
        Blueberry, 244
        Butterscotch-Peach, 247–248
        Chocolate Pecan, 245
        Frozen Orange, 247
        Ice-Cream-Sundae, 246
        Jiffy Cheese, 244–245
        Pastry to Freeze, 251–252
        Peppermint Pink, 248–249
        Strawberry, 249
        Strawberry and Rhubarb, 250
    pudding-cakes, 260–262
        Apple Pan Dowdy, 260–261
        Cheese-Apple, 261
        Cranberry Dessert, 262
    recipes, 238–262
    See also Fruit
Deviled Crab, 91–92
Deviled Ham Salad, 221
Deviled Lamb Chops, 25–26
Dewberries
    freezing instructions, 112
    season for, 109
Dip, Avocado, 152
Dressing for Fruit Salad, Frozen, 214

Duck(s)
  Breast of, Elaine, 52
  Claret, Wild, 97–98
  halved or quartered, 35
  Madeira, Wild, 97
  Roast Wild, 96
  roasting, 37
  timetable for thawing in refrigerator, 33
Dutch Holiday Bread, 179–180

Easy Elegant Date Roll, 239–240
Eggplant
  freezing instructions, 131–132
  Pasqualino, 143
  season for, 126
Eggplant Pasqualino, 143
Eggs, 152, 264–265
  Artichoke Omelet, 142
  Midnight, 20–21

Fats, using, 201
Favorite Chocolate Sauce, 242
Fiberboard containers, 5
Figs
  freezing instructions, 114–115
  season for, 109
Fish, 54–66
  Baked
    Bass with Shrimp Stuffing, 63
    Steaks with Creole Sauce, 64–65
    Stuffed Whole, 62–63
    Sword-, 65–66
  and Chips, Portuguese, 61
  Fillets, 57–58
  freezing rules, 56–57
  Mousse
    with Lobster Sauce, Halibut, 60–61
    Tuna, 216–217
  Pan-Fried Trout, Perch, or Catfish, 62
  Poached Salmon Steaks, 65
  Rolls with Anchovy Sauce, 59
  Soup, Provincetown, 59–60
  Stock, 58
  See also Shellfish
Foldovers, 183–184
Freezer Rye Loaves, 197–198
Freezer Sticky Pecan Buns, 198–199
French Bread, 178–179
Fresh Mushroom Soup, 169
Fried Chicken, 43–44
Fried Clam Fritters, 81
Fried Clams, 80–81
Fried Oysters, 84–85
Fritters, Fried Clam, 81–82

Frosting
  Chocolate, 228
  Sea Foam, 255
Frozen Cheese Balls, 214–215
Frozen Cranberry Salad, 212
Frozen Dinner Rolls, 196–197
Frozen Dressing for Fruit Salad, 214
Frozen Fruit Medley, 212–213
Frozen Fruit Salad, 213
Frozen Lobster Salad, 215–216
Frozen Orange Pie, 247
Frozen Venison Stew, 104–105
Fruit, 107–123
  Apples Crestwick, 119–120
  Bread, 189–190
  Cake, 256–257
    California, 257
  Cherry Delight, Quick, 120
  Cookies, 229–232
    Cranberry, 229–230
    Date Whirls, 230
    Holiday, 231
    Raisin, Soft, 231–232
  Cranberry Sauce, 120–121
  freezing instructions, 109–118
  juices, 115
  Medley, Frozen, 212–213
  Nectarines in Red Wine, 121
  packing directions, 108–109
  Peaches, Butterscotch, 121–122
  Raspberry Panama, 122
  recipes, 119–123
  Rhubarb Sauce, 122–123
  Salad
    Cranberry, Frozen, 212
    Frozen, 213
    Frozen Dressing for, 214
  seasonal chart, 109
  serving suggestions for frozen, 119
  -Stuffed Wild Goose, 100
  Stuffing, 38
  See also Desserts; specific fruits
Fruit Bread, 189–190
Fruit Cake, 256–257
Fruit-Stuffed Wild Goose, 100
Fruit Stuffing, 38
Funnel, for preparation, 7

Game, 95–106
  Apricot Sauce for, 106
  Brunswick Stew, 102–103
  Duck(s), Wild, 96–98
    Claret, 97–98
    Madeira, 97
    Roast, 96
  freezing instructions, 94–96
  Goose, Fruit-Stuffed Wild, 100
  Grouse with Orange Sauce, 99

Game (*cont.*)
  Pheasant a la Mrs. Deeds, Cream-
    Braised, 98–99
  Rabbit, 100–101
    Cream-Braised, 100–101
    Sherried Wild, 101–102
  Venison, 103–105
    Marinade for Roasts or Steak, 104
    Roast Rack of, 103
    Stew, 105
    Stew, Frozen, 104–105
Garlic Bread, 179
Giblets, 36
Glass containers, 5
Gnocchi, 208–209
Golden Chicken, 44
Goose
  Fruit-Stuffed Wild, 100
  halved or quartered, 35
  roasting, 37
  timetable for thawing in refrigera-
    tor, 33
Gravies, in main dishes, 202
Green Beans Manchu, 144
Green peppers, *see* Peppers
Greens
  freezing instructions, 132
  season for, 126
  serving suggestions, 139
Grog, Pumpkin, 147–148
Grouse with Orange Sauce, 99

Halibut Mousse with Lobster Sauce,
    60–61
Ham
  -Bean Bake, 204–205
  Salad, Deviled, 221
  Stuffing, 38
Ham-Bean Bake, 204–205
Ham Stuffing, 38
Hamburgers for Sandwiches, 21
Harvard Beets, 128–129
Hawaiian Muffins, 193
Herbed Marinade, 40
Herbs, 263
Holiday Fruit Cookies, 231
Hollandaise, Blender, 140–141
Homemade Chicken Pie, 47–48
Honey Butter, 219
Hong Kong Baked Chicken, 41
Horseradish Butter, 219
Hot Crab-Meat Sandwiches, 93
Hot Crab-wiches, 225
Hot Lemon Shrimp, 69
Hot Lobster, 88

Ice-Cream
  Pumpkin, 241
  Roll, 240–241

Ice-Cream (*cont.*)
  Sauce(s), 242–243
    Butterscotch Almond, 243
    Chocolate, Favorite, 242
    Strawberry, 243
  -Sundae Pie, 246
Ice-Cream Roll, 240–241
Ice-Cream-Sundae Pie, 246
Individual Barbecued Meat Loaves, 23–
    24
Iowa Pork Chops, 29–30

Jiffy Cheese Pie, 244–245
Juices
  fruit, 115
  tomato, 137

Labeling, 6–7
Lamb, 25–26
  -Barley Soup, 165–166
  Chops, Deviled, 25–26
  Roast Leg of, 26
  storage time, 12–13
Lamb-Barley Soup, 165–166
Leftovers, freezing, 202–203
Lemon rind, 263
Lentil Soup, Mission, 106–107
Lima Bean Casserole, 144–145
Livers
  chicken, 36
  storing uncooked, 14
Lobster, 86–90
  Bisque, 87–88
  boiling, 86
  Canapés, 87
  freezing, 86–87
  Hot, 88
  Salad, 89
    Frozen, 215–216
  Sauce, 61
  Thermidor, 88–89
Lobster Bisque, 87–88
Lobster Canapés, 87
Lobster Salad, 89
Lobster Sauce, 61
Lobster Thermidor, 88–89
Loganberries
  freezing instructions, 112
  season for, 109
Luncheon Sausage, 207

Macaroni, cooking *al dente*, 201
Maggie's Meat Loaf, 22–23
Main dishes, 200–210
  Beef, Cheese, and Noodle Combo,
    205–206
  Boston Baked Beans, 203–204
  casseroles, 205–208
  freezing rules, 200–201

Main dishes (*cont.*)
  Gnocchi, 208–209
  Ham-Bean Bake, 204–205
  Luncheon Sausage, 207
  Pancakes Aloha, 209
  Pork Suey Casserole, 206
  recipes, 203–210
  reheating frozen, 202
  Ruth's Sauerkraut, 207–208
  See also Fish; Meat; etc.
Manhattan Clam Chowder, 80
Maple Butter, 219
Marinade for Venison Roasts or Steak, 104
Marinade Monterey, 40
Marinade Rockport, 39–40
Marjorie's Buttermilk Biscuits, 185–186
Mayonnaise
  Blender, 89–90
  in freezing sandwiches, 151, 218–219
  in frozen salads, 211
Meat, 10–31
  cooking frozen, 14
    in foil, 14
  freezing instructions for uncooked, 10–14
  Loaf(-ves)
    Individual Barbecued, 23–24
    Maggie's, 22–23
  See also Beef; Pork; etc.
Meatballs
  Superb, Cocktail, 158
  Tomato, 22
Melons
  freezing instructions, 115
  season for, 109
  serving suggestions, 119
Midnight Eggs, 20–21
Midwest Chili with Beans, 170–171
Milk, 264
Mission Lentil Soup, 166–167
Mobile Pickled Shrimp, 71–72
Molasses-Cream Cookies, 234
Mousse
  Halibut, with Lobster Sauce, 60–61
  Strawberry, 241–242
  Tuna, 216–217
Mrs. Marshall's Refrigerator Rolls, 184–185
Muffins
  Bran-Raisin, 195–196
  Hawaiian, 193
Mushroom(s)
  freezing instructions, 132–133
  a la Limpet, 146
  Sauce, 223
  season for, 126
  Soup, Fresh, 169
  Stuffing, 38

Mushroom Sauce, 223
Mushroom Stuffing, 38
Mushrooms a la Limpet, 146

Nectarberries
  freezing instructions, 112
  season for, 109
Nectarines
  freezing instructions, 115–116
  in Red Wine, 121
Nectarines in Red Wine, 121
New England Clam Chowder, 79
Noodle Combo, Beef, Cheese, and, 205–206
Nut(s), 264
  Bran Bread, Date and, 190–191
  Cake, Very Good Banana-, 252–253
Nylon bags as containers, 5

Oatmeal
  cookies, 232–233
  -Raisin Bread, 181–182
  Slices, 232–233
Oatmeal-Raisin Bread, 181–182
Oatmeal Slices, 232–233
Okra
  freezing instructions, 133
  Sautéed, 146
  season for, 126
Old-Fashioned Ranger Cookies, 233
Old-Fashioned Yellow Sponge Cake, 258–259
Omelet, Artichoke, 142
Onion(s)
  freezing instructions, 133–134
  season for, 126
  Soup, 164–165
  Tart, 210
Onion Soup, 164–165
Onion Tart, 210
Orange
  Baked Pork Chops with Yams, 28–29
  -Cinnamon Bread, 180–181
  Pie, Frozen, 247
  Refrigerator Cookies, Choco-, 228–229
  rind, 263
Orange Baked Pork Chops with Yams, 28–29
Orange-Cinnamon Bread, 180–181
Oyster(s), 82–86
  Casino, 84
  Cocktail, 83
  freezing raw, 82–83
  Fried, 84–85
  Pie, Turkey and, 52–53
  Sautéed, 85–86
  Scalloped, 83–84
  Stew, 85
  Stuffing, 38

Oyster Cocktail, 83
Oyster Cocktail Sauce, 83
Oyster Stew, 85
Oyster Stuffing, 38
Oysters Casino, 84

Packaging, 4–7
Pan-Fried Trout, Perch, or Catfish, 62
Pancakes Aloha, 209
Parkerhouse Rolls, 197
Parsley, 263
Pastry(-ies)
  Cheese, 154
  crusts, 202
  Foldovers, 183–184
  to Freeze, 251–252
  Triangles, Pie, 47–48
  See also Bread; Pie
Pastry to Freeze, 251–252
Pâté, 159–160
  de Foie Poulet, 159
  Pork and Veal, 160
Peach(es), 107–108
  Butterscotch, 121–122
  freezing instructions, 115–116
  Pie, Butterscotch, 247–248
  season for, 109
  serving suggestions, 119
Peas
  freezing instructions, 134
  season for, 126
  serving suggestions, 139
Pecan
  Buns, Freezer Sticky, 198–199
  Loaf, Southern, 258
  Pie, Chocolate, 245
Peppermint Pink Pie, 248–249
Peppers
  freezing instructions, 135
  season for, 126
Perch, Pan-fried Trout, Catfish, or, 62
Pheasant a la Mrs. Deeds, Cream-
    Braised, 98–99
Pickle Relish Butter, 219
Pie, 243–252
  Blueberry, 244
  Butterscotch Peach, 247–248
  Cheese, Jiffy, 244–245
  Chicken, Homemade, 47–48
  Chocolate Pecan, 245
  Clam, 77
  Ice-Cream-Sundae, 246
  Onion Tart, 210
  Orange, Frozen, 247
  Pastry
    to Freeze, 251–252
    Triangles, 47–48
  Peppermint Pink, 248–249
  Pork, Vermont, 26–27

Pie (cont.)
  Strawberry, 249
  and Rhubarb, 250
  Turkey and Oyster, 52–53
Pie Pastry Triangles, 47–48
Pineapple
  freezing instructions, 116
  season for, 109
Plastic containers, 5
Pliofilm wraps, 5–6
Plums
  freezing instructions, 117
  season for, 109
Poached Salmon Steaks, 65
Polyethylene wraps, 5
Pork, 26–30
  Chops, 12, 28–30
    Iowa, 29–30
    Tappan, 29
    in Tomatoes, 30
    with Yams, Orange Baked, 28–29
  Pie, Vermont, 26–27
  Spareribs, Barbecued, 27–28
  storage time, 12–13
  Suey Casserole, 206
  and Veal Pâté, 160
  See also Ham; Sausage
Pork and Veal Pâté, 160
Pork Chops in Tomatoes, 30
Pork Chops Tappan, 29
Pork Suey Casserole, 206
Port Sauce, 103
Portuguese Fish and Chips, 61
Potato(es)
  Bread, 177–178
  freezing instructions, 135–136
  pasta, 208–209
  Patties, 177–178
  season for, 126
Potato Bread, 177–178
Potato Patties, 147
Poultry, 32–53
  broiling suggestions, 39
  freezing instructions, 32–37, 43
  roasting suggestions, 37
  See also specific birds
Pretzels, 265
Provincetown Fish Soup, 59–60
Prunes, 117
Pudding-cakes, 260–262
  Apple Pan Dowdy, 260–261
  Cheese-Apple, 261
  Cranberry Dessert, 262
Pumpkin(s)
  Cookies, Chewy, 235
  freezing instructions, 136
  Grog, 147–148
  Ice Cream, 241
  season for, 126

Pumpkin Grog, 147–148
Pumpkin Ice Cream, 241
Pyroceram, 5

Quick Brunch Bread, 193–194
Quick Cherry Delight, 120

Rabbit, 100–101
  Cream-Braised, 100–101
  Sherried Wild, 101–102
Raisin
  Bread, Oatmeal-, 181–182
  Cookies, Soft, 231–232
  Muffins, Bran-, 195–196
Raspberry(-ies)
  freezing instructions, 117
  Panama, 122
  season for, 109
  serving suggestions, 119
Raspberry Panama, 122
Refreezing thawed foods, 8–9
Relish
  Butter, Pickle, 219
  Salad, 217
Rhubarb
  freezing instructions, 117–118
  Pie, Strawberry and, 250
  Sauce, 122–123
  season for, 109
Rhubarb Sauce, 122–123
Rice
  Chicken Fried, 45
  converted, 202
  Shrimp and, 70–71
  Soup, Chicken-, 168
Rich Coffee Cake, 192
Roast Leg of Lamb, 26
Roast Rack of Venison, 103
Roast Wild Duck, 96
Rock Cornish hens, timetable for thaw-
    ing in refrigerator, 33
Rolls
  Apple, 186–187
  Biscuit, 197
  Cloverleaf, 197
  Frozen Dinner; 197
  Mrs. Marshall's Refrigerator, 184–185
  Parkerhouse, 197
Roux, 264
Ruth's Sauerkraut, 207–208
Rye Loaves, Freezer, 197–198

Salad(s), 211–217
  Cheese Balls, Frozen, 214–215
  Corned Beef, 220–221
  Crab-Meat, 92

Salad(s) (cont.)
  Cranberry, Frozen, 212
  freezing rules, 211
  Fruit, 212–214
    Dressing for, Frozen, 214
    Medley, Frozen, 212–213
  Ham, Deviled, 221
  Lobster, 89–90
    Frozen, 215–216
  recipes, 212–217
  Relish, 217
  seafood, 215–217
  Shrimp, 71
  Tuna Mousse, 216–217
Salmon
  Steaks, Poached, 65
  Tidbits, Smoked, 161
Sandwich(es), 218–225
  Beef, 221–224
    Bake, 222–223
    Barbecued, 221–222
    Loaf, Savory, 224
    Salad, Corned, 220–221
  Canapés, 151
    Lobster, 87
  Cheese Rolled, 156
  Chicken
    Chickburgers, 224–225
    Salad, 221
  combinations and fillings that freeze
    well, 220–221
  Crab
    -Meat, Hot, 93
    -wiches, Hot, 225
  flavored butters for, 219–220
  freezing rules, 218–219
  Ham Salad, Deviled, 21
  Hamburgers for, 21
  recipes, 221–225
Sandwich Bake, 222–223
Sauce(s)
  All-American, 246
  Anchovy, Fish Rolls with, 59
  Apricot, for Game, 106
  Béarnaise, 15–16
  Butterscotch Almond, 243
  Cheese, 141
  Chocolate, Favorite, 242
  Clam
    Cocktail, 76
    White, for Spaghetti, 82
  Cranberry, 120–121
  Creole, Baked Fish Steaks with, 64–
    65
  Hollandaise, Blender, 140–141
  ice-cream, 242–243
  Lobster, 61
  in main dishes, 202
  Mushroom, 223

Sauce(s) (*cont.*)
  Oyster Cocktail, 83
  Port, 103
  Rhubarb, 122–123
  Shrimp Cocktail, 68–69
  Sour Cream and Cucumber, 141
  Spaghetti, 20
    White Clam, 82
  Strawberry, 243
  Tartar, 81
  for vegetables, serving suggestions, 139–140
  Vinaigrette, 140
Sauerkraut, Ruth's, 207–208
Sausage
  Luncheon, 207
  storage time for uncooked, 13
  Stuffing, 38
Sausage Stuffing, 38
Sautéed Okra, 146
Sautéed Oysters, 85–86
Sautéed Scallops, 73
Savory Beef Birds, 17
Savory Sandwich Loaf, 224
Scallop(s), 72–75
  Broiled, 73
  Brother Girard, 74
  Casserole, 75
  Chowder, 74–75
  freezing raw, 72
  Sautéed, 73
Scallop Casserole, 75
Scallop Chowder, 74–75
Scalloped Oysters, 83–84
Sea Foam Frosting, 255
Shellfish, 66–93
  freezing rules, 56
  See also specific kinds
Sherbet, Cranberry, 239
Sherried Chicken Breasts, 42
Sherried Wild Rabbit, 101–102
Shrimp, 66–72
  Beer, 68
  Cocktail, 68–69
  cooked, 67
    recipes, 67–72
  Hot Lemon, 69
  Marinara, 70
  Mobile Pickled, 71–72
  raw, 66–67
  Remoulade, 69–70
  and Rice, 70–71
  Salad, 71
  Spicy, 67–68
  Stuffing, Baked Bass with, 62
Shrimp and Rice, 70–71
Shrimp Cocktail, 68–69
Shrimp Cocktail Sauce, 68–69
Shrimp Marinara, 70

Shrimp Remoulade, 69–70
Shrimp Salad, 71
Smoked Salmon Tidbits, 161
Snappy Cheese Rolls, 155
Soft Raisin Cookies, 231–232
Sophisticated Spoonburgers, 25
Soup(s), 162–172
  Apple, 171–172
  Chicken
    Broth, 167–168
    -Rice, 168
    -Vegetable, 168–169
  Fish, Provincetown, 59–60
  freezing rules, 162–163
  Lamb-Barley, 165–166
  Lentil, Mission, 166–167
  Lobster Bisque, 87–88
  Mushroom, Fresh, 169
  Onion, 164–165
  Tomato-Vegetable, 165
  Turkey Broth, 169–170
  See also Chowder; Stock
Sour Cream and Cucumber Sauce, 141
Southern Pecan Loaf, 258
Spaghetti Sauce, 20
  White Clam, 82
Spareribs, Barbecued, 27–28
Spice Box Cookies, 236
Spiced Banana Tea Loaf, 191–192
Spicy Shrimp, 67–68
Spinach, serving suggestions, 139
Sponge Cake, Old-Fashioned Yellow, 258–259
Steak Chatelaine, 18–19
Stock
  Beef, 163–164
  Fish, 58
  freezing rules, 162–163
  See also Broth
Stockinette, using, 6
Strawberry(-ies), 107
  freezing instructions, 118–119
  Mousse, 241–242
  Pie, 248
    and Rhubarb, 250
  Sauce, 243
  season for, 109
  serving suggestions, 119
Strawberry and Rhubarb Pie, 250
Strawberry Mousse, 241–242
Strawberry Pie, 249
Strawberry Sauce, 243
Stuffed Baked Clams, 78
Stuffings, 38
Squash
  Bread, 188–189
  freezing instructions, 136–137
  Puff, 148
  season for, 126

Squash Bread, 188–189
Squash Puff, 148
Swedish Cabbage Rolls, 24–25
Swordfish, Baked, 65–66

Tabasco Butter, 219
Tableware, as containers, 5
Tart, Onion, 210
Tartar Sauce, 81
Tins, as containers, 5
Tomato(es)
    freezing instructions, 137–138
    Meatballs, 22
    Pork Chops in, 30
    season for, 127
    -Vegetable Soup, 165
    Zucchini and, 137
Tomato Meatballs, 22
Tomato-Vegetable Soup, 165
Topper Cake, 259–260
Topping, whipped, 265
Trout, Pan-Fried Perch, Catfish, or, 62
Tuna Mousse, 216–217
Turkey
    Broth, 169–170
    halved or quartered, 35
    and Oyster Pie, 52–53
    roasting, 37
    timetable for thawing whole in refrigerator, 33
Turkey Broth, 169–170
Turnips
    freezing instructions, 138
    season for, 127

Variety meats, instructions for storing uncooked, 13–14
Veal
    Pâté, Pork and, 160
    Profile, 30–31
    storage time, 12–13
Veal Profile, 30–31
Vegetable(s), 124–148, 201
    Artichoke Omelet, 142
    Corn Treat, 142–143
    Eggplant Pasqualino, 143
    freezing instructions, 124–138
    Green Beans Manchu, 144
    Lima Bean Casserole, 144–145
    Mixed
        freezing instructions, 132
        Medley, 145

Vegetable(s) (cont.)
    Mushrooms a la Limpet, 146
    Okra, Sautéed, 146
    Potato Patties, 147
    Pumpkin Grog, 147–148
    recipes, 142–148
    Sauce(s), 139–141
        Blender Hollandaise, 140–141
        Cheese, 141
        Sour Cream and Cucumber, 141
        Vinaigrette, 140
    seasonal chart, 126–127
    Soup
        Chicken-, 168–169
        Tomato-, 165
    Squash Puff, 148
    suggestions for serving frozen, 139–140
    See also Main dishes; Salad(s); specific vegetables
Vegetable Medley, 145
Venison, 103–105
    Marinade for Roasts or Steak, 104
    Roast Rack of, 103
    Stew, 105
        Frozen, 104–105
Venison Stew, 105
Vermont Pork Pie, 26–27
Very Good Banana-Nut Cake, 252–253
Vinaigrette Sauce, 140
Vitamin C (ascorbic acid), using, 108–109

Waxed paper, using, 7
White Bread, 175–176
White Clam Sauce for Spaghetti, 82
Whole Wheat Bread, 176–177
Wild Duck Madeira, 97
Wild Ducks Claret, 97

Yams, Orange Baked Pork Chops with, 28–29
Youngberries
    freezing instructions, 112
    season for, 109

Zucchini
    freezing instructions, 136–137
    season for, 127
    and Tomatoes, 137